We live in [...] internationalised. Imperialism b [...] world economics. In this [...] ow the Fourth International, founded in 1930 by [Revolutionary] Marxist militants, nuclei, currents and organizations, answered the problem of the construction of anti-capitalist, revolutionary political formations. As Ernest Mandel's biographical essay explains, Frank was secretary to Leon Trotsky in 1932-1933. This book draws on Frank's experience as a central leader of the Fourth International through to 1979.

Daniel Bensaïd's appendix explains the following 30 years of the Fourth International life. Two contributions develop its perspective of establishing a new independent political representation of the working class that takes into account the diversity of the working class in defending a resolutely class-based programme: a statement by founders of the French LCR explaining its decision to dissolve into the NPA; and the key resolution adopted by the Fourth International's 2009 world congress.

Resistance Classics

October Readings: the development of
the theory of permanent revolution
D. R. Rayner Lysaght (Ed.)

Building Unity Against Fascism:
Classic Marxist Texts
Leon Trotsky, Daniel Guérin, Ted Grant

The Long March of the Trotskyists: Contributions
to the history of the Fourth International
Pierre Frank, Daniel Bensaïd, Ernest Mandel

Women's Liberation and the Socialist Revolution:
Documents of the Fourth International
Penelope Duggan (Ed.)

Forthcoming

Marxism and Anarchism
Karl Marx, Frederick Engels, Leon Trotsky

Introduction to Marxist Economic Theory.
Third Edition
Ernest Mandel

The thought of Leon Trotsky
Denise Avenas, Michael Löwy, Jean-Michel Krivine

The united front & the Transitional Programme
Leon Trotsky, Daniel Bensaïd, John Riddell

CONTRIBUTIONS TO THE HISTORY OF THE FOURTH INTERNATIONAL

The Long March of the Trotskyists

About the Notebooks for Study and Research

The Notebooks for Study and Research are published by the International Institute for Research and Education. The Notebooks focus on themes of contemporary debate or historical or theoretical importance. Lectures and study materials given in sessions in our Institute, located in Amsterdam, Manila and Islamabad, are made available to the public in large part through the Notebooks.

Since 1986 we have published 50 issues in English. Since 1998 they have been published as a book series in collaboration with publishers in London. For many years we had a parallel series in French, the *Cahiers d'étude et de recherche* (currently under review). Different issues of the Notebooks have also appeared in languages besides English and French, including German, Dutch, Arabic, Spanish, Japanese, Korean, Portuguese, Turkish, Swedish Danish and Russian.

CONTRIBUTIONS TO THE HISTORY OF THE FOURTH INTERNATIONAL

The Long March of the Trotskyists

Contributions to the history of the Fourth International

Pierre Frank

Introduction by Marijke Colle

With contributions by Daniel Bensaïd & Ernest Mandel

International Institute for Research & Education, Amsterdam
Resistance Books, London

THE LONG MARCH OF THE TROTSKYISTS

Both the International Institute for Research and Education and Resistance would be glad to have readers' opinions of this book, its design and translations, and any suggestions you may have for future publications or wider distribution.

Our books are available at special quantity discounts to educational and non-profit organizations, and to bookstores.

To contact us, please write to: Socialist Resistance, PO Box 62732 London SW2 9GQ, Britain, email contact@socialistresistance.org or visit: www.socialistresistance.org

Published by Resistance Books, October 2010
Printed in Britain by Lightning Source
ISBN 978-0-902869-80-6

The translations in this volume may be republished under http://creativecommons.org/licenses/by-sa/2.0/

First French-language edition © French section of the Fourth International, 1973.
English translation, and chapter 8, © Inprecor 1978.
Appendix 1 © IIRE, 2008.

Published as issue 50 of the Notebooks for Study and Research.
ISSN 0298-7902

Contents

Preface Marijke Colle 11

Introduction Pierre Frank 13

Chapter 1: **Historical Continuity** 16

Chapter 2: From 1923 to 1929. **The Bolshevik-Leninist Faction in the USSR** 18

    Policy in the USSR 19

    The Anglo-Russian Committee (1926) 21

    The second Chinese revolution (1925-27) 23

    Permanent revolution vs. socialism in one country 25

Chapter 3: From 1929 to 1933. **Formation of the International Left Opposition** 27

    Defence of the USSR 29

    The united front against the Hitler danger 30

    Fight to reform the Communist International 32

Chapter 4: From 1933 to 1938. **Preparing for the Fourth International** 35

    The 'Declaration of the Four' 38

    The first draft of a transitional programme 39

    'Entryism ' 41

    The rise of fascism and the war 42

Chapter 5: From 1938 to 1948. **From the Founding of the Fourth International to the Second World Congress** 47

    Founding of the Fourth International and the Transitional Programme 47

    The ordeal of the world war 51

The Second World Congress _____ 56

Chapter 6: From 1948 to 1953. **From the Second World Congress to the Split** _____ 59

    Post-war upheavals _____ 60

    The crises in the Trotskyist movement _____ 64

    The Third World Congress (1951) _____ 68

    A tactical turn in building revolutionary parties _____ 71

    Critique of the Third World Congress _____ 74

Chapter 7: From 1953 to 1968. **Splits & Reunification** 78

    The 1953-54 split _____ 78

    The Fourth and Fifth World Congresses (1954 and 1957) _____ 80

    Crises and regroupments (the Sixth World Congress) _ 85

    The International Committee _____ 90

    The International Reunited _____ 92

    The Reunification Congress ('Dynamics of World Revolution Today') _____ 93

    Attacks against the reunited International (the splitters) _____ 96

    The degeneration of the Ceylonese section _____ 98

    The campaigns of the International (The Second Congress after reunification) _____ 103

Chapter 8: From 1968 to 1978. **The Turn in the World Situation** _____ *109*

Chapter 9: 1978. **The 'Long March' of the Trotskyists** _____ *124*

Chapter 10: **Those Who Died So That the International Might Live** _____ *134*

Appendix: 2010 World Congress. **Role & Tasks of the Fourth International** *Fourth International* _____ *148*

Appendix: 2008. **From the LCR to the NPA** *Members of the LCR* _____ *163*

Appendix: From 1979 to 2007. **Trotskyisms: What I know** *Daniel Bensaïd* _____ *167*

   Changing times _____ 167

   The new century _____ 174

   The start of a new chapter _____ 175

Appendix: 1963. **'For Early Reunification of the World Trotskyist Movement'** *Socialist Workers Party resolution* **179**

Appendix: 1940-1944. **Trotskyists and the Resistance** *Ernest Mandel* _____ *188*

Postface: Who was Pierre Frank? *Ernest Mandel* __ **196**

   Declaration of the Fourth International and the Ligue communiste révolutionnaire _____ **198**

THE LONG MARCH OF THE TROTSKYISTS

Preface
Marijke Colle

Internationalism emerged in the 19th century and became "proletarian internationalism" as expressed through the successive Internationals from the First to the Fourth.

A first European gathering of workers organisations was build after the defeat of the 1848 revolutions. The Second International was constructed by the new social-democratic mass parties again mainly in Europe. It was the betrayal of its own internationalist ideas by the leaderships of the Second International at the beginning of the First World War and the victory of the Bolshevik Revolution in Russia that constituted the motive for the formation of the Third International. The Stalinist degeneration of the Soviet Union, the seizure of power by Hitler and the defeat of the Spanish civil war, were the main reasons to found the Fourth International at the worst possible moment in the history of the twentieth century.

This book focuses on the fight for the building of this Fourth International during the twentieth century.

As we have now plainly entered the XXIst century, a new internationalism has clearly developed. We saw the Zapatistas Uprising in the Mexican state of Chiappas in 1994, the massive demonstration against the WTO Ministerial Conference in Seattle (1999) and successive World Social Fora, of which the latest took place in Belèm (2009).

The economic and institutional developments of our globalised world have stimulated a new world wide resistance against the Washington consensus and the neoliberal agenda.

This new international network of activists has a truly planetary dimension. It is the answer to the generalised commodification and privatisation in a globalised capitalist system.

The anti-globalisation movement is also much larger than the "working class" or "workers movement" as it encompasses the feminist movement, ecological movements, the farmers' movement, cultural struggles, etc.

However, this new internationally structured network and movement is not homogenous. It is not producing a global criticism of the world capitalist system as such. Its alternative projects are not always precise.

THE LONG MARCH OF THE TROTSKYISTS

The diversity of the anti-globalisation movement is a source of rich debates but also sometimes a factor of weakness. From those NGOs which have a tendency to work towards reforms of international bodies to more radical movements, the anti-globalisation movement or network is certainly not directly comparable with the international workers' movement in the 20th century.

But in its diversity and pluralism, this international movement represents the first global reaction to the consequences of neoliberal globalisation and militarism. In this movement, we see organisations which produce radical answers to the problems they are working on, from CADTM (cancellation of the debt of the countries of the global South) to Via Campesina (a farmers' international response to the devastation brought about by agribusiness worldwide).

Socialism in the 21st century will certainly be the result of programmatic clarifications: a new and more democratic vision on the fight against exploitation and all kinds of oppressions; and above all of victorious struggles for power.

Members of the Fourth International have been fully involved in the building of these global movements: against the climate crisis; for women's rights; in the anti-war movements; or in the campaign against the debt crisis. Our internationalism must now involve the discussion about a new International, incorporating the historical lessons from the experiences of the workers' movement of the past two hundred years, but it must above all open up the debate on a strategy to confront and overturn the new global imperialist world order.

CONTRIBUTIONS TO THE HISTORY OF THE FOURTH INTERNATIONAL

Introduction
Pierre Frank

Up to the present, no study has been written on the history of the Trotskyist movement. Some work is presently being done in the universities, but it bears only on certain periods or on very limited aspects of the movement. The principal aim of this book is therefore to give today's young militants some knowledge of the past of the Trotskyist movement. The first part of this work served as material for a course at a school conducted by the French section of the Fourth International in 1948, and was published at that time. It appears here without any appreciable changes, with additional material to cover the ensuing period.

Within the limits of a work of this size, we wanted to give what seemed to us the most essential aspects of the history of the Fourth International. Until now the Trotskyist movement, for reasons connected with the size of its forces, has exercised its influence on the class struggle principally in the domain of ideas, by its analyses and its elaborations of perspectives and programmes. Generally speaking, it has not been able to lead mass mobilisations and mass actions based on its programme and its slogans; the objective reasons for this are given in this book. Thus a history of the Fourth International has to describe above all the positions taken by the organisation in the gigantic social struggles that have characterised the world in the course of the half century of the Trotskyist movement's existence. In addition, such a history has to show how the Trotskyist movement, in the course of these struggles, defended and enriched the formulations of revolutionary Marxism, as developed from the time of Marx down to the early congresses of the Communist International. We have done our utmost to illuminate the most important stages in the life of the Fourth International, the problems it had to resolve, the debates that took place, and the positions that were reached.

We have limited this book to the history of the international movement and have not treated the history of its sections, except where a particular section at a particular time played an especially significant role in the history of the International.

The history of the Trotskyist movement scarcely poses any problem in connection with what historians call 'periodisation'. The transition from capitalism to the world-wide victory of socialism, inaugurated by the October Revolution, is turning out to be much longer and more complex than anyone had imagined in 1917; no other political movement has followed this transitional period as closely as has the Trotskyist movement, whose successive stages coincide with the very stages of that history itself since 1923.

The Trotskyist movement was born in the USSR at the close of the revolutionary wave that followed the First World War, when a period of relative stabilisation of capitalism began. It expanded internationally during the great economic crisis that began in 1929. It moved towards the construction of a new revolutionary International after the debacle of the German working class movement in 1933, and founded the Fourth International on the eve of the Second World War. It reoriented itself in accordance with the tremendous upheavals of the post-war period. And today the Trotskyist movement has entered a new phase in line with the turn inaugurated on a world scale in 1968.

In this book we have done no more than mention the mountains of slander heaped on Trotsky and the Trotskyist movement. We have never yet dealt with this question in depth. Because of the vast proportions the calumny assumed, and the after-effects that still remain, this question will no doubt constitute an important subject for future historians. A century ago Karl Vogt and others furiously slandered Marx and his supporters, calling them the *Schwefelbande* (devil's gang) within the movements for emancipation. How tiny and pale were those vilifications compared to those underwritten by powerful states, heaped high in an effort to make the Fourth International appear the *Schwefelbande* of the Twentieth Century.

This work leaves aside a good number of questions. Given the aim and the size we had set for this book, we could not go into numerous details. There was no possibility of using extensive quotations without requiring three to four times the number of pages. We had to stick to essentials. We hope that we have succeeded in correctly setting forth how the Trotskyists advanced internationally in the domain of theory and practice, in the defence of positions previously taken, and in the elaboration -- difficult in every epoch, and rendered still more arduous by the conditions under which the movement has fought -- of new positions in the face of new problems posed by the changes taking place all over the world.

The author of this book has participated in this 'long march' of the Trotskyists for more than forty years, first becoming part of the international leadership of the Trotskyist movement in 1931. Although this work very largely expresses the views of numerous leading members of the International, it cannot be considered an 'official' history of the Fourth International. We do not think that for

Marxists there can be an 'official' history, even of their own organisation. The organisation is an instrument of political combat, which inevitably necessitates a line of action determined according to the rules of democratic centralism. History, to a great extent, serves to determine politics; its determination cannot be placed at the service of politics. For having abandoned Marxism on this question, as on others, Stalinism has obliged the historians under its thumb to write 'official' histories, forcing them in fact periodically to rewrite history as a function of the line of the moment. They have succeeded only in accumulating historical falsifications as well as in proving their growing incapacity to draw objective lessons from history.

Chapter 1: Historical Continuity

The Trotskyist movement, born in 1923 at the onset of the Stalinist degeneration, has taken part ever since in all the great events of our age, thus assuring the *continuity* of revolutionary Marxism on a world scale. Between the Communist League and the First International, there was a lapse in time of a dozen years in the field of organisation -- although political continuity was assured by Marx and Engels personally. Between the First and Second International, there was also a gap of almost fifteen years -- the political continuity being assured by Engels, who established a kind of international centre by corresponding with leaders of parties in the most important countries. The years of World War I fell between the Second and the Third International. This time it was the Bolshevik Party and Zimmerwald that assured the maintenance of the Marxist movement.

Our movement was born within the Third International. From 1923 to 1933 we fought -- within its ranks or outside -- as a faction of the Communist International, trying to wrest its leadership from the hands of the centrists and place it once again on the path of revolutionary Marxism. When objective conditions no longer made it possible to pursue this aim, we proceeded directly to the building of new parties and a new revolutionary International, taking as our point of departure the first four congresses of the Communist International. There was no break, no gap in the continuity of the revolutionary movement, and that despite the enormous ebb in the labour movement starting in 1923, despite the degeneration of the October Revolution, despite the infamous role exercised by Stalinism within the working class.

Congresses and resolutions of a revolutionary organisation are not mere matters of form. They do a good deal more than define policy for the immediate period. They record, for the collectivity constituted by the party, its experience, its rules of action, the framework in which -- while renewing its membership with the passage of time -- it continues to evolve. Should the organisation cease to exist, all this remains as historical data that will certainly be used by those who, at some later date, will want to rebuild the revolutionary party. But only as historical data! They would inevitably have to grope about, sometimes for a very long time, to re-establish, to re-create, an adequate framework for the organisation. The degeneration of the Third International and the resulting dispersion of forces have enormously hindered the progress of our movement, which has experienced numerous crises. But it is enough to imagine for a moment what would have happened if the thread had been broken -- if there had no longer been, at a given moment, an international Marxist centre -- to realise by how much the difficulties would have been multiplied, to have an idea of the even greater obstacles revolutionists would have had to overcome in order to re-establish a firm political movement and to rebuild an international leadership.

History will not fail to point out that it was Trotsky, through the sum total of his works, who made the greatest contribution to this task of maintaining historical continuity. Although the names *Communist-Internationalist* and *Bolshevik-Leninist* have been borne by our various organisations, the name Trotskyist will most probably be -- and correctly so -- the one that history will give us.

Chapter 2: From 1923 to 1929. The Bolshevik-Leninist Faction in the USSR

The revolutionary period opened by the Russian Revolution of 1917 was followed from 1923 to 1929 by an ebbing of the revolutionary tide and a period of relative stabilisation of capitalism. The European economy was recovering; American capitalism gained world ascendancy, replacing British capitalism, which experienced its first big crisis in 1926. In China the struggle of the colonised masses against imperialism began its great and tragic course. In the Soviet Union, economic progress was smell; a bitter internal political struggle went on, in the course of which the bureaucracy succeeded in shifting the axis of Soviet policy from world revolution to 'socialism in one country'. In several European countries, Socialist parties were in power, while the Communist International was in crisis, traversing the first stages of its bureaucratic degeneration.

The first period of our movement extended from 1923 to 1929. During that period, there was indeed no international Bolshevik-Leninist movement: there was a Bolshevik-Leninist faction of the Communist Party of the Soviet Union, but liaison with individuals or groups of supporters in other countries was confined to correspondence. There was no real, collective international elaboration of political thought and action.

From the moment of its birth, the Bolshevik-Leninist faction in the USSR evinced one of the essential characteristics of our movement -- *internationalism*. The faction was created in 1923 on the basis of an understanding of the changes in the international situation; its principal battles in the course of these six years bore as much on specifically Soviet questions as on problems of the world revolution.

The point of departure was the *turn in the world situation after the defeat of the German revolution in October 1923*[1]. The German CP was losing ground, while the Social Democracy was moving ahead. Trotsky, against the majority of the Political Bureau of the Bolshevik

---

[1] See Pierre Frank's NSR *Revolution and Counter-revolution in Europe*.

Party (the Zinoviev-Kamenev-Stalin troika), maintained that the international situation had changed from top to bottom, that the revolutionary wave of the post-war period was spent, that a period of relative stabilisation of capitalism had started, and that all this imposed new tasks for the Communist international and its sections in capitalist countries -- as well as for the problems of building socialism in the USSR.

From 1923 to 1929 the Bolshevik-Leninist faction in the USSR fought on three main questions:

- The policy of the leadership in the USSR.
- The Anglo-Russian Committee (1926).
- The second Chinese revolution (1925-27).

Policy in the USSR

We shall limit ourselves here to a few lines on this question, since it has been thoroughly treated by Trotsky in his *Draft Programme of the Communist International: A Criticism of Fundamentals*, and *The Revolution Betrayed*.

The establishment of the New Economic Policy (NEP) after the end of the civil war and the waning of the labour movement had a very great effect on social relations in the USSR, as well as on the ranks of the Bolshevik Party. Political passivity developed in the ranks of the workers. Part of the best revolutionary elements had lost their lives on the field of battle. Another part, which had reached command positions in the Red Army, found executive positions in the state and in the economy, where they applied the methods of command inherited from the army. With the NEP as a base, capitalist elements developed in the cities and in the countryside. The relationship of forces was evolving in a direction opposite to that of the revolutionary period. These factors gave the state apparatus increased independence and power. The entire last portion of Lenin's political activity was devoted to denouncing this danger. We have, he said, a workers state with bureaucratic deformations. Just read his report to the Eleventh Congress of the Russian party to see to what extent he denounced these evils![2]

The bureaucratisation of the state was accompanied and abetted by a bureaucratisation of the Bolshevik Party. As a revolutionary instrument, the latter was rusting away. A layer of *parvenus*, satisfied with what had already been obtained, gained the upper hand. These social layers and the state apparatus found their most responsive

---

[2] Lenin, Collected Works, Vol. 33, pp. 263-324

political expression in the organisational Secretariat of the party, in the person of that 'old Bolshevik' Stalin. The last conversations between Lenin and Trotsky were concerned with organising a faction to conduct the struggle against this party Secretariat. Lenin's last two letters to the Central Committee, known as 'Lenin's Testament', point out the danger of a split and propose to dismiss Stalin from the post of party secretary.[3]

In October 1923 Trotsky, pointing out the mounting dangers, proposed a 'new course', to be characterised by a struggle against the bureaucratisation of the party and in favour of the following: admitting young proletarian elements, who had proved themselves, into the leading bodies of the party; making these bodies elective; a plan for industrialisation; a certain number of measures to set the poor peasants against the kulaks.

In the beginning, this 'new course' was not openly rejected by the majority of the Political Bureau; but the latter did nothing to implement it. On the contrary, the Zinoviev-Kamenev-Stalin leadership (at that time these names were mentioned in that order) initiated a violent struggle against 'Trotskyism', bringing up -- and distorting -- twenty-year-old differences between Lenin and Trotsky, long outdated by events. Later Zinoviev and Kamenev admitted they had invented 'Trotskyism' for this occasion.

The Moscow Opposition -- the first faction gathered together by Trotsky to struggle for a 'new course' -- which consisted in large part of veteran militants of the revolution and the civil war, and constituted the first organisation of our movement, was prevented by bureaucratic methods from getting a hearing in the party, after having won some preliminary success in the Moscow cells.

Unbeknown even to some of its initial protagonists, the fight on the question of past differences concealed the struggle of the bureaucratic layers against internationalist revolutionary policy. As

---

[3] These two letters were banned in the USSR. Nevertheless, on two occasions, Stalin could not avoid mentioning their existence. Since the Twentieth Congress of the CPSU, publication in the Soviet Union of these letters (see Lenin, *Collected Works*, Vol. 36, pp. 594-96) and other of Lenin's writings, as well as the 'Journal of Lenin's Duty Secretaries' (ibid.. Vol 42, p. 480), has completely confirmed what Trotsky wrote, namely that in the last period of his life, Lenin had sought and obtained Trotsky's support to fight a weakening in the foreign-trade monopoly, the repressive measures taken by Stalin against the 'nationalist' faction of Georgian Bolsheviks led by Mdivani and, above all, to fight the bureaucracy in the party -- particularly its political spokesman, Stalin -- at the next party congress. Illness, then death, prevented Lenin from so doing.

the policy followed by the leadership of the Bolshevik Party slid more and more to the right, in 1925-26 Zinoviev and Kamenev broke with Stalin, who then pursued that policy with Bukharin, Rykov, and Tomsky as allies. The rightist policy was supposed to 'integrate the kulak into socialism', which would be achieved 'at a snail's pace' (Bukharin); industrialisation was denounced as an absurdity ('the peasant needs a cow, not a phonograph', declared Stalin).

The Opposition formed in 1926 by the Zinoviev-Trotsky bloc, forced to meet clandestinely, struggled to impose an industrialisation programme and a policy directed against the kulak, the Nepman, and the bureaucrat. A five-year plan was finally accepted in 1927 by the Bukharin-Stalin leadership, but the very limited yearly increases projected in the plan indicated the scepticism and hostility of that leadership. Under pressure from the Opposition, another plan was prepared, with higher yearly goals.

Towards the end of 1927, and without any confidence, the bureaucracy launched the first five-year plan. Early in 1928 -- less than three months after having broken party unity and exiled the Opposition to Siberia -- a frightened Stalin acknowledged the kulak danger, broke with the rightist Bukharin faction, made a sudden zigzag to the left, and began an ultra-left policy (the five-year plan had to be completed in four years, agriculture had to be 100 per cent collectivised, etc.). Put into practice in a bureaucratic way, by force of decree, and in a brutal manner by a party shorn of any real political life, this orientation brought the country to the brink of catastrophe.

The old Bolshevik Party -- after elimination of the left and right oppositions -- subsisted only as the political machine of the bureaucracy. The revolutionary cadres were exiled or exterminated. From that date on, the bureaucracy's domination increased and its policy developed in a series of zigzags, ranging from the most contemptible opportunism to the most unbridled ultra-leftism. In the final analysis, however, its general direction was very strongly opportunistic. The ultra-left zigzags have now ceased.

The Anglo-Russian Committee (1926)

The affair of the Anglo-Russian Committee marks the beginning of the Stalinist faction's policy of dissociating the fate of the USSR from that of the world revolution. It was on this question that they began the policy of putting pressure on foreign governments as a substitute for revolutionary struggle in defence of the USSR. This was done particularly through political combinations and subterfuges in which Communist parties abandoned part of their revolutionary programme on the pretext of thus attracting larger masses than they could mobilise by themselves.

The centre of world reaction right after the First World War was still British imperialism, despite the fact that its decline had already begun and despite the phenomenal rise of American capitalism. British imperialism's policy was all the more anti-Soviet in that the Russian Revolution set an extremely attractive example for the colonial peoples oppressed by the Empire. From a political point of view, the British labour movement was developing considerable strength. In 1924 the Labour Party had formed a minority government, although the Tories and Liberals soon found it opportune to oust it. Around 1926 a turn to the left occurred in the British trade unions.

The British CP was very weak -- it still is today -- and the Minority Movement it had activated in the trade unions was also rather weak. In order to counter British imperialism's threat to the USSR, Stalin proposed to the Political Bureau of the Bolshevik Party that efforts be made to establish a committee of English and Russian trade unions under the pretext of working towards rebuilding trade union unity on an international scale. A united front of Russian and British trade unions for the establishment of worldwide trade union unity was politically admissible, although it presented the danger of being mostly a summit operation, difficult for the rank and file to control. For Stalin, however, the real object of this Anglo-Russian Committee was to turn it into the 'centre of the struggle against imperialist war' -- the political centre of the struggle for the defence of the USSR. In answer to Trotsky, who was at the time still a member of the Political Bureau and who stressed the necessity of relying only on the revolutionary struggle of the proletariat, Stalin retorted: 'What can you do with your English Communists?'

The dispute concerning the aims of the Anglo-Russian Committee did not remain merely a battle of words. The class struggle in Great Britain gave it a tragic content. The leftward swing of the British workers was expressed by the miners' struggle against any wage cuts, giving rise to a strike that was supported by the British working class as a whole. In May 1926 a nine-day general strike forced the British Empire to its knees. This was the first manifestation of the crisis of British capitalism (a crisis that reached full bloom after the end of the Second World War). But British capitalism was able to pull itself out of this grave difficulty thanks to the British trade union leadership's betrayal: they ended the general strike and let the miners continue the struggle alone for several months.

For any revolutionary with the most elementary knowledge of the Leninist position on the united front, this betrayal would have demanded an immediate break by the Russian unions from the Anglo-Russian Committee -- plus an appeal to the British workers to stand up against their leadership. But considering the essential object of the Anglo-Russian Committee to be the 'defence of the USSR', and conceiving the latter as a task separate and distinct from the revolutionary struggle of the masses, Stalin kept the committee -- whose activity for months and months was reduced to nothing but talk, anyway -- in existence. When the militant members of the British Communist Party and the Minority Movement denounced the reformist leaders of their unions as traitors, the latter therefore had an easy reply at hand: "That's not what the Russians think -- and you can't very well accuse *them* of being reformists and traitors. There they are, in the same committee with us!' This policy disarmed and demoralised the British CP as well as the Minority Movement, which eventually disappeared.

Several months after the general strike, the leaders of the British trade unions, having thoroughly exploited the committee (which was no longer of any use to them) for their own purposes, denounced the financial aid provided to the striking miners by the Russian unions as an interference in the internal life of their organisations, and used this excuse to break up the Anglo-Russian Committee.

The Bolshevik-Leninist Opposition had exposed Stalinist policy on the question of the Anglo-Russian Committee and had conducted a very strong campaign for breaking from this committee at the time of the betrayal of the general strike.

The second Chinese revolution (1925-27)

A big upsurge occurred in the revolutionary movement in China in the period 1925-27. The merchant and industrial bourgeoisie, whose political party was the Kuomintang[4], tried to exploit this revolutionary upsurge for their own purpose -- the unification of China. At that time the country was divided into a certain number of provinces governed independently by warlords, who were continually at war with each other to extend their dominions.

In the years following the First World War, a Chinese Communist Party had been established around Chen Tu-hsiu[5], a

---

[4] The Chinese nationalist party. In pinyin, Guómíndǎng.
[5] In pinyin, Chén Dúxiù (1879 –1942). He was a leading figure in the anti-imperial Xinhai Revolution and the May Fourth Movement for Science and

Peking professor who had been active in revolutionary struggles in China since about 1910. The young Chinese CP lacked experience of any kind, and it was the leadership of the Communist International that bore complete responsibility for the CCP's policies during that period. The Soviet bureaucracy, the political expression of which was Stalinism, was hostile to the development of an autonomous revolutionary struggle by the proletariat and poor peasants, in whom the Stalinists had no confidence. To serve the needs of its nationalist policy, the bureaucracy favoured a policy of alliance with the Chinese bourgeoisie. In order to justify such a class-collaborationist policy, the Stalin-Bukharin leadership elaborated the theory of a 'bloc of four classes' for China (a combination of workers, peasants, intellectuals, and capitalists -- the last-named being considered 'progressive' in a colonial or semi-colonial country), developed the concept of two-class worker and peasant parties, and the necessity for a 'revolution by stages' with the 'democratic dictatorship of workers and peasants' as an intermediate stage between capitalism and the dictatorship of the proletariat.

Put into practice, this policy of class collaboration resulted in an order to the Chinese Communist Party to enter the Kuomintang. The Chinese CP thus renounced an independent policy and, in particular, opposed the creation of soviets during the ascending period of the revolution; it was also opposed to the development of the agrarian revolution, so that the landholdings of Kuomintang army officers could remain intact. For months and months the Communist International and its sections praised the Kuomintang leaders to the skies as allies of the proletariat and champions of the anti-imperialist struggle. The head of the Kuomintang armies, Chiang Kai-shek, was particularly singled out for praise, being depicted as the 'hero' of the Chinese revolution (see *l'Humanite,* late 1926, early 1927).

As the Kuomintang armies neared Shanghai in their march from the commercial South to the North, the workers rose up and seized the city. Their class instinct led them to refuse Chiang Kai-shek's troops entry into Shanghai. But, on orders from the Communist International, the Chinese Communists prevailed upon the workers to allow Chiang Kai-shek and his soldiers to enter the most industrialised centre of China. No sooner was he installed than Chiang Kai-shek set about the wholesale slaughter of the Communist movement of China.

Democracy. Along with Li Dazhao, Chen was a co-founder of the Chinese Communist Party in 1921. He was its first Chairman and General Secretary.

A little later the Chinese Communists, still under orders from the Stalinist leadership of the Third International, resumed the same policy of collaboration with a wing of the Kuomintang, the 'left Kuomintang' led by Wang Ching-wei, with the same result. When Chen Tu-hsiu, secretary of the Chinese CP, joined the Left Opposition, he revealed that Borodin, a representative of the Communist International, had declared that 'the worker must be the coolie of the Kuomintang'.

The Bolshevik-Leninist faction in the USSR conducted a struggle of increasing intensity against the Stalinist policies in China; the peak of this struggle coincided with the peak of the entire struggle by the Soviet Bolshevik-Leninists against Stalinism.

Permanent revolution vs. socialism in one country

The three principal questions on which the struggle of the Left Opposition in the USSR was based can, on the theoretical level, be subsumed into one single question: the struggle for permanent revolution against the theory of 'socialism in one country'; the struggle for maintaining a policy of world proletarian revolution against the nationalist, reactionary policy of the Soviet bureaucracy. This fight, begun in 1923, had nothing to do with a power struggle between individuals -- as some people, obviously incapable of any political insight whatsoever, still think; nor did it have anything to do with a struggle between two revolutionary schools of thought with divergent views on the strategy to follow for the victory of world socialism -- as certain bourgeois political leaders and journalists still write, whether through ignorance or through their desire to depict Stalinism as a revolutionary bogeyman. This fight was, primarily and above all, *a struggle between two political formations representing two different social groups.* The Left Opposition consciously represented the fundamental historical interests of the world proletariat; the Stalinist faction represented the interests of the party and state bureaucracy, anxious to stabilise, consolidate, and, subsequently, increase its privileges. Inasmuch as the leaders of that faction had come out of the Bolshevik Party, for most of them the slide did not take place on a conscious level -- in the beginning, at any rate. But they became prisoners of the social layers whose political spokespersons they were, and in a few years this faction became the most conscious, and the most dangerous, counter-revolutionary force *inside* the working class movement.

THE LONG MARCH OF THE TROTSKYISTS

The climax of the struggle in the USSR occurred on the tenth anniversary of the October Revolution, in November 1927, when the Oppositionists participated in the official Moscow and Leningrad demonstrations under their own slogans, with their own banners and placards against the kulak, the Nepman, and the bureaucrat. For months the Stalinist faction had been accumulating frame-up charges against the Opposition, which had been reduced to clandestine activity. The former had especially sought to plant provocateurs inside the organisation. To avoid being quietly disposed of, it was necessary to take political action out in the open. The tenth anniversary served as a pretext for the Stalinist faction to consummate the split in the party and exile the Bolshevik-Leninist militants to Siberia. [6]

In the following year, the Left Opposition in the Soviet Union continued its struggle in an organised fashion; its centre was set up by Trotsky, in exile in Alma Ata. That was why Stalin decided to expel him from the Soviet Union.

After 1929, the Trotskyist Opposition in the USSR, our mother section, found itself more and more cut off from its principal leader, Leon Trotsky; as a result, the organisational axis of our movement shifted. From that time on we had but little information about our faction, which was subsequently crushed by the Stalinist repression.

Some information about the political life of Opposition leaders in the Verchne-Uralsk 'isolator', long before the Moscow trials, can be found in Anton Ciliga's *Au pays du grand mensonge* (In the Country of the Big Lie). This information, however, must be taken with reservations -- considering that it comes from a man who broke with Bolshevism and passed into the camp of petty-bourgeois liberalism.

The most important document of the Bolshevik-Leninist Opposition in the USSR for the period under discussion is *The Platform of the Left Opposition* (1927), drawn up in agreement with the Zinovievists (whose first capitulation took place right after the Fifteenth Congress of the Bolshevik Party).

One more word about our faction in the USSR: its leading elements included not only old Bolsheviks whose names are well known for their role in the October Revolution, but also an entire group of young cadres trained during the years of the Revolution and civil war, some of whom were well-developed Marxists who never for one moment capitulated. To be cut off from them was a great Loss to our movement.

---

[6] Ten years later, during the Moscow trials, Stalin for the first time made the claim that an attempt at 'insurrection' had been involved.

Chapter 3: From 1929 to 1933. Formation of the International Left Opposition

The years 1929-33 marked the greatest economic crisis in the history of capitalism. Tens of millions of people were thrown out of work -- or never even got a job after leaving school. The social crisis thus brought on ended not in a gain for socialism but in the victory of fascism in Germany. Colonial revolts and revolutions were on the increase; the Chinese Communists set out on their 'long march '. In the Soviet Union the period of the five-year plans began under the leadership of Stalin, who succeeded in strangling the Bolshevik Party. In this period, despite their policy of class collaboration (the theory of the 'lesser evil'), the Socialist parties were generally not in government. The Communist parties followed an ultra-left sectarian policy (the 'third period'). The combination of the two policies -- Socialist and Communist -- paralysed the proletariat.

Stalin expelled Trotsky from the Soviet Union early in 1929. Even at that time he would have got rid of Trotsky in a more permanent way, except that -- as Zinoviev and Kamenev revealed after the troika broke up -- he feared an assassination might boomerang against him; his position was still far from secure, while Trotsky still had considerable authority in the USSR. Inside the USSR itself, Trotsky would never have discontinued his activity. He had refused to make an agreement to that effect when Stalin had demanded it. It was after this refusal that Stalin saw only one solution -- to forbid any relationship, any contact, between Trotsky and the USSR. That was the purpose Trotsky's exile was intended to serve. Let us not forget that in the past Stalin had considered the pre-1917 revolutionary emigration as something of little importance. Later Stalin was to admit that he had made a mistake in exiling Trotsky. It was probably from that moment on that Stalin started the preparations for Trotsky's assassination.

Upon his arrival in Turkey, Trotsky set himself the task of creating an international Bolshevik-Leninist faction to fight against the disintegration of the international revolutionary movement. As early as 1924, centrifugal currents had been appearing in the Communist International and in most of its sections, but, except in the USSR, practically no group (apart perhaps from the Bordigists in

Italy) had developed distinct political positions of its own -- its own well-rounded programme. On the contrary, during the 1924-29 period a series of numerically tiny groups had been formed, generally without solid ties to the working class, quarrelling amongst themselves, and without any real political cohesiveness. This can very well be explained by the fact that the Communist parties had arisen from currents of very diverse origin in the working class movement, and there had not been enough time before the onset of the degeneration to re-educate and unify these parties on the basis of the theoretical, political, and organisational experience of Bolshevism. As soon as the ebb in the revolutionary movement appeared, as soon as the impact of the Bolshevik Party's degeneration was felt in the Communist International, reactions on the most diverse political bases occurred amongst those who avoided getting caught up in the Stalinist corruption. Thus in France, between 1924 and 1929, half-a-dozen different oppositions appeared, all of them very heterogeneous.

Immediately upon his arrival in Turkey, Trotsky addressed a letter to all of the groups and individuals who found themselves in opposition to Stalinist policy. Signed 'Gurov', the letter projected an international regroupment and asked each of them what their positions were on the three basic questions: the USSR, the Anglo-Russian Committee, and the Chinese revolution. In this letter and in other documents that followed shortly thereafter, *Trotsky distinguished three fundamental currents in the Communist International* around which the different groups were, or would be, gathered -- in a more or less clear-cut fashion:

(a) The Left Opposition, which defended the fundamental political and organisational policies of Leninism advocated by the Bolshevik-Leninists in the Soviet Union.

(b) The right opposition, oriented by the right wing of the Bolshevik Party (Bukharin) and composed of groups opposed to Stalinism, not because of its fundamental policy, not on the question of 'socialism in one country', but more particularly because of its 'ultra-left' errors. These groups, the most important of which was that of Brandler in Germany, each tried to have an independent national policy, with the result that they found themselves moving towards the social-democratic left.

(c) In the centre, *the Stalinist faction*, the bureaucratic wing in the service of the Kremlin.

In his letters, Trotsky also specified that the problem of the internal regime of the party, no matter how important it was, nevertheless had to be considered subordinate to fundamental political problems, and *there could be no question of entering into a bloc with the right* (Brandlerites) because, while we had the same criticism of the party regime that they did, there was complete and total disagreement between us and them on the essential political problems, on the general political orientation.

The 1929-33 period of our international movement was essentially a period of *principled delimitation and formation of cadres*. That was the period in which a large number of our sections were formed and in the course of which we learned, if such an expression can be used, to 'talk Trotskyist'. It was during this period in France that the group which published *La Vérité* (The Truth) was established (September 1929) and organised the Ligue Communiste (Communist League) in 1930. It was in April 1930 in Paris that the first International Conference of Bolshevik-Leninists took place, which was to give birth to an international centre, very weak at the time, that would become the International Secretariat. The development of our movement led to the Copenhagen Conference of 1932, attended by Trotsky, and to a 1933 conference that adopted the 'eleven points' summarising our basic programme. Let us take a look at the principal problems confronting the Trotskyist movement at that time.

Defence of the USSR

Beginning in 1929, the opponents of Stalinism were faced with the problem of *defence of the Soviet Union,* occasioned by incidents that occurred during the summer of 1929 on the East China railroad.

At that time, the Trans-Siberian Railway included a section that passed through Chinese territory.[7] Agreements did exist between the USSR and China on the management of the railroad on Chinese territory. These agreements had been established by the two countries on an equal footing, after Lenin's government had voluntarily repudiated all treaties concluded by Tsarism that were of the 'unequal treaty' type between the imperialist powers and China. After the victory of the counter-revolution in China, Chiang Kai-shek wanted forcibly to expel the Soviet managers of that part of the railroad. From the strategic point of view, that constituted a great danger for the USSR, since the Pacific port of Vladivostok would thus be cut off from all of Siberia. In answer to Chiang, the Soviet government sent the Red Army to enforce the rights of the Soviet state, at which point denunciations of 'Soviet imperialism', and other arguments we have often heard since, took place among a number of opponents of Stalinism. It was more or less at this time that Hugo

---

[7] Since then, a line has been built that goes only through Soviet territory.

Urbahns, leader of the Hamburg insurrection of 1923, began to expound theories on the existence of 'state capitalism' in the USSR.[8] It was at this time that Trotsky wrote *The Defence of the Soviet Union and the Left Opposition,* the first fairly complete examination of a question that was to be raised many times thereafter.

In this pamphlet Trotsky defines the class nature of the Soviet state, product of the October Revolution. The aim of any war against the USSR would be to destroy the bases of the society (collective ownership of the means of production, etc.) rather than its repressive regime. The defeat of the USSR would also bring in its wake colonisation of the country by imperialism, which would thus be assured a new lease of life. This defeat would result in profound demoralisation of the masses throughout the entire world. But defence of the Soviet Union does not at all consist in accepting or supporting Stalin's policy. On the contrary, the latter is one of the greatest dangers threatening the USSR -- Stalin hunting around the world for 'allies', to the detriment of the world revolution. This policy must be bitterly denounced, even in time of war. 'For the defence of the Soviet Union, always! For the defence of Stalinism, never!' *The only real defence of the Soviet Union in the event of world conflict is the revolutionary struggle of the international proletariat in all the capitalist countries, 'allies' or not of the USSR.*

The united front against the Hitler danger

The main struggle waged by the Left Opposition from 1930 on was the struggle for the *united front in Germany* against the rise of fascism. The Left Opposition's policy was radically opposed to the Stalinist policy of the 'third period', which can be summarised as follows: capitalism has entered a period of final crisis; *consequently* (by virtue of Stalinist logic), the entire bourgeoisie is turning fascist, and along with it its party in the working class, the social-democratic party, which is becoming a social-fascist party; *consequently,* the danger of war against the USSR is becoming imminent; and *consequently* the masses are becoming radicalised, placing on the agenda general strikes, revolutionary days, leading to armed insurrection. The political consequence of this 'logic', of this theory of 'social fascism', was that there could be no possible question of entering a united front with a social-fascist party; on the contrary, it

---

[8] The theory of 'state capitalism' was really not new. It had been created right after the October Revolution by Social Democrats like Otto Bauer. Karl Kautsky, etc.

was necessary to fight this social-fascist party, to cut right through it, in order to get at the bourgeoisie and at fascism, the 'twin of social fascism'.

This international policy of Stalinism had its most dreadful repercussions and its most horrible results in Germany, where the workers, faced with the Hitlerite gangs, found themselves divided. Still worse, in certain cases (the plebiscite in Prussia) the Stalinists voted together with the Nazis against the Social Democrats. Another fact: following the assassination of some thirty Berlin workers on 1 May 1929 by police led by the Social Democratic prefect Zoergiebel, the Communist Party declared that all Social Democrats were also Zoergiebels who had to be struck down. Children of Social Democrats were then 'little Zoergiebels', and the order was given to Communist children's organisations to beat up Social Democratic children at school. Shortly before Hitler came to power, members of the German CP and the Nazis had common picket lines during the strike of the Berlin public transport system, which was run by a Social Democratic municipality. This 'third period' policy created a rift between Social Democratic workers and Communist workers and rendered the German proletariat helpless in the face of the rise of the Nazis.

The Left Opposition led an international struggle against the line of 'social fascism' and in favour of a united front of the German Communist and Social Democratic parties in order to stop Hitler. That campaign was based on a series of pamphlets by Trotsky: *What Next?*, *The Only Road*, *Letter to a German Communist Worker*, *Germany: The Key to the international Situation*. The development of the situation and our intervention led the Stalinists, who had wanted to avoid the issue, to take a position on the Nazi danger. In France the CP leadership called an information conference of the Paris region, at which the then secretary, Semard, branded the German question 'the Trotskyite hobbyhorse'. A public meeting of the CP at Bullier Hall was the scene of violent fist-fights between Stalinists and Trotskyists.

Later, forced to respond to the workers' anxiety about the fascist threat, as well as to serve the Kremlin's diplomatic manoeuvring between the democratic countries and Hitlerite Germany, the Communist International organised the 'Amsterdam Committees' for the fight against fascism. It was one of the first experiments with a 'mass'-type organisation controlled by the Stalinists. Our organisation 'participated' in these Amsterdam and Paris (Pleyel Hall) Congresses in order to expose them as subterfuges. They were just that -- on many counts. The Stalinists separated the fight against war and fascism from the revolutionary struggle for power.9 In that way, they spread the idea that the rise of fascism could be stopped and imperialist war prevented *within the capitalist system*. Even at that time the policy of 'peaceful coexistence' was already taking its toll. This policy was not invented by Khrushchev, as many bourgeois, social-democratic and pro-Chinese observers pretend. In the *Criticism of the Programme of the Communist International*, written by Trotsky in 1928, there is a denunciation of this policy of 'peaceful coexistence'. The differences between Khrushchev and Stalin related not to the basis of this policy -- that is, obtaining a global agreement with the capitalists in order that the Soviet Union might quietly build 'socialism in one country' but to the different conditions under which they attempted to implement this policy. In both cases the interests of the revolutionary struggles of the masses were subordinated and even sacrificed to the needs of the Kremlin's diplomacy. It must be noted that the same leaders of the Chinese CP who so strongly denounced this policy when carried out by the Soviet leaders are, for the same reasons of 'socialism in one country', now proceeding along the same lines with regard to Chile, Iran, Sri Lanka, Sudan, etc.

Under the banner of Leninism and the October Revolution, Stalinism reintroduced social-democratic and opportunistic ideas. The door was opened to collaboration with the 'anti-fascist' bourgeoisie or bourgeois 'friends of peace', and the Kremlin took its first steps on the road to the Popular Front in France and Spain. In their attempts to build 'mass'-type class collaborationist bodies like the 'Amsterdam Committees', the bureaucracy perpetrated a massive confusion in the working class. They claimed they were building a united front through this method of organisation, whereas they were in fact only regrouping people who had accepted their leadership in advance. Thus did they distort -- in the minds of revolutionary workers and in the masses -- the concept of a united front among working class organisations.

Fight to reform the Communist International

As we said, a great number of our sections originated in this period, which was also marked by numerous internal crises in our movement. Since there were no large-scale workers' struggles taking place in many countries and since our movement did not have much

---

9 It is obvious that a revolutionary party must conduct specific campaigns and actions against fascism and imperialist war, but these actions must be anti-capitalist in character.

of a mass base, personal aspects of our internal discussions often assumed undue importance. But the personal elements of these fights were closely bound to, were grafted onto, political and organisational problems. All these crises were *phases of the struggle to establish connections with the masses and to build revolutionary leaderships.* Only philistines, only centrists, can sneer at these fights instead of trying to understand them. In this period, an attempt at collaborating with the Bordigists, in the same international organisation, proved fruitless. The Copenhagen Conference registered the impossibility of our being in the same movement, under the given circumstances.

During this entire period, we were opposed to building a new International and new revolutionary parties. *The essence of our political line was to struggle to reform, to regenerate, the Communist International and its sections.* Although expelled, we considered ourselves a faction of the Communist International and of the Communist parties, a faction struggling to put these organisations back on the correct revolutionary road. In that period we came up against tendencies that wanted to form a new International, that said there was no longer anything that could be done with the Communist International and its sections. Our answer was that our attitude towards working class organisations could not be dictated by subjective considerations such as our expulsion, nor even solely by the policy followed by the leadership of those organisations. The birth and continued existence of revolutionary parties and of a revolutionary International correspond to a historical situation, to given objective conditions that cannot arbitrarily be dismissed with a few strokes of the pen. The Communist International and its sections had at their command the historic capital rising out of their origin, their connection with the Russian Revolution, their years of struggle in working class movements. These organisations had deep roots in the masses. Stalinism was squandering the historic capital of the Third International, but only great historic events could show whether it was definitively finished, doomed from a revolutionary point of view, despite our efforts to regenerate it.

From 1923 on, we had seen the Left Opposition in the Communist parties grow, with (and by means of) every revolutionary upsurge of the workers. We had no grounds for saying that the bureaucratisation of these parties was irreversible. It should not be forgotten that the CPs of that era, although already led by Stalinists, were quite different from the political machines of today. They were still revolutionary formations. Finally, in our struggle against the policies of the 'third period', we had warned that a defeat of the German proletariat and a victory for Hitler could constitute precisely the historic event likely to change our course with regard to the Communist International. We must bear in mind the world situation at that time. The European working class constituted the majority of the world working class; the colonial movements had only just begun.

For Trotskyists, the International cannot be an arbitrarily created organisation; it must be the concretisation, the embodiment of all the principles of revolutionary Marxism and of the vanguard of a historical epoch. The First International marked the epoch when the working class movement for the first time disengaged itself from bourgeois and petty-bourgeois republican currents and organised itself independently on a class basis, even if it lacked clarity on a theoretical level. The Second International before 1914 marked the epoch of capitalist ascendancy and the expansion of bourgeois democracy in various countries, in which the working class movement in these countries organised itself in mass parties and mass trade unions. In this epoch Marxism became the dominant political current in the working class movement.

The Third International -- in its first five years, the only ones when it was truly the Communist International -- marked the epoch of the October victory, the first assaults of the socialist revolution in the whole world. As long as the Third International contained revolutionary forces potentially capable of throwing off the bureaucratic yoke and regenerating it, the Trotskyist opposition was totally hostile to the building of another pole. It considered that to do so would be to divert and dissipate revolutionary forces in a project divorced from what was still the international centre of the socialist revolution. But when the German proletariat was defeated by Nazism, when the Communist International unhesitatingly underwrote Stalin's policy -- which bore such a heavy responsibility for this defeat -- then it became useless to attempt to revive a body which had been shown to be lifeless. The epoch had arrived for a new revolutionary International. How long its gestation would last could not be predicted. But in any case it was necessary to start work immediately.

It should be noted that later on, when we turned towards the construction of a Fourth International and new revolutionary parties, practically none of the people who had condemned our policy of reforming the Third International and had taken a position against us in favour of creating a Fourth International practically none of these people joined us in this task. Most of them continued to form ultra-left groupings. This proves that there were much deeper differences between us and those who criticised us at that time than the possible reform of the Communist International. Actually, these divergences stemmed from totally different concepts of the party and its relationship to the working class.

Chapter 4: From 1933 to 1938. Preparing for the Fourth International

A slight economic recovery occurred from 1933 to 1938, due largely to preparations for a new world war. The spread of fascism in Europe was barely held in check by the mass movements in France (June 1936) and in Spain, where fascism unleashed a civil war that was to end in tragedy for the working masses. In the Far East, Japan embarked on what was to prove a hopeless war against China. In the Soviet Union, execution of the five-year plans was accompanied by a monstrous lowering of the standard of living and suppression of the rights of the working masses, by the extermination of the Bolshevik cadres and the entire revolutionary vanguard. The dissension of the previous years between Socialist and Communist parties was replaced by a policy of 'unity' in order to build 'popular fronts'. This class collaboration with sections of the bourgeoisie had results as disastrous for the cause of socialism as those of the preceding period.

The economic crisis of 1929 had important political consequences, beginning in 1932-33. At the end of 1932, Franklin D. Roosevelt became president of the United States. In an effort to revive the economy, he inaugurated the New Deal, which proved favourable to development of the trade union movement in the United States -- in a proletariat hitherto under the sway of craft unionism, where workers in the huge plants had not been organised. The rise of the Congress of Industrial Organisations (CIO) would take care of that. But aside from the United States, this change had no immediate repercussions, the American proletariat's big step forward on the political level still remaining to be taken. No doubt this will be the result of the next great crisis, which in the United States will not necessarily be exclusively economic in origin.

Hitler came to power in Germany early in 1933 as a result of the combination of the policies of the two working class leaderships, reformist and Stalinist. For different reasons and in different ways, both were opposed to united action by the workers. Both engendered inertia, passivity, and lack of resistance in the German proletariat as a whole, in face of the growing Nazi movement. Both acted like competing shopkeepers and placed their interests as opposing cliques above the interests of the class they claimed to represent.

A turn in our general orientation took place when Hitler came to power. We abandoned the struggle to reform the Third International and set our sights on building a Fourth International and new revolutionary parties. This decision was not taken in one stroke. We began in the early months of 1933 by abandoning the struggle to reform the German CP, because it was obvious that a party which had failed in so serious a situation was historically doomed. (See Trotsky's article,'The German Workers Will Rise Again -- Stalinism, Never!') We were waiting to learn the reactions in the other CPs and in the Communist International. These reactions were negligible, and the Executive Committee of the Communist International unanimously approved a report by Heckert endorsing the whole previous Stalinist policy in Germany -- even though, in their heart of hearts, most of the leaderships of the CPs were hostile to these policies. Stalinism had definitively triumphed in the Communist International. As the revolutionary International of the proletariat, the Comintern was dead.

Following this vote of the ECCI, an International Plenum of our movement during the summer of 1933 almost unanimously decided on the change in our international orientation. Until then we had spoken in terms of reforming the Communist International, reforming the Bolshevik Party, and reforming the Soviet state, without always making a distinction among them in our statements. The orientation towards building new revolutionary parties and, by extension, a new party in the USSR, called for a clarification of our position vis-a-vis the Soviet state. At that time we made a careful distinction between reforming the Bolshevik Party, henceforth an impossibility, and the still possible reform of the Soviet state, which remained a proletarian state. Later, in 1935, our point of view developed on this question too, and led to our affirming the necessity of a political revolution in the USSR as a degenerated workers state -- a political, not a social, revolution, because what was needed was not a fundamental change in the Soviet Union's production relations but the destruction of the omnipotence of the bureaucracy and the re-establishment of workers democracy.

We were dealing with a country where property relations were different from those of a capitalist country and corresponded to those of a transitional society towards socialism (collectivisation of the means of production, monopoly of foreign trade, planned economy), but where the working class and the toiling masses were deprived of power and of all democratic rights which could enable them to reform and correct the situation. Trotsky reminded us of the history of bourgeois revolutions, recalling particularly that in spite of all that the great French Revolution had achieved, two more revolutions -- in 1830 and 1848 -- were needed to complete this revolution from the bourgeois point of view. He thought that the October Revolution too would need to be completed by a revolution which would aim not to change the basic property relations but to re-establish socialist democracy in the workers state.

'The revolution which the bureaucracy is preparing against itself will not be social, like the October revolution of 1917. It is not a question this time of changing the economic foundations of society, of replacing certain forms of property with other forms. History has known elsewhere not only social revolutions which substituted the bourgeois for the feudal regime, but also political revolutions which, without destroying the economic foundations of society, swept out an old ruling upper crust (1830 and 1848 in France, February 1917 in Russia, etc.). The overthrow of the Bonapartist caste will, of course, have deep social consequences, but in itself it will be confined within the limits of political revolution... The proletariat of a backward country was fated to accomplish the first socialist revolution. For this historic privilege, it must, according to all evidences, pay with a second supplementary revolution -- against bureaucratic absolutism.' (Trotsky, *Revolution Betrayed*, Chapter IX)

Trotsky's idea of a new, political revolution in the Soviet Union remained for long a purely theoretical notion, specific to the Trotskyist movement. With the international crisis of Stalinism, however, this notion has passed from the realm of theory and has begun to be outlined in reality. Thus others as well as Trotskyists have adopted it, although often in a confused fashion.

The preceding period of our history had been chiefly characterised by the grounding of our movement in the bedrock of principle. In the new period, we added to it a large measure of *organisational flexibility*. At the time of our struggle to reform the Third International, we assiduously separated ourselves from all currents that had an equivocal attitude, no matter how tiny, on this question of reform. But declaring that the Third International was no longer capable of being reformed meant placing on record an enormous setback to revolutionary consciousness, and it was not possible to tell in advance what a new International and new revolutionary parties would be and in what ways they would be established. Certainly we intended to try to gain acceptance for our programme, as being the most complete expression of the proletariat's experience to date; but we could not foresee how we would reach this goal, i.e. what organisational paths the construction of revolutionary parties would follow. Nor could we foresee what the evolution of our relationships with other revolutionary currents in the working class movement would be. Two experiments were made in this regard -- one limited in scope, the other much larger.

The 'Declaration of the Four'

From July-August of 1933, the question of regroupment of the revolutionary forces was placed before us in concrete form following the calling by the British ILP (Independent Labour Party) of a conference open to all organisations outside the Second and Third Internationals, for the purpose of examining the world situation and the situation of the labour movement in light of the Nazi victory. We decided to participate in this conference to make our position known and to try to get together all the organisations that were willing to promulgate -- to the working class of the world the need for a Fourth International. This participation was somewhat similar to that of the Bolsheviks, in other circumstances, at Zimmerwald and Kienthal. The result was the 'Declaration of the Four' -- a document signed by our international organisation, the League of Internationalist Communists; by the German SAP (Sozialistische Arbeiterpartei -- Socialist Workers Party); and by two Dutch organisations, the RSP (Revolutionair-Socialistische Partij -- Revolutionary Socialist Party) and the OSP (Onafhankelijke Socialistische Partij -- Independent Socialist Party).

The SAP consisted of some of the left socialists who, critical of its reformist line, had broken with German Social Democracy in 1931-32. Shortly before Hitler came to power, leadership of the SAP passed into the hands of Walcher and Frölich, two former leaders of the Communist right opposition (Brandlerites) who had broken with the latter to join the SAP. The Dutch OSP corresponded in origin to the German SAP. The RSP was led by Henricus Sneevliet, a Communist leader for many years, who had come into conflict with the Communist International over trade union policy in Holland, where he was an official of the NAS (Nationaal Arbeiders Syndikaat -- National Workers Union), a labour federation that included Communists and anarcho-syndicalists. In his struggle against the latter, Sneevliet had been led to organise his union faction into a political party.

The 'Declaration of the Four' proclaimed the need for a new International, for new revolutionary parties, and defined the main points on which they should be built. While it did not set forth our whole programme, the Declaration did contain our essential points. On a world scale the results of the 'Declaration of the Four' were minimal. In Holland, nevertheless, the two organisations held common rallies, and then merged to form the RSAP (Revolutionair-Socialistische Arbeiderspartij -- Revolutionary Socialist Workers Party). Later this party joined our movement, then split with us during the Spanish revolution, when it supported the POUM (Partido Obrero de Unificacion Marxista -- Workers Party of Marxist Unification). The opposition to this line in the RSAP was based on the youth, led by Sal Santen. During the war, it was these youth who organised the Dutch section of the Fourth International. Sneevliet, who led the RSAP and who broke with the movement for the Fourth International on the question of the war in Spain, nevertheless remained extremely close to us. He died a hero during the war, shot by the Nazis.

As for the leaders of the German SAP who lived in exile, they behaved like inveterate centrists. Shortly after having signed the 'Declaration of the Four', they became the bitterest enemies of Trotskyism and were at the bottom of all the centrist groupings (the London Bureau, etc.) that spread indescribable confusion among the vanguard in the period preceding the Second World War. After the war, Walcher became a functionary in East Germany; Frölich, on the other hand, was a sympathiser of our movement.

The first draft of a transitional programme

Before going into the second experiment, by far the more important in building the revolutionary party, a few words should be said on the political situation resulting from Hitler's accession to power. The Nazi victory cut off the prospect of revolution in Germany for an entire period. Throughout the rest of Europe, reaction was sharply on the rise, but not without resistance. In Austria, where the working class was completely under the influence of the Social Democracy, the clerical reaction, led by Dollfuss, propelled the workers into armed struggle under Social Democratic leadership, and they fought for one week in February 1934. The crushing of the Austrian proletariat by Dollfuss opened the way to the Nazi victory in Austria -- the fascists took power after killing Dollfuss and eliminating his party.

THE LONG MARCH OF THE TROTSKYISTS

The centre of the European working class movement shifted to France after 1933. Hitler's victory upset the equilibrium established in Europe at Versailles in 1918; this, in turn, laid bare the most formidable crisis in government that France had ever experienced -- a crisis that continues to this day. For the first time, it was apparent to all that France was no longer a first-rate power. To re-establish its position, or rather to maintain it, French capitalism had no other recourse but to lower the standard of living of the masses -- which could only be done by inaugurating a 'strong state'. French capitalism tried to get rid of parliamentary forms by means of the reactionary coup of 6 February 1934. But from the point of view of the bourgeoisie, the blow was struck prematurely. The French working class, literally whipped into action by this blow, awoke to the fascist danger, and there was a great deal of political tension in the country as a result.

Against the growing fascist danger, we advocated a *united front of working class organisations* in France. But to implement this, a *programme of action* was needed on the basis of which the working masses could mobilise to extricate themselves from the situation into which capitalism had plunged them. It was in that spring of 1934 that the first Bolshevik-Leninist programme of action was drawn up with Trotsky's collaboration. This document is of interest mainly because it constitutes the very first draft of a transitional programme. The following year, the Belgian comrades drew up a similar programme (against the decree laws in their country), and comrades in other countries followed suit. Thus the *Transitional Programme* adopted in 1938 by the founding congress of the International, far from being an improvisation, was the fruit of various earlier experiences in the different sections of the International.

As we have said, the French Trotskyist organisation, the Ligue Communiste, waged a systematic campaign for the united front. In the week following 6 February, a united front was established between the Ligue and the Seine Federation of the Socialist Party, which was under the influence of Marceau Pivert. Mass pressure for united action intensified after February 1934. In July of the same year, the Socialist and Stalinist leaderships, forced to respond to the pressure from below, signed a pact for unity in action. This pact did not rest on any concrete revolutionary policy; but the very fact that the two leaderships, who had fought each other so violently for so many years, called on the working class to counterpose a common front to the fascist gangs aroused enormous enthusiasm in the masses.

This pact had another result that concerned us. At the very moment that our campaign for an SP-CP united front was to a certain extent successful, paradoxically enough the consequences of this victory were unfavourable for our organisation. All the sympathetic response we had met with, partly in the CP and much more in the SFIO,[10] which had recruited a substantial number of workers, often former CP members -- all this sympathetic response was lost to us. This was not due to hostility, but rather to a lack of political clarity on the concept of a revolutionary party and the need for such a party -- especially in the united front and to the very strong attraction exercised by the CP-SP united front. Our meetings were no longer attended; our organisation became very much isolated, as it had been before. Inevitably, a crisis developed. We searched for a way out of this isolation; for a way to establish connections with, and links to, a mass movement the likes of which had never before been seen in France and which was growing larger with each passing day; for a way to be with the masses in action.

'Entryism '

Our second big organisational experiment, aimed at building a revolutionary party, took place at this point. In our efforts to move towards a stronger organisation, we were to pass through a stage in which the Trotskyist group would temporarily lose its organisational independence by entering a mass working class party. Trotsky himself raised the question of the Ligue Communiste entering the SFIO. The move was decided on in September-October of 1934. This policy, called *entryism,* was subsequently extended to other countries. At first it aroused a great deal of disagreement within our international organisation, even causing splits. It was with a great deal of resistance that the October 1934 International Plenum ratified the policy of the French Trotskyists' entering the SFIO. Since then the majority of the organisation has considered this tactic admissible.

For an entire initial period, the activity of the Bolshevik-Leninist Group[11] in the SFIO was conducted with remarkable political clarity. This attracted numerous young people, particularly the whole Jeunesses Socialistes (Socialist Youth) tendency, organised under the name Jeunesses Socialistes Revolutionnaires (Revolutionary Socialist Youth), into the organisation's ranks, thus renewing its membership.

---

[10] 'Section Francaise de l'Internationale Ouvritre -- French Section of the Second International, official name of the Socialist Party.
[11] The name adopted by the Trotskyist organisation when it joined the Socialist Party.

On the other hand, our exit from the SFIO while the Popular Front was being organised took place under very unfortunate circumstances, and the split among the Bolshevik-Leninists occurring at that time caused us to lose part of the benefits obtained from our entry.

In other countries, notably Belgium and the United States, entryism had better results. In Belgium, where the organisation had a working class base in the Charleroi Basin, it acquired a strong mass base in the Borinage. In the United States, the Socialist Party never recovered from the blow it suffered when the Trotskyists left.

On the contrary, Nin and Andrade in Spain, who had opposed the entry of the French Trotskyists into the SFIO, did not delay in uniting -- on an incorrect programmatic basis -- with the Worker-Peasant Bloc in Catalonia, thus forming the inveterately centrist POUM.

The rise of fascism and the war

On an international scale, this entire period was dominated by the rise of fascism and the approach of the new imperialist war, despite high peaks of workers' struggles, notably the movements of June 1936 in France and a few other countries, and the civil war in Spain. In the course of this period, three large struggles dominated the activity of our international movement:

1. The struggle against the Popular Front policy, with especial reference to Spain and France. With a tenacity born of desperation, our organisations fought the class collaborationist policy by means of which Stalinists and social-democrats -- this time united, not divided -- prepared the worst of catastrophes for the working class movement. The Popular Front constituted the first big period of class collaboration for the Stalinists. On that occasion, however, they were not (except in a very limited fashion in Spain) seeking ministerial posts. This came later, and became widespread in another period of class collaboration by the Stalinists -- the period following the close of World War II.

The united front and the Popular Front incorporate two very opposite conceptions. Since the Third Congress of the Communist International in 1921, the united front has meant the unity in action of big working class organisations to achieve more or less extended common aims. Before 1933 the Trotskyists advocated the united front between the CP and the Social Democrats in Germany against the rise of Nazism. The united front of the mass organisations of the working class is a generally positive fact -- if, however, the revolutionary yeast can act in it. This is never the case with the Popular Front, which is a political combination -- a bloc of working class reformist parties with wings of the bourgeoisie. In these cases the bloc is realised on a bourgeois programme, a class collaborationist programme.

The Stalinists justify such a line by pretending that the working class must not isolate itself from the petty bourgeoisie, that it must not frighten it by socialist demands and aims, by the use of force, etc. The aim of the Popular Front policy, according to the Stalinist~, is to cajole the petty bourgeoisie, to accustom it to march with the workers parties, and to create a broader and broader 'democracy' finally culminating in socialism.

All these arguments are wrong. One should not identify the petty bourgeoisie with parties -- like the Radical Party in France which are capitalist parties whose electoral base is made up of the petty bourgeoisie. It is not true that the working class becomes more attractive by diluting its programme. It is not true that the Petty bourgeoisie is essentially parliamentarist, electoralist, hostile to force. The example of the Nazis in Germany shows this only too well. The Nazis used the most brutal force and a 'socialist' demagogy, not fearing in the slightest to put the word 'socialist' in the name of their party. The petty bourgeoisie cannot be attracted by sweet words. This social layer has no political stability; it is attracted by those who show strength. Every worker who has been on strike has a clear experience of this. When strikers are determined, small shopkeepers often sympathise with them; when they are hesitant, undecided, the latter immediately turn against them. The Popular Fronts never ceased to be characterised by their hesitations and their softness, owing to the presence and pressure of bourgeois politicians. The working class can only win a section of the middle classes to its side, and neutralise another section, by being strong, decided and determined.

2. *The struggle against centrism.* This struggle was characterised by a denunciation of the policy of the London Bureau and centrist organisations such as the Spanish POUM, the English ILP, the German SAP, and the Norwegian NAP.[12] The struggle against centrism also required entering the PSOP[13] -- an unhappy experience

---

[12] The NAP (Norsk Arbeiderpartiet -- Norwegian Labour Party) was a mass party that broke with the London Bureau and subsequently fulfilled the traditional social-democratic role in Norway.

[13] The PSOP (Parti Socialiste Ouvrier et Paysan -- Workers and Peasants Socialist Party) was formed by the 'revolutionary left' tendency in the SFIO, which Blum expelled when the Popular Front fell apart. The PSOP was led by Marceau Pivert, who joined the 'old house' after the war and became an assiduous anti-Trotskyist.

because of the French Trotskyist movement's state of disintegration at the time.

In Marxist literature, the characterisation 'centrist' is applied to all tendencies or groups that fluctuate between revolutionary Marxism and reformism. Some very diverse organisations are thus included in this category. There have even been some mass organisations of a centrist nature, for example, the Independent Socialist Party of Germany (USPD -- Unabhtingige Sozialistische Partei Deutschlands), which broke with the Social Democracy during the First World War and part of which participated in forming the German Communist Party in 1920.

The struggle against centrism is one of the most difficult and yet essential tasks of revolutionary Marxists. Reformism has an unmistakable shape, and the struggle against it is comparatively easy -- at least with working class militants who do not rely only on day-to-day demands, especially in periods when capitalist contradictions are crudely revealed. Centrism, however, needs more than theoretical denunciations in order to be fought efficiently. To carry out this task requires very great flexibility, because centrism takes the most varied and oscillating forms. It easily adopts a revolutionary vocabulary, mostly adopted from Marxism, but its actions usually fail to correspond with its words. It should not be forgotten that Kautsky's centrism dominated the Second International for twenty years, and it took August 1914 for Lenin himself to grasp it thoroughly. And for many years the Communist parties, before they became completely bogged down in reformism, followed a centrist policy which duped very large sections of the masses.

Centrist currents often go out to win large sections of the masses by offering short cuts, throwing overboard part of the revolutionary Marxist programme. Not to believe in short cuts, to defend the revolutionary Marxist programme as a whole, is regarded as evidence of 'sectarianism' by the centrists. But up to now no victorious revolution has travelled such a road; and, far from having proved the necessity to simplify revolutionary Marxism, the experience has enriched it. This will be even more true for the victory of socialist revolutions in countries with a more developed economy and much more complex social structures. No-one will triumph with a second-hand programme, with leaderships unable to answer the more complex problems raised by revolutions in such countries. It may perhaps be more tempting, in the light of the difficulties encountered by the Trotskyist movement, to set out on a seemingly shorter road with a lighter theoretical and political burden. But all those who have acted thus -- and there have been many of them in half a century --

have come to nothing. They have only hindered the process of building revolutionary parties and disoriented numerous militants, particularly when the weakness of the Trotskyist organisations prevented them from vigorously opposing these centrist experiences.

In the period preceding the Second World War, these small centrist groupings sought to break the masses away from the old parties, without, however, developing a cohesive programme as a basis for a new, revolutionary International (that's what they called the 'sectarianism' of the Trotskyists!). They did not, of course, attain their objective. But they did succeed -- and that was their main activity -- in raising all kinds of obstacles to theoretical and political clarification among the vanguard militants who were disgusted with the old parties and disoriented by a terrible decline in the working class movement. During the Second World War, the London Bureau showed no sign of life. The same held true for the SAP and the PSOP. In England, the ILP was nothing more than an empty husk.

3. The struggle against the Moscow trials was one of physical defence, a struggle, literally, for the very existence of our movement, a struggle against an avalanche of slander, of frame-ups, of widespread brutality and Stalinist crimes against Trotskyist militants, in a whole series of countries outside the Soviet Union. (In France, Leon Sedov, Rudolf Klement; in Spain, Erwin Wolf, Moulin; in Switzerland, Ignace Reiss.)

From 1936 to 1938, three big trials took place in Moscow, in which the role of prosecuting attorney was played by the ex-Menshevik Vishinsky, who became foreign minister after the war. In the first trial, the defendants (Zinoviev, Kamenev, I.N. Smirnov, etc.) 'confessed' to having plotted against Stalin out of *greed for power*. In the second trial, the defendants (among whom were Pyatakov and Yagoda, organiser of the first trial) 'confessed' that they and the defendants in the preceding trial had conspired to *re-establish capitalism* in the Soviet Union. In the third trial, the accused (Bukharin, Rakovsky, etc.) 'confessed' that they all, including those executed following the previous trials, had for a long time been *spies in the service of the (German) Gestapo, the (British) Intelligence Service, the Mikado,* etc. In addition to these 'trials', this period saw the execution, also as plotters, of the most important heads of the Red Army (Tukhachevsky, Gamarnik, Putna, etc.).

In all these trials, the main defendants were Trotsky and his son Leon Sedov. Trotsky was pictured as a counter-revolutionary agent -- from time immemorial! These trials served to prepare the groundwork for the assassination of Trotsky and Leon Sedov and for the liquidation of the Bolshevik Old Guard who, in the difficult period

THE LONG MARCH OF THE TROTSKYISTS

of the war then looming on the horizon, could have become the centre of a revolutionary opposition to the Stalinist faction. Despite our campaigns, despite the irrefutable evidence placed before the Dewey Commission[14] proving that these trials were infamous political machinations, Stalin attained his objectives -- with the seal of approval of representatives of American big business, such as Ambassador John E. Davies.

This period as a whole was characterised by great demoralisation in the vanguard of a working class more and more on the downgrade. For our movement, the most painful example of this was the fragmentation of the French Trotskyists, which reached such a state that at one point the International declared it could no longer accept responsibility for their actions.

*   *   *   *   *

In 1936 an international conference of supporters of the Fourth International was held. Trotsky wanted the birth of the Fourth International announced then and there, but his proposal was not accepted by the conference, which called itself merely 'Movement for the Fourth International'.

---

[14] A commission of socialist-minded and liberal intellectuals formed to investigate the charges against Trotsky made in the Moscow trials of 1936-37. It was headed by John Dewey, the most reputable bourgeois philosopher and educator in the United States, and brought in a not-guilty verdict for Trotsky.

Chapter 5: From 1938 to 1948. From the Founding of the Fourth International to the Second World Congress

Munich 1938 was only a short prelude to a new world war. For six years millions of men were mobilised, shoved into regiments, armed, shipped from continent to continent, and hurled against one another in murderous combat. The contradictions among the capitalist powers prevailed over the contradictions between capitalism as a whole and the Soviet Union, so that at the beginning of the war the Kremlin was allied with Nazi Germany in a pact that would give way, in two years' time, to agreements with the imperialist democracies. This collaboration would contribute to giving the Resistance an ambiguous class character. In the course of the war, mass movements began to get beyond the control of the major powers. Taking advantage of defeats suffered by the metropolitan countries, colonies began to revolt. Towards the end of the war, the Soviet Union had a sphere of influence in East Europe, the social character of which would only be definitively determined in the following period. The Socialist International succeeded in committing suicide at the beginning of the war; the Communist International was dissolved by Stalin in 1943. The old working class parties, Socialist and Communist, tightly regimented during the war, emerged from the conflict with an increasingly right-wing political line.

Founding of the Fourth International and the Transitional Programme

In 1938, with the world darkened by the monstrous shadow of war and fascism, the International Conference met again. The meeting took place at the same time that the temporary capitalist compromise was signed in Munich. Again Trotsky raised the question of founding the Fourth International. It was to this conference that Trotsky submitted the *Transitional Programme* -- which was to serve, for an entire historical period, as the basis for the Fourth

International's activities. The conference also adopted a resolution, 'Class Struggle and the War in the Far East', characterising China's struggle against Japan as a war of national liberation and supporting China in its struggle.

At this conference the objection could ·gain be heard that it was too early to announce the formation of the Fourth International, that such a decision would not be understood by the masses, etc. in short, all the arguments that had led to the unfavourable decision in 1936 were still being used on this occasion.

These objections were similar to those expressed at other moments when decisive steps had to be made by the working class movement. At the time of the break with the Second International and the founding of the Third International, for instance, the objection was raised that there was no mass Communist Party other than the Bolshevik Party which was in government. Against the founding of the Fourth International, the considerable ebb of the working class movement and the absence of Trotskyist organisations with a mass base were invoked as reasons. But what is to be done to transform circumstances in order that they should become favourable and create organisations with a mass base? It is impossible to renounce the programme and the organisation until the objective conditions are transformed in a favourable way. Indeed, these objections only serve to conceal an opposition to the programme and a refusal to fight for it in extremely difficult conditions.

That is why Trotsky was so very insistent on this question. That is why he pushed it right to the point of including an undisguised polemic against those who were opposed to announcing the establishment of the Fourth International in the final chapter of his *Transitional Programme*.[15] He did so because, for him, the most important consideration was not the numerical size of our forces, nor the readiness of a more or less large sector of the workers to understand our decision; but above and beyond all, it was a question of political perspective and political continuity. Trotsky was acutely aware that the workers movement in general, and our movement in particular, was about to enter an extremely difficult Period -- the imperialist war -- in the course of which we would be subjected to extraordinary pressures by the class enemy and by powerful centrifugal forces. These pressures could well disintegrate and destroy an organisation as weak in numbers as our own. Looking

---

[15] But the sceptics don't keep quiet: "Has the time to announce its birth arrived as yet?" "The Fourth International", will be our reply, "doesn't need to be 'announced'. It is alive and in battle."

back, in examining what happened in our movement during the war, it can be seen that entering the war period without having proclaimed the founding of the Fourth International would have allowed all the outside pressures and all the centrifugal forces which appeared during that time to operate a thousand times more intensively.

In face of the difficulties stemming from national isolation and clandestinity, how many members, subject to all kinds of pressures, might have failed to use as the point of departure in making political analyses the necessity of defending and maintaining the organisation and the programme it outlined before the war? How many would have had a tendency to work up a new programme, to wonder what might be the new ideas they should adopt! At the beginning of this work, we mentioned the importance of historical continuity in the revolutionary movement. In announcing the founding of the Fourth International, Trotsky was essentially aiming at assuring this continuity during a perilous period. It was not at all 'too soon', but rather in the nick of time, that the Fourth International was founded, at the 1938 conference. The decision to create *The World Party of Socialist Revolution* -- the name the Fourth International adopted -- rendered an inestimable service to the working class movement.

The importance of the *Transitional Programme* has often been stressed. It answers these crucial questions: How can humanity be extricated from this nightmare of crises, of world wars, of continuous chaos in which it has been floundering for some forty years? How can the transition to socialism be assured?

The *Transitional Programme* is, at one and the same time, a programme for organising the workers in the struggle to win power and a programme to be put into operation immediately after the workers take power.9 At the end of the Nineteenth and the beginning of the Twentieth Century, when capitalism was in its ascendancy, the socialist parties had a two-part programme: the *maximum* programme, which expressed the demand for a socialist society in some vague future period; and the *minimum* programme of immediate demands, a programme of reforms that did not pose the question of the conquest of power. As early as its Third Congress, the Communist International had put forward the idea of a transitional programme: 'Instead of the minimum programme of the reformists and centrists, the Communist International struggles for the concrete needs of the proletariat, for a set of demands which, in their entirety, organise the proletariat and constitute the stages of the struggle for the dictatorship of the proletariat; each of these demands expresses an urgent need of the broad masses, even if these masses do not as yet consciously stand for the dictatorship of the proletariat' *(Theses on Tactics)*.

The *Transitional Programme* is not what can be called the fundamental programme of the Fourth International. The latter comprises the sum total of the teachings of the struggle for socialism, from the very beginning of the working class movement. This programme does not appear in any single printed document, but is found in several basic texts (the Marxist classics, the first four Congresses of the Communist International, basic documents of the Left Opposition and of the Fourth International, etc.). In this historical context, the *Transitional Programme* is its most important political part, the part which, proceeding from the basic teachings, formulates a programme for mobilising the masses in actions appropriate to their level of class consciousness, in order to lead them, through the education they receive by means of these actions, to the highest level -- the conquest of power. This programme comprises a series of immediate, democratic and transitional demands corresponding to the needs of the broadest sectors of the toiling masses, and to the logic of the development of the class struggle. Its key item is the slogan of *workers government*. As was the case at the Third and Fourth Congresses of the Communist International, this slogan is used in the *Transitional Programme* not as a synonym for the dictatorship of the proletariat, but as a transitional government formulation, which has to be adapted to the masses' organisational situation and degree of class consciousness at a given moment. A programme lacking any perspective for a government of the toiling masses taking anti-capitalist measures is not a transitional programme.

In the years since the *Transitional Programme* was written, its validity was particularly demonstrated in the immediate post-war period, when circumstances obliged the traditional organisations to advance certain of its slogans, although they were careful to avoid moving on to anti-capitalist slogans and to calling for a workers government. For some years now, its validity has also been evidenced in the fact that the idea has been picked up by reformists and centrists, but with the purpose of emasculating it. They use it to offer the masses a so-called new road -- basically reformist -- by which society can be moved from capitalism to socialism without revolutionary upheavals.

Given its nature, the *Transitional Programme* cannot and should not be considered holy writ. The foundation on which it stands, however -- the principle of a mobilisation of the masses towards the conquest of power, on a programme of combined demands remains unalterable. But the demands and the way they follow on from each other must in each instance be adapted to the particular conditions of time and place.

As early as 1938, the *Transitional Programme* illustrated the characteristics of the three areas in which the socialist revolution would be continued after the war: the advanced capitalist states, the colonial and semi-colonial countries, and the workers states (at that time there was but one, the Soviet Union).

The ordeal of the world war

Shortly before the war, the International Secretariat was transferred to America. The war brought considerable losses to our movement -- first and foremost, the assassination of Trotsky several weeks after he had written the Manifesto of the Emergency Conference (May 1940). There was also a wholesale slaughter of our comrades in the European countries: in France, Marcel Hic and Pierre Tresso (Blasco), former member of the Political Bureau of the Italian CP; in Belgium, Leon Lesoil and A. Leon.; in Greece, Pouliopoulos; the German comrade Widelin -- to ate only the names of a few leading comrades. But our dead in the Second World War can be counted by the hundreds. *Our European sections, for the most part, were changed from top to bottom, and their leaderships almost wholly replenished by youthful elements.* To this must be added the organisational break-up resulting from measures taken by the bourgeois states (censorship, travel restrictions, etc.) which confined most of our sections to a narrow national life in an atmosphere of enormous, reactionary political pressure, of biased news accounts, without an international centre capable of functioning normally -- even to the slightest extent.

The International Secretariat in America could keep in contact with only a few countries in the 'Allied' camp (and even that with great difficulty). Several years were to pass before a European Secretariat could be established among sections in countries occupied by Germany. Despite these extraordinarily great difficulties, we were able to ascertain, when international connections were re-established in 1946, that most of the sections, beyond frontiers and fronts, had followed a common general line on essential questions. This, of course, did not happen without a certain number of internal struggles and crises in several Trotskyist organisations, principal among which were the following:

1. In the United States. At the beginning of the war, Shachtman and Burnham, under the pressure of a petty bourgeoisie indignant over the Nazi-Soviet Pact, questioned our position on the USSR. Discussion on the point was begun and lasted seven months, covering all the fundamental questions, from problems of Marxist philosophy to problems of building a proletarian party. A petty bourgeois tendency grouped around Shachtman broke with the Socialist Workers Party[16] to form an organisation that continued to move farther and farther from our programme before disappearing completely. Following this split, a special international conference was held in America in May 1940, which condemned the political line and activity of the splitters and adopted a manifesto drawn up by Trotsky -- *The Proletarian Revolution and the Second Imperialist War*. This manifesto was written at the time when Hitler's offensive was driving into Holland, Belgium, and France. Stalin was then in a *de facto* alliance with Hitler. It was also at that time that the first attempt was made by Stalin's agents to assassinate Trotsky.

This document recalls the immediate causes of the war. It denounces the positions defended by the big powers, and the lies of 'fatherland' and 'democracy' being used to fool the masses. It also unmasks the 'peace offensive' being conducted by Hitler and, whilst exposing the fatal policy and role of Stalin, it calls for the defence of the Soviet Union. Many chapters are devoted to the problems of the colonial countries (China, India, Latin America). The role of the social-democratic, Stalinist and centrist leaderships of every ilk are unveiled at length. Finally the manifesto concludes with an appeal for the Fourth International, for a struggle in which two alternatives are at stake: socialism or slavery.

About a month later, on 30 June, Trotsky wrote an article about the fact that the German troops occupied the whole European continent up to the Atlantic. This article, 'We Do Not Change Our Course', contained in particular the following lines:

'In the wake of a number of other and smaller European states, France is being transformed into an oppressed nation... (Imperialist democracy) cannot be "saved" from fascism. It can only be replaced by proletarian democracy. Should the working class tie up its fate in the present war with the fate of imperialist democracy, it would only

---

[16] At that time the Socialist Workers Party was the American section of the Fourth International. Passage of the Voorhis Act in 1940, forbidding labour organisations to belong to an International, resulted in the formal disaffiliation of the SWP, but has never ceased to remain rigorously faithful to the Trotskyist programme. (By 1990, after Frank's death, the SWP has ended its affiliation with Trotskyism and the Fourth International.)

assure itself a new series of defeats... True enough, Hitler boastfully promises to establish the domination of the German people at the expense of all Europe and even of the whole world "for one thousand years". But in all likelihood this splendour will not endure even for ten years... Consequently the task of the revolutionary proletariat does not consist of helping the imperialist armies to create a "revolutionary situation" but of preparing, fusing and tempering its international ranks for revolutionary situations of which there will be no lack. The new war map of Europe does not invalidate the principle of revolutionary class struggle. The Fourth International does not change its course.

2. In the case of the *German* section (more exactly, the emigre committee leading that section), we witnessed a truly tragic degeneration of a group demoralised by years of exile. The first document to reveal this degeneration was called the 'Three Theses' (1941). The basic concept embodied in this document is that fascism constitutes a new historical period succeeding imperialism, one in which humanity is dragged so far backwards that, instead of remaining in the era of world wars and proletarian revolution, it finds itself thrown back into the era of wars for national liberation and of democratic revolutions of the 1848 type!

3. In *France* we saw the two Trotskyist groups, the POI (Parti Ouvrier Internationaliste -- Internationalist Workers Party) and the CCI (Comité Communiste Internationaliste -- Internationalist Communist Committee), both start off by going off the track -- in opposite directions -- under pressure from the class enemy. After a political struggle in both groups had enabled them to overcome their respective deviations, unification could take place through the founding, early in 1944, of the PCI (Parti Communiste Internationaliste -- Internationalist Communist Party), the French section of the Fourth International.

In a pamphlet entitled 'Problems of the World Party of Revolution and Reconstruction of the Fourth International', dated 28 February 1966, the group 'Voix Ouvrière' (Workers Voice) whose views are now defended by the 'Lutte Ouvrière' (Workers Struggle) group -- categorically condemned the Fourth International for the patriotic attitude adopted by one of the Trotskyist groups during the war, and for the fact that the Fourth International supposedly did not move to criticise this policy when the reunification of the French movement and the founding of the PCI took place in 1944. Here is what this pamphlet says: 'The unification of the different Trotskyist groups (POI, CCI, October Group) took place in the beginning of

THE LONG MARCH OF THE TROTSKYISTS

1944. The chauvinist policy of 1940 was blithely passed over, everything was forgiven and forgotten, and, better yet, they had always been right'(p.8). It adds:'...And when after the war the Fourth International ratified the policy of the French section, it became clear that it, too, was opportunistic' (P· 10).

Unfortunately for these comrades, their statements are not correct. In February 1944, under the German occupation, a European conference of the Fourth International was held. One of the items on its agenda was the French reunification and the formation of the PCI. This conference did not 'blithely pass over' but proceeded seriously to criticise the positions previously taken. The positions adopted at this European conference served as the basis for reunification in France. The documents of the European conference were published in a clandestine issue of *Quatrième Internationale* (Fourth International). We cite below Point XXIX of 'Theses on the Condition of the Working Class Movement and Perspectives for the Development of the Fourth International', which deals with this question and which explains as completely as anyone could desire what happened at that time. We are very sorry that these comrades did not verify their statements before making them.

'XXIX. Above all else the present war has subjected the Fourth International movement to the most difficult and decisive ordeals. On the one hand, we had to defend ourselves, on the basis of internationalist principles, against the danger of catching the nationalistic and patriotic fever that, at the beginning, was epidemic among the masses; on the other hand, we had to defend ourselves against the terrorism of the bourgeoisie. Under pressure of the conditions created in France and elsewhere after the defeat of French imperialism, a certain weakening in the internationalist behaviour of some sections became apparent. The French section primarily -- in its day-to-day policies often expressed the nationalistic influence of the petty-bourgeois masses who were exasperated by the defeat of their imperialist masters.

'The position taken by the French section on the national question, the theses issued in the name of the European Secretariat of the Fourth International, at that time exclusively controlled by the French comrades, represent a social-patriotic deviation that must once and for all be openly condemned and rejected as incompatible with the programme and general ideology of the Fourth International.

'Instead of making a distinction between the nationalism of the defeated bourgeoisie (which is an expression of its imperialist interests) and the "nationalism" of the masses (which is only an expression of their reaction to, and resistance against, exploitation by the imperialist occupiers), the POI leadership deemed progressive the struggle of its own bourgeoisie; did not, right from the start, separate itself from Gaullism; and was satisfied to clothe the latter in more "revolutionary" terminology. By placing the French bourgeoisie -- a defeated imperialist power -- on the same plane as the bourgeoisie of colonial countries, the POI leadership acquired a completely false concept of the national question. It spread dangerous illusions about the character of nationalist organisations, which, far from being able to serve as hypothetical "allies" for the revolutionary proletariat, will prove to be the counter-revolutionary vanguard of imperialism.

'In the same way, starting out with the entirely correct premise that it was necessary to take part in the mass struggle and to win large layers of the working class away from the baneful influence of nationalism, the POI leadership permitted itself to be drawn into making dangerous ideological and tactical concessions. It did not understand that the most important consideration in winning the masses lay in the crystal-clear and revolutionary language of the international class struggle, as opposed to the confused and treacherous language of social patriotism.

'It should be added, however, that just as this condemnation of a right-centrist deviation is called for, so also must the Fourth International vehemently condemn the sectarian "left" deviation as evidenced, for example, in the policies of the French CCI on the national question. Under guise of safeguarding the heritage of Marxism-Leninism, the CCI obstinately refused to make any distinction between the nationalism of the bourgeoisie and the mass resistance movement.

'In dismissing as "reactionary and nationalist" the struggle for their everyday interests waged by the proletariat and petty-bourgeois masses when this struggle is directed against the imperialist occupiers and uses petty-bourgeois slogans, sectarianism paralyses the precise revolutionary efforts needed to combat nationalist ideology, and automatically isolates itself from real mass struggles.

'The social-patriotic deviation was, nevertheless, energetically opposed from the beginning by the healthy resistance of the revolutionary rank-and-file of the French section, as well as by the rest of the international organisation.' (Quatrième Internationale, No. 6-7, April-May 1944, pp. 8-9)

The errors made at this time are explained by the huge pressures of a totally different order to those of peace time -- which were weighing upon militants who carried on the struggle, a struggle which was far from being simply a verbal one with the possibility of only extremely limited errors. Serious as these errors may have been, however, they remained at the level of errors and never became betrayals. They were corrected by the movement itself, which -- one should never forget -- defended the banner of the Fourth International at the cost of immense sacrifices.

The Second World Congress

As soon as international relationships had been re-established, the International Secretariat in America and the European Secretariat jointly organised an International Conference. Held in the spring of 1946 with a dozen sections participating, this conference assumed the powers of a congress, electing a new International Executive Committee and a new International Secretariat. It set a political orientation and assigned the new leadership bodies the task of preparing a world congress. These decisions were ratified by the sections that had not been able to attend the conference. The new orientation, resulting from the new world situation, consisted in the task of changing our sections, which until then had been propaganda groups, into parties linked to mass struggles -- and aiming to lead these struggles.

Preparation for the Second World Congress took almost two years. It entailed a lively struggle to maintain fundamental positions, especially against tendencies that wanted to revise our position on the question of the USSR. Twenty-two organisations from nineteen different countries were represented at the Second World Congress. It showed that, generally speaking, our movement had emerged from the war with increased strength although as yet unable to make a breakthrough in any particular place. It also showed that our movement had especially broad possibilities in those countries with relatively young working class movements in the Far East and in Latin America, for example. New statutes presented by Sherry Mangan were adopted.

Three main political points, in addition to an evaluation of the organisation's progress since its founding congress, were on the agenda of the Second World Congress. The first point was the international situation in the three years following the end of the Second World War, for which the report was presented by Michel Pablo. The congress noted the preponderant strength of the United States compared with the rest of the world; the difficult problems of reconstruction, both in Europe and in the Soviet Union; and the onset of the 'cold war'. It assessed the situation of the working class movement, the sharpening of the class struggle, and assigned the sections of the Fourth International the task of strengthening themselves in order to form mass parties.

A document on 'The Struggle of the Colonial Peoples and the World Revolution', presented by Pierre Frank, stressed the point that because of the new relationship of forces among capitalist states, we were witnessing a new division of the colonial world, with the United States taking over from the former imperialist countries, now weakened and unable to maintain their former domination. But the document also noted the policy of strategic retreat adopted by the imperialists in a large number of colonial countries, whereby they moved from the old forms of direct rule to new forms of indirect domination, with the help of layers of the indigenous bourgeoisie. Thus the congress clearly saw from the very beginning the new orientation that imperialism would follow, in the direction of what was later called neo-colonialism, while at the same time conducting colonial wars wherever it deemed it had absolutely vital strategic interests to defend.

The congress devoted a very large part of its work -- in fact, the major part -- to the discussion of a document entitled 'The USSR and Stalinism', presented by Ernest Mandel. The Soviet Union's expansion on the heels of its victory over German fascism, the occupation by Soviet troops of several East European countries, the enormous abuses and crimes committed in the course of this occupation, without the bourgeois social structure of these countries having been changed -- all this had caused innumerable debates everywhere on the class nature of the Soviet Union. The document approved by the delegates at the congress reaffirmed Trotsky's definition of the Soviet Union as a degenerated workers state, but it showed the stage which that degeneration had reached. It pointed out that the contradictions within the Soviet Union were sharper than ever; it dissected the Stalinist political line, indicating that the bureaucracy was more and more acting as an absolute brake on economic progress; and it concluded that the task before us, now that the war was over, was to overthrow the bureaucratic regime. A good part of the document was devoted to a study of the 'Soviet buffer states', i.e., those East European countries occupied by Soviet troops, and it concluded that these countries had retained the structure and function of a bourgeois state. Several pages of the document dealt with the Communist parties, stressing the slide towards reformism they had taken -- a very steep slide compared to the pre-war period. In conclusion, this document examined the significance of the world discussion on the question of the Soviet Union, and replied to the 'state capitalist' or 'bureaucratic collectivist' theories.

The question of the class nature of the Soviet Union and the question of the defence of the Soviet Union had been continuously raised inside the Trotskyist movement and had provoked many splits. The Second World Congress marked the end of the great debates on these questions inside the Fourth International. Afterwards, on the basis of the definition of the Soviet Union as a 'degenerated workers state', the debates took place on the transformations which took place there, their significance, and their consequences in relation to political tasks. In all the debates on the class nature of the Soviet Union, deep divergences of methodology were in the background concerning the way to analyse states, movements, and political formations. Out of these developed no less deep divergences on the political level. Thus most of those who fought the Trotskyist positions on these questions found themselves more or less frankly in the camp of imperialism against the Soviet Union during the 'cold war', in the name of the struggle of 'democracy' against 'totalitarianism'. The most monstrous example in this field was, I think, Shachtman himself, who eventually joined the American Socialist Party and defended US imperialism in the Vietnam War.

In retrospect, it can be seen that the main function of the Second Congress had been to reaffirm the fundamental principles of Trotskyism as opposed to the various centrifugal tendencies that had appeared during the war and immediately thereafter. It was an absolutely indispensable task, but that was as far as the congress could go. Coming events would confront the International with problems and tasks not touched on there.

Chapter 6: From 1948 to 1953. From the Second World Congress to the Split

At the Second World Congress, held in April-May 1948, several sections, especially in Europe, found themselves replenished and strengthened by new forces acquired in the aftermath of the war. In some cases, these sections began to be a factor in the political life of their countries. Thus, despite the growth of the old parties (especially the Communist parties) during that period, the perspective of a further development of the Fourth International's sections was adopted by the congress, which raised the slogan, 'Forward to building mass Trotskyist parties!'

But the situation was in the process of developing in a totally unexpected direction. The few signs pointing to this development were still too weak at the time of the congress to permit a correct evaluation -- too weak even to give us an inkling of where it was going. The post-war revolutionary wave in Western Europe seemed to be momentarily halted, but actually it had begun to subside. The 'cold war' had only just started. The Soviet blockade of West Berlin would start several weeks later. The 'Prague coup', i.e., the seizure of power by the Czechoslovak Communist Party, was only a few weeks old. The social changes within the so-called people's democracies were only beginning to take shape. There was no way to foresee the break that was to take place two months later between Yugoslavia and the Soviet Union.

Important events and totally unexpected developments occurred immediately after the Second Congress and for some years thereafter. Their results were unpredictable; the world was assuming a shape that had never been envisaged or even imagined by the most eminent, the most perspicacious, the most farsighted Marxists. These upheavals raised extremely complicated theoretical and political problems. Moreover, we were confronted, not with a single event that could have been judged per se, but with numerous events spread out over several years and not necessarily connected with each other. These events finally, after several years, resulted in a world picture totally different from what had previously been seen, even since the First World War and the October Revolution.

Certain Marxist tenets seemed to be placed in doubt by some aspects of the situation. As a result, a multiplicity of assessments and theories proclaiming the bankruptcy of Marxism appeared. Marxists could not answer these arguments with a pure and simple repetition of basic tenets, treating the latter as eternal truths independent of time and space. Such an approach would not have been worthy of Marxists. The primary task of the Fourth International was to place the basic teachings of revolutionary Marxism in juxtaposition with the new world picture, to redefine the situation, to re-evaluate perspectives and tasks. Neglecting such a task would have meant leaving the field free both for the apologists of the Communist parties and for the innumerable revisionists on the left and on the right.

For the sake of clarity, this exposition will not treat events in chronological order but will first point out the major changes that took place as a whole -- in order to arrive at the overall picture that emerged at the end of a few years. In this way, theoretical problems that were raised and difficulties that had to be resolved will stand out. The actions of the Fourth International can thus be set forth in context, making it possible to judge them on an objective basis.

Post-war upheavals

Let us first review the main events and the basic changes that occurred from 1947-48 to about 1960.

The 'cold war' began in 1947. Soon -- after the breach in the American monopoly on atomic energy in 1949 -- the development of nuclear weapons and the atomic arms race between the United States and the Soviet Union would begin. The problem of world war was thenceforth posed in new terms, not new on a social level, but new because of the availability of vast powers of destruction, so huge that they were in a completely different dimension from so-called conventional weapons.

In 1947 the Communist Information Bureau (Cominform) was created. At the same time, the 'cold war' led the Soviet Union (in order to protect its buffer states) to effect a social change -- by military-bureaucratic means -- in the East European countries its armies had entered during the war. Despite a few measures aimed at those members of the propertied classes who had collaborated with the Germans, the army had left the bourgeois social structures of these countries intact. The 'cold war' forced the Kremlin to liquidate the bases of capitalism in those countries and to transform them into workers states.

In June of 1948 the first great crisis of Stalinism erupted, in the shape of the Soviet-Yugoslav split. The Yugoslav Communist Party was expelled from the Cominform on charges reminiscent of the pre-war Moscow trials -- the Yugoslavs were fascists, spies, etc. But, for the first time, the Kremlin's hegemony over the workers states and the Communist parties as a whole was challenged by a party that had led the armed struggle during the war and had, against Stalin's advice, pursued that struggle until it had established a workers state. Stalin extended his repression in the East European workers states in order to prevent any spreading of the Yugoslav split. But the Yugoslav affair was his first big setback, at the very moment that the Soviet Union was at the peak of the glory reaped from its resistance during the war and its victory over Hitler's armies.

October 1949 saw the victory of the Chinese revolution -- that too despite the advice Stalin gave the Chinese Communist Party's leadership, namely, to make a deal with Chiang Kai-shek. The collapsing Kuomintang regime took refuge on the island of Taiwan (Formosa), where it would thenceforth survive only by grace of US military aid. The victory of the Chinese revolution had immense repercussions, which have developed through the years and which we shall summarise as follows:

1. A huge shift in the overall relationship of forces on an international scale, to the advantage of socialism.

2. A tremendous impetus to the colonial revolution, which thenceforth would spread from one colonised continent to another; outbreak of the Korean war in 1950; continuation of the Vietnamese revolution, first against French imperialism, later against American imperialism; extension of the colonial revolution to Latin America and victory of the socialist revolution in Cuba in 1959; extension of the colonial revolution to the Middle East, to North Africa in the 1950s, then to Black Africa from 1960 on.

3. Extension of the crisis of Stalinism.

In the course of the post-war period, enormous upheavals also occurred in the economically developed capitalist countries, in the capitalist countries based on a colonial structure, and in the workers states. Let us review them.

In a great many colonial countries, we witnessed a quasi-withdrawal by the imperialist nations (principally Britain; others, to a lesser extent), in which these colonies acquired formal political independence while at the same time an economic hold on them was maintained. These new -- and indirect -- forms of domination constitute what has been called *neo-colonialism*. In several cases, American imperialism has supplanted the colonising imperialism in its function of economic hegemony. Indigenous bourgeois leaderships of a special type appeared (Peronism, Nasserism, Sukarnoism, etc.). Sometimes they played along with mass movements -- a dangerous game. In the case of Cuba, the revolution won victory under a leadership which, although it did not originate in the working class movement -- and certainly not in the official Communist movement -- made the revolution a socialist one. Finally, in the colonial movements there are a number of leaderships that either try to seesaw between West and East, or gravitate for a time around the workers states without, however, effecting their countries' social transformation into workers states.

The growth and development of colonial revolutionary movements persisted. But receiving neither sufficient solidarity from the working class in the imperialist centres, nor a correct political line from the workers states, it was difficult for them -- with the exception of Cuba in Latin America -- to find a political orientation that would permit them to resolve, in the least costly way, the problems posed by the economic and social backwardness of their countries.

The Soviet Union's isolation, unbroken since 1917, had come to an end -- in the West (the 'people's democracies' of Eastern Europe) as well as in the East (China and the Democratic Republics of Vietnam and Korea). Then, on the American continent, socialist Cuba was born.

To the Soviet Union were added workers states which, with the exception of Czechoslovakia and East Germany, were less developed economically than the first workers state. Following a rocky period of post-war reconstruction in which Stalinism, faithful to its concept of 'socialism in one country', shamelessly pillaged the neighbouring countries, the Soviet Union's progress was so tremendous that it became the world's second greatest economic power. In the new workers states of Eastern Europe, the new forms of property ownership also, generally speaking, brought about great economic progress. This, however, did not serve to improve the living standard of the masses to any considerable extent. In their initial period, these states had the same internal regime that the Soviet Union had experienced under Stalin. But the growth of the new relationships of production did not entail the growth of Stalinism. The Latter proved incompatible with the former. The crisis of Stalinism thus began to become evident under the impact of various factors -- the police state's ever greater brake on the Soviet Union's economic progress; the contradiction between the needs of the other workers states and the Kremlin's policies; the rising revolutionary tide throughout the world. The Communist parties were no longer inevitably and automatically aligning themselves with Moscow. China was to play a very special role in the crisis of Stalinism.

In Western Europe, the Communist parties, which had generally increased in size at the war's end, did not succeed (with exceptions such as France, Italy, etc.) in becoming rooted in the working class. The social-democratic parties remained, or again became, the majority working class parties.

As noted above, the crisis of Stalinism began with the Yugoslav events in 1948. The crisis, for all practical purposes, has never since stopped growing (onset of 'de-Stalinisation' after Stalin's death in 1953; East Berlin events in June 1953; Twentieth Congress [of the CPSU] and events in Poland and Hungary in 1956; Sine-Soviet conflict; Czechoslovak crisis; etc.).

The absence of a revolutionary victory in the economically developed countries was not without influence, for a time, on the 'de-Stalinisation' process. Among other things, it determined the protracted nature of this process and the fact that it was largely kept under control by the Kremlin bureaucracy. For the most part, the 'socialist camp' remained under Moscow's hegemony. China's break with Moscow shook the Kremlin's authority in the Communist world to a tremendous extent, without contributing to any decisive advance for revolutionary Marxism.

In the highly developed capitalist countries, some very surprising phenomena occurred. There was a general agreement among economists -- both bourgeois economists and those in the labour movement, Marxist or not -- that following a post-war period of reactivation and reconstruction, a serious economic crisis would occur. Marxists, basing themselves more particularly on Lenin's concepts of imperialism, believed that the loss of the colonies would contribute to the disintegration of the imperialist centres. Yet, far from disintegrating, for about fifteen years the capitalist world experienced boom, an unprecedented economic prosperity interrupted not by crises but only by 'recessions' of varying but always limited size and duration. This led to what was called the 'consumer society' or 'neo-capitalism', which on the surface seemed no longer to correspond with the capitalism that Marx had analysed. In this unparalleled prosperity, the European workers movement, the oldest organised movement with the oldest Marxist tradition, experienced stagnation and even a pronounced political decline. The social-democratic parties tended, even formally, to renounce socialism in order to become 'people's parties'; the Communist parties 'social-democratised' themselves; the left social-democratic tendencies dissolved; the revolutionary vanguard steadily dwindled. The socialist movement, born in Europe more than a century ago, raised in the perspective that a socialist revolution in Europe would precede the economic, political, and social development of other areas of the world, no longer corresponded to this image of yesteryear.

In the course of the First World War and in the early years of the October Revolution, Lenin and Trotsky had foreseen the possibility of victorious socialist revolutions in the colonial countries, paralleling those in Europe. But from 1948 onward, revolution was in full swing on capitalism's periphery, while in the imperialist centres the workers movement was, or appeared to be, at a lower ebb than ever before in its entire history. And finally, in the countries where capitalism had been overthrown, the bureaucracy seemed to be entrenched, with the working class passively submitting to its domination.

A capitalism deprived of its colonies yet flourishing more than ever, with a working class shorn of political aspirations and almost exclusively preoccupied with its standard of living; in the workers states an extension of the new relationships of production, with bureaucratic domination maintained and without any workers' mobilisations; in the colonial countries a revolutionary upsurge, based essentially on the peasantry -- all this largely explains the proliferation of theories denying, in one way or another, the historical mission of the proletariat as formulated by Marx, whether in classically capitalist countries, colonial countries, or workers states (the class nature of the last-named also gave rise to a multiplicity of theories). It was not possible to grasp the totality of the process immediately. In the midst of the tremendous pressures brought to bear on the entire world, and inevitably on the Trotskyist movement, delay was unavoidable.

The crises in the Trotskyist movement

It was impossible to deny these contradictory events and to cite, in lieu of explanation, all the great classics of revolutionary Marxism on the revolutionary mission of the proletariat, etc. In order to answer pertinently the profusion of theories successfully and to be able to act, it was necessary to proceed to an examination of the situation with the help of revolutionary Marxism, to seek therein the key that would permit an explanation of this new situation, to see what adjustments, rectifications, and enrichment had to be brought to revolutionary Marxism. This was possible only while participating in the class struggle at the same time, testing the evaluations of the new situation in the fire of battle. And this is what the Fourth International tried to do, in a situation rendered all the more difficult by the fact that it was operating in a political scene such as no revolutionary tendency had ever before encountered. In addition to the enormously complex picture of the world that has been sketched here, the International was faced with the obstacle of two old, organised workers movements, which came to life only when fighting revolutionary currents. The 'workers state' factor, which from 1917 on had given a new dimension to working class politics and which, in the form of Stalinism, had for so many years influenced the working class movement, introduced -- together with the existence of several workers states in the underdeveloped areas of the world -- increasingly complex effects.

In order to understand the problems and tasks with which the Fourth International was faced, in order to understand the positions it took during the years in which these changes occurred, in order to judge its activity as objectively as possible -- it is quite necessary to grasp the size and scope of the changes produced in the aftermath of the Second World War. It is quite necessary to grasp this state of affairs in order to have a Marxist explanation of the internal difficulties the Fourth International experienced, especially its crises and its splits.

A detailed history of the Fourth International will not fail to examine each of the crises and splits, to study their various stages, the primary and secondary positions defended by this or that current or faction, the role of individuals, etc. But such a historical study can have value only if it is written from a Marxist view of the total picture, with a correct appreciation of the general causes at the root of these crises and splits, and of the main orientations which, aside from any specific position, conflicted with each other. It is this philosophy of crises, as it might be termed, that we will indicate here as an indispensable prerequisite. A number of our adversaries, incapable of doing this, find themselves reduced to mumbo-jumbo in describing this period of crises and splits, embellishing their account with more or less inane bits of gossip.

Let us start with a point that is not without significance. A big to-do has been made, and is still being made, about the crises the Trotskyist movement has gone through. 'What, another crisis! Another split!', invariably exclaimed those who were often more content to fight the Fourth International on that basis than to discuss its ideas. We have no need to deny the oft-times painful nature of the crises in our movement. Nevertheless, this characteristic, which for a long time seemed peculiar to the Trotskyist movement and which could be looked down on with cynical amusement from the lofty seats of the big organisations, is today prevalent in all kinds of movement organisations, big and small. Actually, what was really abnormal in the working class movement was monolithism -- that 'unity' achieved by smothering all independent political thought within organisations laying claim to Marxism, the most critical school of thought in the world. The history of the working class movement proves that, more often than not, it has been racked by struggles between divergent theoretical and political tendencies and currents. This was normal, because without continually testing theories, positions, and orientations, by measuring them against reality, no progress in revolutionary thought and action can be envisaged. There was all the more reason for the movement to undergo such struggles, faced as it was with a world in constant upheaval, in which 'something new' appeared, as it still does, each day. Although differences are a perfectly normal phenomenon, it does not follow that discussing them must necessarily and frequently end in splitting the movement. It is therefore necessary to look into the objective or subjective reasons that contributed to this state of affairs. In the history of the Trotskyist movement, both objective and subjective factors played their role.

Objectively, the splits were caused in large measure by the fact that differences on analyses or on the orientations to follow in order to build the revolutionary party were rendered all the more acute because the organisation was numerically weak, with very weak roots in the masses. Most often the differences boiled down to opposition on the tactics to adopt to overcome that precise situation. The entire world is more than ever subject to the pressure of colossal forces that tear up not only tiny vanguards, but bourgeois and petty-bourgeois groups, workers' mass organisations, etc., as well (it would be easy to draw up an impressive list). The international Trotskyist movement's theoretical base is an invaluable instrument for resisting the divisions that antagonistic forces tend to produce. But a theoretical base, no matter how powerful, is not without limits, especially in face of material forces that can at certain times assume considerable size in a few countries or groups of countries. As we shall see, in every crisis and split it is easy enough to uncover which factor (in the given circumstances) assumed undue proportions for a group of members -- to the point where they left the International.

Subjectively, the situation was aggravated in numerous cases by the fact that since the organisation was tiny, it was viewed by some as a secondary factor, to which too much importance should not be attached. Cutting it in half did not seem to matter much, numerically speaking, especially for those who believed that they had found the orientation which would lead to rapid growth. These feelings were rendered all the stronger in view of the disproportion between the objectively revolutionary character of the situation the important tasks this set -- and the clearly inadequate forces and means at our disposal, a disproportion that continually weighed (and still does) on our movement. Such feelings are the exact opposite of those that prevail in mass organisations, where the members, responsible to large masses and aware of the role of the organisation per se, are loath to initiate splits -- even when serious differences arise within these organisations.

We are not saying that crises and splits can be explained solely by the above-mentioned factors. Factors of a personal nature, for example, also played a role. But in order to have a clear understanding of history, the most general elements have to be placed in the forefront; without them the actions of other factors could not acquire significant weight. Within a period of about fifteen years, the most important changes in history took place; changes embodying the transition from capitalism to socialism while the major revolutionary forces were still under reformist or Stalinist leadership; changes, moreover, affecting essentially the most backward, not the most economically advanced, countries in the world. This situation favoured the rise of multitudinous theories denying the validity of Marxism. It also gave rise to tendencies and currents in the Trotskyist movement that to a certain degree held a distorted view of the situation; believed they could bank essentially on one or another aspect of the situation; and did not believe they had to consider the Fourth International, as constituted, a political force. As is always the case, those who broke away were not aware of the process they were part of -- nor where it would lead them.

It is also worth noting that, with rare exceptions, those who broke with the Fourth International and did not take part in the 1963 reunification soon found themselves -- if not politically nonexistent -- with reduced forces, despite any expectations they might have had or the forces at their disposal when they left. Nor should we view this as an accidental result. Rather must we examine the causes of this phenomenon -- not causes of a personal nature, because there was no lack of determination or capability on the part of the individuals involved. This situation must be attributed to:

1. The fact that they embarked on a politically incorrect course.

2. Their separation from the international movement, which, by its very international nature, was best able to resist the colossal forces at work in the world and to correct its own errors when they occurred.

The International is not a fetish; it does not generate miracles. But, despite its numerical weakness, the very nature of the organisation, centralised and democratic at the same time, makes it a force that can best prevent any national distortion and resist the pressures exerted throughout the world by all kinds of forces (state powers, mass movements with all kinds of leaderships, etc.).

The Third World Congress (1951)

As already mentioned, the break between the Kremlin and the Yugoslav leadership occurred right after our Second World Congress. In vain were Moscow's efforts to isolate the Yugoslav leadership, to find a substantial opposition to Tito, even to attempt a coup against that leadership. In his famous report to the Twentieth Congress of the CPSU in 1956, Khrushchev described Stalin's state of mind when he decided publicly to announce Tito's excommunication. Said Khrushchev: 'I remember when the conflict between the Soviet Union and Yugoslavia first began to be artificially blown up. One day, upon arriving in Moscow from Kiev, I was invited to see Stalin. Showing me a copy of a letter recently sent to Tito, Stalin asked: "Have you read this?" Without waiting for a reply, he added: "All I have to do is lift one little finger and there'll be no more Tito. He will go down." ' But this was the first time since he had got rid of all the political currents within the Communist parties that Stalin, now at the very height of his authority, underwent defeat and witnessed a Communist Party and a workers state rising against him.

As soon as this split became public knowledge, the leadership of the Fourth International understood that the international crisis of Stalinism would for the most part thenceforth be out in the open; that the Kremlin's incompatibility with a living revolution was clearly evident; that it was necessary to help the Yugoslavs resist the Stalinist attacks; and that the Yugoslav conflict would sooner or later have big repercussions -- which should be utilised to build new revolutionary leaderships -- inside the Communist parties and the workers states.

The Trotskyist organisations very quickly mobilised to help the Yugoslav revolution answer the torrent of slander emanating from Moscow and the Communist parties. Campaigns were launched in numerous countries. Leaflets, pamphlets, meetings were used in the fight against Stalinism. In several countries it was the Fourth International's organisations that initiated the youth brigades that went to Yugoslavia -- brigades of inquiry, support and work in the service of the Yugoslav revolution. These brigades were relatively successful, with an enrollment of several thousand young people. For Stalinism, the Yugoslav affair was a wound that never healed.

For a short period, the sections of the Fourth International, profiting from the Yugoslav crisis, became stronger. But this process was interrupted during 1950 when, at the beginning of the Korean war, the Yugoslav leadership -- which until then had made progress in many areas of domestic policy (self-management, etc.) and in its criticism of part of the Stalinist past -- took a disgraceful position on the international scene. In the United Nations General Assembly, Yugoslavia voted for UN military intervention against North Korea. This position succeeded in alienating many of Yugoslavia's defenders. The hopes of recruiting a larger revolutionary vanguard because of the Soviet-Yugoslav dispute were thus destroyed, until such time as the crisis of Stalinism would erupt elsewhere.

While the crisis between Yugoslavia and the Kremlin was taking this turn, the victory of the Chinese revolution was becoming an international factor requiring a reassessment of the situation. It could be stated, and correctly so, that this victory would inevitably entail a much bigger crisis of Stalinism than did the Yugoslav affair, for somewhat similar reasons. But there was no reason to believe that the crisis would erupt in the immediate future.

China had just got rid of the Chiang Kai-shek government on the mainland; it found itself threatened on its Korean frontier, while American imperialism was turning Taiwan into a fortress against the new republic. The new Chinese government could not get along without Soviet aid, for a time at least. The 'cold war', the Korean war, Yugoslavia's international policy, the Sine-Soviet cooperation -- all showed that the perspectives of the Second World Congress were no longer satisfactory. A re-evaluation of the situation was called for. Moreover, the sections, no longer making the progress they had made during the post-war period, were meeting with mounting difficulties. This also necessitated a re-examination of the orientation of our activity.

A plenum of the International Executive Committee held in November 1950 decided to convoke the Third World Congress. This plenum adopted theses on the international perspectives of the Fourth International to be submitted for discussion prior to the Congress, which was held in August 1951. These theses were adopted without any serious opposition, except for that of the majority of the French section.

Seventy-four delegates from twenty-five different countries attended the Third Congress. The main document the congress adopted, by a vote of 39 to 3 with one abstention, consisted of 'Theses on the International Perspectives and the Orientation of the Fourth International'. These theses were devoted to an examination of the international situation where, with the victory of the Chinese revolution, the global relationship of forces had developed to the disadvantage of world capitalism and in favour of the socialist cause. They began by stressing the increasing preparations of various kinds being made at that time for a new world war: the creation and delineation of alliances, the 'cold war', the armaments race, etc. The theses did not dismiss the possibility of temporary compromises between the United States and the Soviet Union, above all because of the Kremlin's conservative policy, but they projected such a new world war in the relatively near future. They added that, by its nature, this war would be a 'war-revolution', in which an imperialist victory would be problematical. Linked to this perspective on the war was the point of view that the arms race economy would have catastrophic consequences on the economic situation: inflation, lowering of the workers' standard of living, etc.

In addition, these theses underlined the economic progress beginning to be made in the Soviet Union and in the so-called people's democracies once post-war reconstruction had been achieved. The theses did not foresee any expansion of Stalinism, despite the economic progress, and ruled out any historical future for Stalinism, i.e. the Soviet bureaucracy. From what had happened in Yugoslavia and China, these theses concluded that the Communist parties, even when they had a reformist policy, were not exactly classical reformist parties; that they were not as yet mere instruments of the Kremlin under any and all circumstances; that, under certain conditions of exceptional mass movement, they could even be drawn into going beyond orientations corresponding to the policies of the Kremlin and beyond their strictly reformist objectives. These theses insistently stressed the concrete, contradictory relationships in operation between the masses, the Communist parties, and the Soviet bureaucracy; and they stated that the Trotskyists had to take advantage of these contradictions, and, in order to do so, had to become part of the real mass movement, especially where Communist parties were mass organisations.

In addition to these theses and to a political resolution applying them to the immediate situation, the Third Congress adopted three other important resolutions. The first dealt with the 'people's democracies'. Restating a document adopted by a session of the International Executive Committee held in April 1949, the resolution characterised the East European states as 'bureaucratically *deformed* workers states'. Unlike the Soviet Union, a workers state born of a proletarian revolution but which had bureaucratically degenerated, these states were essentially a result of the Kremlin's military-bureaucratic intervention, supported at best by a limited and bureaucratic mobilisation of the masses. These 'people's democracies' had never experienced a true revolution and were born with bureaucratic deformations.

For the particular case of Yugoslavia, which had gone through a genuine revolution, a special resolution was adopted that traced the various phases of the revolution from the time of the partisan struggle. This resolution noted the contradiction between Yugoslavia's progressive development in numerous respects and its rightist international policy. It exposed the dangers this policy might hold for the country domestically, including the opportunities it afforded the forces of capitalist restoration. But the resolution went on to indicate that the restoration of capitalism could never be accomplished in a 'cold' way. This 1951 resolution shows that the Fourth international's response to Chinese and Cuban charges that capitalism has been 'restored' in Yugoslavia, in Czechoslovakia, etc., was not improvised for the occasion.

The last resolution, on Latin America, had as its main feature the first Marxist explanation of the nature of Peronist-type governments. Thanks to the Second World War, these governments of the 'nationalist bourgeoisie' had developed -- at the particular expense of foreign imperialism and the oligarchy (landholders and comprador bourgeoisie)-- by involving large sectors of the working class (to different degrees in different countries, and in exchange for minimal concessions) in the anti-imperialist struggle under the leadership of this nationalist bourgeoisie.

A tactical turn in building revolutionary parties

Complementing the analysis and the perspectives projected by the Third World Congress, at a subsequent plenum (February 1952) the International Executive Committee adopted a resolution on tactics for building Marxist revolutionary parties, for the first time generalising and enlarging on the concept of 'entryism' in a certain number of mass Communist or Socialist parties. This new entryist tactic took its inspiration from examples or tactics previously advocated by Lenin and Trotsky, as well as from the line followed by Marx in 1848 in the German revolution and later during the formation of the First International.

In *Left-Wing Communism: An Infantile Disorder,* Lenin expressed no definite opinion because he lacked sufficient data, but he warned against a single answer to the question, 'Should we join the Labour Party?' -- an answer that would follow from principles such as, 'The Communist Party must keep its doctrine pure and its independence of reformism inviolate'. He indicated that in this area it was necessary to 'know, study, seek, discover' each country's peculiarities in order to apply the general and fundamental principles of communism in each case.

THE LONG MARCH OF THE TROTSKYISTS

As explained in an earlier chapter, in 1934 Trotsky had made clear that for an organisation whose limited numbers made it essentially a propaganda group, constructing a revolutionary party capable of independent action and capable of mobilising the working class in action could necessitate temporarily entering a reformist or centrist group -- in order to win, through adequate work, forces among the currents moving to the left by helping them in their political experiences. The entryism of the pre-war period resembled a raid in the Socialist parties.

After the war, the International had come out in favour of the British Trotskyists entering the Labour Party. This was not the same kind of 'entryism' that was practised before the war in the SFIO, or the Belgian Workers Party (Parti Ouvrier Belge), or the Socialist Party in the United States. The tactic for Great Britain rested on the structure of the labour movement of the country, above all on the close link between the political party and the trade unions, which means that, for the British workers, the Labour Party is their party and the Conservative Party is their bosses' party. The workers are faithful to their party even when they do not agree with its leaders or the policies of its leaders.

The new entryist tactic rested both on long-term and conjunctural perspectives.

At the time the Third World Congress was being held, Bevan's left opposition had appeared in the Labour Party, after Labour had been in office a few years. The international and national situation was then favourable to the formation and development in Britain of a mass centrist tendency moving towards the left. Considerations of a conjunctural type flowed from the general theses of the Third World Congress. The prospect of a new world war and the growing economic difficulties in store for capitalism would, we thought, favour the growth of Bevanist-type tendencies within the social-democratic parties on an international scale -- and also give rise to mass left-wing tendencies within the Communist parties. Thus we had to help such tendencies in an experience that would lead them, through phases unforeseeable at that time, to the formation of revolutionary Marxist parties.

The long-range considerations were based on a premise relating to the European workers movement, namely the persistence of the old, reformist workers parties and the lack of growth of the Communist parties after the First World War -- with some exceptions. It could be deduced from this premise that the bond between the working class and these parties was not due primarily to their programme or policy, but to the length of time these parties had been embedded among the workers, to the fact that they constituted for the workers a more or less valuable instrument but at least an instrument available to them on a day-to-day basis in capitalist society; that the workers were not inclined to leave these parties for new formations untested in action.

This organisational inertia on the part of the working class in the European countries would also be evident, to a lesser degree, during revolutionary periods -- the political development of the class proceeding at a faster pace than its development on the organisational plane. No major social crisis in a European country could fail to involve a major crisis for the mass workers parties in that country, especially the dominant workers party. Sustained activity in the mass parties, more especially in the main mass party in each country, was thus placed on the order of the day.[17]

The Leninist theory of the revolutionary party defines the essential features that such a party must have. But it cannot define the precise methods of building the party, because these will depend on general historical conditions and the specific circumstances in each country. The revolutionary party can develop itself only on the basis of class struggles in which there emerges a political vanguard capable of leading the working class in overthrowing the capitalist regime.

In the case of small groups created on a programmatic basis (as has generally been the case for the sections of the Trotskyist movement), it is not conceivable that they can transform themselves into vanguard parties really linked to the masses solely through individual recruitment. No party has ever been built in this way. All parties have been formed not merely through individual recruitment but also by a process involving fusions, the evolution of mass currents, splits, etc., which took place in response to important political events. Thus most of the Communist parties were created as a result of developments inside the old Socialist parties in response to the policies they followed during the First World War and to the victory of the October Revolution.

The Fourth International has never envisaged that it will become a mass International through a gradual, linear development of its sections. Thus in recent years these sections have adopted tactics corresponding to the particular conditions created by the very uneven

---

[17] In the discussion on entering the Labour Party, the emphasis was on the structural aspects of the workers movement. In the Third Congress discussion, the emphasis was placed on conjunctural aspects; structural conditions were taken up again only towards 1954-55.

political maturation inside the youth and the bulk of the working class in many countries of Europe.

The 'entryist' tactic was elaborated precisely because of a combination of circumstances never experienced by revolutionary Marxists in the past: they existed in extremely small numbers, had very limited means of propaganda, and faced parties which encompassed the overwhelming majority of the class, depriving them almost of the right to exist. Where could potential currents arise in a new situation? Our intention was to reject any ultra-left idea that the unorganised workers were in their mass more politically advanced than the organised ones. We concluded that, without renouncing one iota of our programme, we must at all costs participate in the mass organisations. The 'entryist' tactic as it was tried was undoubtedly risky, but revolutionary Marxist politics is not like a recipe book in which all dangers have been eliminated. All those who accused us at that time of capitulation have been shown to be wrong; indeed, with the changes in the political situation, many of them have in fact ended up in the political camp of these old parties, unlike the sections of the Fourth International. In its entryist tactic, the International made a distinction, then, between the Socialist parties, where at that time relative internal democracy allowed for the organisation of tendencies, and the Communist parties, which did not tolerate the least manifestation of divergent points of view. In the former, entryism was envisaged as being total; while in the latter, where it was necessary to use 'trickery and lies' (as Lenin had advised in connection with remaining in the reactionary and reformist mass trade union organisations), the tactic provided for maintaining an independent sector that would publicly explain the positions of the Fourth International in full.

Critique of the Third World Congress

The theses and resolutions of the Third World Congress represented an initial attempt to answer questions raised by the post-war upheavals mentioned earlier -- upheavals that continued to occur. It would thus be useful to see what aspects of the theses were subsequently confirmed and what invalidated. For the verdict to be relevant, we should not overlook the fact that any analysis inevitably includes gaps and errors, life itself bringing into being trends that were only embryonic at the time the analysis was being made or that emerged from the struggle of social forces. The important thing to see is whether the line of action stemming from the analysis was, on the whole, valid for the situation at a given moment; whether it enabled the organisation to react correctly to events while keeping up with each change in the situation in order to take into account the emergence of new factors and new trends -- not to mention correcting any errors in the analysis. Because of the limited scope of this work, only the major political lines will be examined.

The Third World Congress had correctly evaluated the shift in the global relationship of forces at the expense of world capitalism. The congress had even accurately demonstrated that this did not prevent capitalism from maintaining its superiority at that time on the economic plane per se (a superiority it still possesses) and on the military level. Strictly speaking, capitalism's military superiority probably no longer exists on an overall world scale (which obviously does not mean that there is parity in each particular area: army, navy, air force, conventional weapons, nuclear weapons, etc.).

Our understanding of the regroupment around the Soviet Union on the one hand and around the United States on the other was proved correct. The situation began to change in this respect only about fifteen years later, when centrifugal forces assumed increasing weight in each alliance. Nevertheless, even taking into consideration the new factors, we cannot say that new alliances, new constellations are henceforth foreseeable or circumscribed and that the former division may not reappear in the event of a considerable deterioration in international relations.

What the theses stated about the dual role of the Soviet bureaucracy, about the Communist parties, and about the contradictory relationships between the masses, the Communist parties and the Kremlin, was essentially right. Without these considerations, it would have been impossible for us, amid the welter of post-war events, to find an orientation. The explanation of what had occurred in Yugoslavia and China was absolutely valid; moreover, it had been indicated as a possible eventuality by Trotsky in *The Transitional Programme*, in the following terms:

'Of all parties and organisations which base themselves on the workers and peasants and speak in their name, we demand that they break politically from the bourgeoisie and enter upon the road of struggle for the workers' and farmers' government. On this road we promise them full support against capitalist reaction. At the same time, we indefatigably develop agitation around those transitional demands which should, in our opinion, form the programme of the "workers' and farmers' government".

'Is the creation of such a government by the traditional workers organisations possible? Past experience shows, as has already been stated, that this is, to say the least, highly improbable. However, one cannot categorically deny in advance the theoretical possibility that, under the influence of completely exceptional circumstances (war, defeat, financial crash, mass revolutionary pressure, etc.), the petty-bourgeois parties, including the Stalinists, may go further than they themselves wish along the road to a break with the bourgeoisie. In any case, one thing is not to be doubted: even if this highly improbable variant somewhere at some time becomes a reality and a "workers' and farmers' government" in the above-mentioned sense is established in fact, it would represent merely a short episode on the road to the actual dictatorship of the proletariat.

In these lines, Trotsky shows that while fighting as hard as possible to build revolutionary Marxist parties defending the Fourth International, he did not exclude the possibility of exceptional cases in which, because of extraordinary objective conditions, the revolution could win even under a leadership that might not be revolutionary Marxist.

The post-war period has produced a few cases of this type which Trotsky estimated as scarcely probable but not impossible. They cannot be denied except at the risk of complete disorientation on the world arena. But we must also uncover the conditions surrounding these cases, in order to demonstrate their exceptional nature. In that way it will be clearly seen that these are not examples from which we can generalise nor from which we can deduce that the construction of revolutionary parties is not necessary.

Among the sectarian tendencies that appeared in the Trotskyist movement after the war have been groups that have denied the existence of workers states created by exceptional circumstances, under the leadership of a mass movement that was not revolutionary Marxist. Underlying this has been a fear of having to conclude -- by using very formal logic -- that the task of building revolutionary parties was superfluous. But denying facts can only lead to incorrect positions.

On the other hand, the theses of the Third Congress were in error on the prospects for war and on the economic situation. The prospect of a new world war was then brought to the fore by the series of nuclear explosions carried out by the United States and the Soviet Union in order to perfect more and more destructive weapons. All the states, all the political formations in the world, based themselves on such a perspective. The American Secretary of State, John Foster Dulles, even boasted about carrying out a foreign policy 'on the brink of the abyss'.

Nobody at the time imagined that we were about to enter a period of economic prosperity in the capitalist world, the like of which had never before been seen in scope or in duration, a prosperity interrupted only by short, mild recessions. We know of no writer who had even entertained such a notion. The main results of this unforeseen reversal in the economic conjuncture were that the perspectives on the crisis of capitalism and the world war became much more remote than anticipated by the congress's theses, for capitalism is not driven to war as long as the economy is not in dire straits.[18]

On the contrary, the perspectives of the document on the crisis of Stalinism, which the theses postulated as coming to a head not before but during a world war, proved to be wrong because this crisis was much *closer* than anticipated. As for the opponents of the Third Congress's theses, they generally had no real perspective whatsoever on the crisis of Stalinism, even for the long run. In other words, the main error of the theses lay in the relative tempo of the crises of capitalism and Stalinism, the congress having seen the crisis of capitalism as preceding that of Stalinism, while the opposite was to happen.

---

[18] The discussion for the Third Congress barely dealt with the proximity of the war, but with the idea of the 'war-revolution'.

Chapter 7: From 1953 to 1968. Splits & Reunification

At the Third Congress, no principled differences had appeared within the International, such as the disagreement on the class nature of the Soviet Union that had in earlier years torn the movement. Apparently the International was united; the opponents of the congress's theses in the French section (who were subsequently to form the Internationalist Communist Organisation [Organisation Communiste Internationaliste -- OCI] placed the emphasis in their attacks on the tactical conclusions, in which they saw a capitulation to Stalinism, rather than on the analysis itself, only certain parts of which, generally speaking, they criticised.

The 1953-54 split

The error in perspective discussed above would not in itself have caused a split; besides, nobody had proposed any other perspective. Nevertheless, two years after the congress, a split occurred on an international scale, preceded about a year before by a split in the French section.

How can the split be explained? As already indicated, we were on the threshold of an unexpected development, the outcome of which was not clear. It is, therefore, not too surprising to realise, after the fact, that the congress's quasi-unanimity really masked divergent positions and tendencies which had not been expressed, not because of lack of democracy in the organisation, but because the situation was so unclear. The divisions that subsequently surfaced, not only in the form of splits but also inside each of the groupings resulting from the splits, attest to that. With this as a basis, two other factors played an important, if not decisive, role. To begin with, the theses adopted by the congress had not been assimilated by the sections, their leaderships included. It was only with the advent of the split that the situation became completely clear to the leadership of the International. The latter had not at all been aware of this state of affairs; it did not have a clear view of the condition of the organisation as a whole; and it realised all this, belatedly and to its very great surprise, only in 1953, when preparations were being made for the next congress.

In the months following the Third World Congress, relationships between the International and the majority of the French section, which kept refusing to implement the congress's decisions, deteriorated to such an extent that in the middle of 1952 a split took place in the PCI. This split was not to end there: the two organisations claiming to be the French section of the Fourth International soon had their own splits. Disciplinary measures were taken by the International, with the approval of those who, the very next year, would join with those who had been expelled to form the International Committee.

Somewhat later, extremely violent differences erupted in the British section, which, by dint of its systematic work, had made palpable progress inside the Labour Party. So intense was the disagreement that a split took place even before the respective positions were clearly established.

The decisive factor in the split was an internal crisis within the Socialist Workers Party (SWP), the American Trotskyist organisation. At that time the situation in the United States was growing more and more difficult for the vanguard. McCarthyism was on the rise. While a majority of the American organisation maintained fundamental Trotskyist positions, a strong minority was searching for a new path. Without stating its essential positions -- at least in those of its published documents known to the International -- this minority seized upon the Third World Congress's theses and subsequent documents of the International (particularly a discussion document on Stalinism, drawn up in preparation for the next world congress) as weapons in its fight against the majority of the American organisation.

When this internal struggle ended in a split, the majority of the SWP blamed the leadership of the International, with which it disagreed at the time on the question of 'de-Stalinisation'. Moreover, the political differences were overlaid with organisational and even personal suspicions. Finally, there was practically no personal contact, no person-to-person exchange of views, during this period. Thus, without being preceded by an extensive political discussion in the international movement, a split occurred on an international scale. A minority established the 'International Committee of the Fourth International'. As for the SWP minority, no sooner did it break away from the party than it publicly expressed liquidationist positions and openly fought the Fourth International.

The McCarthyism just referred to subjected the SWP to a great deal of pressure and led the party's leadership, embroiled in a fight against the liquidationist current, to resist what it considered dangerous innovations. This happened in 1953 when, immediately after Stalin's death, the first 'de-Stalinisation' measures were taken in the Soviet Union. In preparation for the next world congress (the decision to call this congress had been taken in May 1953), the leadership of the International had prepared a document, 'The Rise and Decline of Stalinism', which, in a way the leadership had not expected, sparked the powder keg. Since this document was adopted at the Fourth World Congress and completed at the Fifth, we shall analyse it later. However, we must say here and now that it excited more than fear in the comrades who were going to form the International Committee: they saw in it a capitulation to Stalinism, the liquidation of the Fourth International, and 'Pabloism'.

This split was by far the most serious of all for the Fourth International. Although all the groups and all the people who have through the years left the organisation cannot be considered lost to us for all time, the other splits proved, by their nature and in actual fact, to be rather splits *away from* the Trotskyist movement. On the other hand, this split was in fact primarily a division of the movement itself into two parts, one continuing the International and the other organised in a committee that acted as a faction. This split profoundly affected the life and development of both sides. Actually, it had the effect, among others, of injecting into the International, into the part continuing the organisation as well as the other, both a disequilibrium and a reinforcement of the centrifugal forces -- during a period which was replete with powerful forces placing unequal degrees of pressure on various sectors of the movement. All this certainly resulted in reinforcing the heterogeneous character of certain tendencies, as well as reducing the authority of the organisation as such and of its centre. During the years of this split, members and groups of the international Trotskyist movement experienced developments that were by no means inevitable. Had this split (which, in our opinion, was not unavoidable) not taken place, the International would have been able to reach the overall appraisal of the post-war world that it acquired at the reunification perhaps faster and certainly in a less costly way.

The Fourth and Fifth World Congresses (1954 and 1957)

Preparations for the Fourth World Congress as well as the congress itself were dominated by the split that had occurred in the meantime. Representatives from twenty-one countries participated in the congress, which was held in July 1954. The congress devoted part of its time to a small group that had waged a violent struggle against supporters of the International Committee but which, right after the split, turned its fire just as violently against the International. This group considered the struggle to create new revolutionary parties unnecessary, did not even stay until the congress adjourned, and then rapidly fell apart.

The most important task facing the congress consisted in subjecting the positions adopted at the previous congress to a thoroughgoing reappraisal. Two principal documents were adopted. One dealt with integrating the Trotskyists into *bona fide* mass movements and reviewed the revolutionary conditions of the era and the essential task of building mass revolutionary Marxist parties. For this purpose, the document insisted on the necessity of merging with the masses *in action, not in programme*. It brought out what was happening within the mass organisations, and pointed out the necessity for the Trotskyist organisations to choose a field of work in these organisations -- it being understood that reforming them was not the question. To the main considerations, the document added considerations appropriate for applying the tactic in various countries.

The other document, presented by Ernest Mandel, was entitled 'The Rise and Decline of Stalinism'. Since it was taken up again and completed at the following congress, we shall come back to it later.

The Fourth Congress served mainly to put a brake on the consequences of the split, to effect a regroupment against the centrifugal tendencies let loose by the split, to consolidate the organisation in the wake of the blow it had just suffered. The congress also adopted a resolution declaring the re-establishment of unity in the Trotskyist movement both possible and desirable, and authorising the International Executive Committee elected at this congress to contact the non-represented organisations -- those of the International Committee -- in order to apprise them of the congress's position on the question of unity.

Shortly after the Fourth Congress, the situation in the International began to improve somewhat, helped in large measure by developments in the international situation.

Beginning in 1955, an unexpected turn in the economic conjuncture became apparent in the advanced capitalist countries. Prosperity began to settle in. This turn called for analysis, and in October 1955 the International Executive Committee provided an initial appraisal. The IEC noted the radical change in the economic conjuncture, the economic prosperity that had been appearing for over a year. The IEC gave a description rather than a theoretical analysis of this phenomenon, and was somewhat cautious as to perspectives.

The most important factor in improving the movement's condition was developments in the Soviet Union and in the workers states of Eastern Europe. In the former, a struggle was going on inside the leadership that had taken over at Stalin's death. Beria was the first to be eliminated. Then Malenkov had to give way to the Bulganin-Khrushchev team. The struggle was to continue for almost another two years. The crisis at the summit, the concessions made by the leadership, opened possibilities for expressing nonconformist views in what had for so long been the citadel of monolithism. And then came 1956 -- the year of the Twentieth Congress of the CPSU, the year of the Polish and Hungarian events. At a closed session of the Twentieth Congress, Khrushchev had delivered a report on the 'Personality Cult of Stalin', in which he denounced many of Stalin's crimes. Khrushchev was not inquiring into the origin of the Stalinist phenomenon; on the contrary, this report sacrificed Stalin as an individual in order to save the power of the bureaucracy. In Poland, strikes followed by a mass movement brought Gomulka, one of Stalin's victims, to the leadership of the party and the state. In Hungary, faced with the breadth of the mass mobilisation and the indecisive attitude of Imre Nagy, the Kremlin repressed the mass movement by a bloody intervention of the Soviet army.

Elsewhere, in the arena of the colonial revolution, hardly had the war between French imperialism and the Vietminh been ended by the Geneva Agreements in July 1954, when the Algerian war began (November 1954). Likewise in 1956 came the Suez crisis, in which the governments of France and Great Britain intervened militarily in collusion with Israel against Egypt, following the nationalisation of the Suez Canal. Under the joint pressure of Washington and the Kremlin, France and Great Britain had to end their military intervention.

All the sections of the International were engaged in two kinds of activity. First of all, they intervened in the international crisis of Stalinism and the Communist parties, which was expressed mainly among students and intellectuals inside those parties but which also reached working class layers. In addition, many sections co-operated more and more in helping the Algerian revolution and, more generally, the colonial revolution.

On the whole this period witnessed a new start for the sections, a certain amount of recruiting, a growing confidence due to the fact that, for the first time, all the things we had been saying about Stalinism for so long in an essentially theoretical way were being verified in actuality on an already considerable scale. Besides a still limited recruitment, the organisation had a wider audience, and its political authority was reinforced. Under these conditions, preparations for the Fifth World Congress got under way in November 1956. This congress was to have an entirely different character from that of its predecessor.

In the course of preparing for the congress, an attempt at rapprochement with the International Committee was made, with a view to reunification in line with the decision of the Fourth Congress. In the wake of the Twentieth Congress of the CPSU, it appeared from a reading of the publications, especially those of the SWP, that differences on the USSR and 'de-Stalinisation' had diminished. This attempt at rapprochement failed, mainly because distrust on the organisational level persisted.

The Fifth Congress, in October 1957, assembled about a hundred delegates and observers from twenty-five countries. Among the fraternal delegates were representatives of the Algerian fighters.

The march of events had permitted far more light to be shed on the problems posed by the post-war upheavals. Three essential questions were dealt with by the congress, the conclusions reached appearing in the following documents: 'Economic Perspectives and International Policies'; 'Colonial Revolution Since the End of the Second World War'; 'Rise, Decline, and Fall of Stalinism'.

The document entitled 'Economic Perspectives and International Policies', presented by Michel Pablo, started off with a thorough discussion of the causes for the unexpected prosperity in the United States and Western Europe. It explained the 'anti-crisis' methods employed by the capitalist states, the role of consumer credit, the public debt, etc. The document went on to explain that the devices used by capitalism to obtain its much vaunted results would eventually bring about increasingly frequent recessions, technological unemployment, and a long-range depreciation of money.

On the economy of the workers states, the document noted its prodigious growth and pointed out that these countries, which had until then stressed the production of capital goods, usually without taking production costs into consideration, would (for social reasons) have to expand their production of consumer goods and would also have to 'rationalise' their economy. Far from advocating solutions such as those presently prescribed by reformers such as Liberman, Trapeznikov, Sik, etc., the document emphasised the basic role of workers democracy, not only as a political factor but as indispensable for development in the economic area.

This document also stressed the fact that although the colonial countries were making economic progress in terms of absolute figures, they were actually regressing in a relative sense compared to other countries; that the result of this would be a growing impoverishment of the colonial masses and consequently the continuation of the objective conditions that were fanning the flames of colonial revolution.

As to the class struggle in the capitalist countries, the document stated that while the economic conjuncture did not allow for revolutionary struggles in the immediate future, in certain countries it could not fail to give rise to trade union struggles linked to the various phases of the economic cycle.

The congress's document on the colonial revolution, presented by Pierre Frank, stressed the fact that it was the dominant feature of the post-war period; it had upset all the perspectives that had been made since the origin of the working class movement, even those made after the October Revolution, because all the perspectives had been based on the victory of the revolution in the West before it could triumph in the East. The document pointed out that the colonial revolution could triumph only as a permanent revolution; that it was thus an integral part of the world revolution; that it constituted at a given stage the link between October and the victory of the world revolution. The document went on to a detailed study of the colonial movements, of the nature of their leaderships (particularly those of a pronounced Bonapartist character), of the policy of the imperialists and of the different workers states (USSR, China) with respect to colonial countries and colonial movements. The document examined the respective roles of the proletariat and the peasantry in the colonial countries. Already emphasised was the importance of guerrilla warfare in colonial countries, not only as a military factor but also as a factor in the organisation and political education of the masses. The congress insisted on the necessity for the Trotskyist movement, especially for the sections in the imperialist countries, to devote a large part of its activity to aiding the colonial revolution.

The Fifth Congress went back to the document 'The Rise and Decline of Stalinism' adopted by the preceding congress and added another section to it entitled 'The Decline and Fall of Stalinism'. The completed document, presented by Ernest Mandel, constitutes one of the most exhaustive texts extant on Stalinism, the workers states, and the Communist parties. Its point of departure is the great historical stages since the October Revolution: the rise in the revolutionary tide from 1917 to 1923, the decline from 1923 to 1943, the new rise beginning in 1943. It reviews the objective conditions surrounding

Stalin's rise in the Soviet Union and the Stalinisation of the Communist parties (isolation and backwardness of the Soviet state, decline of the world revolution) and counterposes the objective conditions of the new situation: the existence of several workers states, the USSR become the second world power, the revolutionary rise throughout the world. Thus it clearly sets forth the conditions underlying the crisis of Stalinism. It demonstrates that henceforth there can be no danger, except in the highly improbable case of defeat in a world war, of a restoration of capitalism in the Soviet Union. The crisis of Stalinism should consequently result in a confrontation between the bureaucracy and the proletariat. The document characterises the 'de-Stalinisation' measures as measures of the self-defence -- not self-liquidation -- of the bureaucracy, showing that those in power are hoping, through these measures, to find a wider base in the bureaucracy itself and to satisfy some of the crying needs of the masses. That part of the document written after the events of 1956 contained an erroneous perspective: it envisaged a sharpening of the crisis of Stalinism in the immediate future. It did not foresee the period that may be called 'reformist', which followed the elimination of the 'anti-party group' by Khrushchev in 1957 and which lasted about ten years. Finally, the document outlined a programme of transitional demands for the political revolution, starting from the demands Trotsky had already formulated in the 1938 *Transitional Programme*, taking into account the data furnished by the new conditions in the Soviet Union and by the Polish and Hungarian events of 1956. The document devotes considerable space to the crisis in the Communist parties, both in the workers states and in the capitalist countries. The subsequent development of the Sino-Soviet dispute would renew this subject and intensify its importance.

The discussions at the Fifth Congress were broad in scope; certain points were strongly debated by various delegates, but there was no tendency struggle. The International had largely recovered; it came out, once again unanimously, in favour of reunification of the international movement. But underneath the unity shown at the congress, new crises were brewing. Friction could already be felt in the International's leadership.

Crises and regroupments (the Sixth World Congress)

The 1953 split had brought the North American movements, among others, into conflict with the International. This resulted in a dangerous disequilibrium within the organisation, where the Asian representation was relatively limited; where, as would later be realised, the Ceylonese section had started to degenerate; and where the European sections were working under increasingly unfavourable conditions, in an atmosphere of growing political apathy. The European sections were, of course, going to devote a large part of their activity to helping the Algerian revolution; but, important as this activity was, it involved only a limited, often not very proletarian, group of people who were sympathetic to the colonial revolution but many of whom had defeatist feelings about a socialist revolution in advanced capitalist countries. There was a striking contrast between what was happening in the colonial countries and the almost complete political stagnation in Europe. In the colonial countries, even when the mass movement suffered defeat, it made a very quick recovery; the revolution was victorious in Black Africa in 1960; it was going to triumph as a socialist revolution in Cuba, in the very jaw of imperialism. In Europe, on the other hand, with the accession to power of de Gaulle in 1958, the proletariat was going to suffer its most severe defeat since the end of the war.

Another phenomenon of major importance also having repercussions in the Trotskyist movement was the Sino-Soviet dispute.

These events affected not only the Fourth International but also that part of the Trotskyist movement regrouped around the International Committee. There, too, various differentiations were taking place. Thus, through a process involving both differentiation and regroupment, the reunification of the International was being prepared. But meanwhile, prior to the Sixth Congress, a serious crisis began to ripen in the International.

Within the International's leadership, divergent points of view became evident, in the first place on tactical problems concerning the European sections that were devoting the major portion of their activity to helping colonial revolutions. Tendencies appeared that considered any effort by the European sections to deal with problems in their respective countries as of little or no value. These tendencies were a reflection in our movement of those currents that had lost all hope in the working class of the European countries; they had been seriously reinforced, especially in France, following de Gaulle's accession to power. The defeat had been a severe one for the working class: the Communist Party had suffered its first big electoral defeat in the second half of 1958, losing a million and a half votes to de Gaulle. Some regarded aid to the colonial revolution not as a task whose importance was determined by the current political conjuncture, but rather as the only thing possible, the proletarian revolution in Europe having been struck off the agenda for a very long period -- if not forever.

In the leadership of the International, a kind of agreement took place at that time between Michel Pablo and Juan Posadas. They united against the 'Europeans' and the members of the international leadership who did not want to abandon political activity within the European mass movement, even though that movement was generally at a very low level of militancy. The early outlines of tendency formations appeared towards the end of 1959, when the International Executive Committee decided to convoke the next world congress. While the documents were in the course of preparation, comrades Pablo and Santen were imprisoned in Amsterdam and prosecuted for their aid to the Algerian revolution. The organisation reacted to these arrests and waged a big campaign for the defence of its members, a campaign linked to the defence of the Algerian revolution.

The arrests gave Posadas the opportunity to launch a violent faction fight against the majority of the members of the international leadership. He mobilised all his forces in Latin America to obtain a majority at the congress. He pretended to be Pablo's spokesperson, and it was at this time that his positions and his statements began to become more and more extravagant. So extreme was his behaviour at the congress that a small group of comrades, forerunners of the Pablo tendency, dissociated themselves from Posadas despite sympathy for his positions. Defeated at the congress, Posadas pursued the struggle inside the International for a few months; then suddenly, shortly before Pablo was set free, he attacked the latter publicly in the Latin American organs available to him and broke with the International.

The Sixth Congress, held early in 1961, had a hundred participants from about thirty countries. Because of the fierce and bitter -- and politically impoverished -- struggle waged by the Posadas faction, the discussions did not allow the International to make any real progress in its thinking; on several occasions it was necessary to refute rather primitive statements on the constant and uninterrupted rise of the revolution and the total inability of capitalism to take measures capable, not of halting the revolutionary thrust, but of containing it for a time. But the documents ratified by the congress were not without importance.

The document on the world economic situation, presented by Ernest Mandel, noted the economic growth in the workers states, particularly China's appearance on the world scene as an industrial power. At the same time, the document refuted Khrushchev's claims, widely believed in that period, to the effect that the USSR would rapidly surpass the USA on the economic plane. As to the capitalist states, the document restated the explanations already supplied on the causes of the 'boom' and expanded them in various areas, especially those related to the proliferation of technological innovation. The document further pointed out the possibilities and the limits of the European Common Market, which was then becoming operative. As to the colonial countries, the document stressed their economic stagnation, if not headlong regression, and stated that economic aid -- whether from capitalist or workers states -- would be insufficient to remedy this state of affairs and thus would not undermine the objective causes giving powerful impetus to the colonial revolution.

The document on the colonial revolution, presented by Livio Maitan, made a special study of the situation in a certain number of colonial zones or colonial countries. A great deal of space was allotted to the Algerian revolution, whose conquest of independence for the country, already discernible, loomed on the horizon. A special resolution was devoted to Cuba, retracing the revolutionary process that had culminated only a short time before in making the island a workers state, the first in the Western hemisphere.

A document on Stalinism, presented by Pierre Frank, noted the 'reformist' character of the period that followed the 1953-57 unrest, and the new contradictions that were beginning to take shape in the workers states. The document also made a study of the new contradictions to which the Communist parties were subject. It pointed out the compromise between the Chinese and Soviet leaderships embodied in the text adopted several weeks earlier by the Moscow Conference of 81 Communist and Workers parties, and concluded that this compromise could not be a lasting one, that the Sino-Soviet crisis would inevitably erupt again.

This was the first congress since 1948 at which the Lanka Sama Samaja Party (Ceylonese section of the Fourth International) was not represented, and its absence was of great concern to the congress. The LSSP had suffered an electoral defeat in March 1960, completely dashing the optimistic prospects it had envisaged and had led the International to share. Instead of moving on to a thorough examination of the causes for this error in analysis and perspective, as the International -- in its internal documents addressed to the LSSP -- attempted to have it do, the leadership of the LSSP had adopted a clearly opportunistic line that the International could not approve. In a public declaration, the Secretariat of the International had dissociated itself from the LSSP's line. The Sixth Congress adopted a resolution, which it made public, disapproving the policy followed by the LSSP after the latter's electoral defeat. The resolution especially criticised the LSSP's vote in favour of the budget of the Sri Lanka Freedom Party bourgeois government, and called on the Ceylonese section to correct its line.

Meanwhile Posadas and his faction (which kept losing ground in Latin America) noisily proclaimed that they supported Pablo, even denying that their faction was separate and distinct from his. Suddenly, after the congress and about two months before Pablo was released from jail, Posadas unleashed a public attack in Latin America against him. Why this unexpected attack -- an attack that surprised Pablo himself at the time it occurred? It soon became clear that even if they were in agreement against those they called the 'Europeans' -- meaning Ernest Mandel, Livio Maitan, Pierre Frank -- and subsequently the 'North Americans', they were absolutely opposed to each other on the question of the Sino-Soviet dispute. This question affected the Trotskyist movement considerably, as well as the working class and mass movements as a whole.

During 1959-60, when the Sino-Soviet conflict began to be publicly revealed as a conflict between two parties in which political differences were of prime importance, the International almost unanimously reacted by giving critical support to the Chinese, whose positions on a certain number of basic questions (colonial revolution, peaceful and parliamentary roads to socialism, peaceful co-existence) were progressive compared to those of the Soviet leadership. At the Sixth Congress, right after the conference of the 81 Communist and Workers parties at which the Chinese and Soviet leaderships had arrived at a compromise, the International was unanimous in its analysis of the Sino-Soviet dispute. In a letter to the congress, Pablo wrote from his prison cell: 'Independently of the inevitable ups and downs of this crisis -- the Sino-Soviet dispute -- and independently of the possible smoothing over of differences, the break between the correctly characterised opportunistic right wing [the Soviet leadership] and the centrist-leaning wing [the Chinese] can be considered deep and lasting...'

But towards the middle of 1961, differing opinions on the Sino-Soviet dispute appeared in the International. After having broken with the International, Posadas not only identified his positions almost completely with those of the Chinese, but even declared that he had inspired them. It is common knowledge that Moscow, by distorting certain of Mao Tse-tung's statements on atomic weapons, made every effort to accuse him, falsely, of wanting nuclear war. But Posadas had no qualms about pushing matters to extreme absurdity, claiming it was necessary for the USSR to launch a preventive nuclear war to assure the triumph of the world revolution. He also picked up the Chinese attacks against Castro and even added to them. While the great majority within the International upheld its positions, Pablo completely reversed his viewpoint. He identified the Chinese positions with Stalinism, and gave almost uncritical support to Khrushchev and especially the Yugoslavs.

The International Committee

A history of the Fourth International must, of course, include the history of the organisations comprising the International Committee and that of the International Committee itself. On this, we apologise for not being able to supply more than brief notes. The primary difficulty stems from the fact that the International Committee really functioned not as a centralised organisation but as a faction with loose ties among its members. According to information supplied by comrades who took part in the International Committee, there were few international meetings of the committee, political positions often being formulated, in the form of documents from national sections, after exchanges of views between the committee's sections. Consequently, after reviewing the conditions mentioned earlier under which the International Committee was formed, we shall deal here with the circumstances that brought it to reunification.

We had said that originally there were political differences, particularly in connection with evaluating the meaning of 'de-Stalinisation' when that process began. There were also suspicions about the role of the international centre in the crisis that divided the Socialist Workers Party in the United States in 1953. For various reasons there had been no clarification of this subject. For some years these suspicions, aimed at Pablo in particular, were a serious obstacle to any rapprochement. But beginning in 1956, the Twentieth Congress of the CPSU and the Sino-Soviet dispute brought the positions of the two groups closer on the question of the crisis of Stalinism.

Moreover, on the problems of the colonial revolution, members and sympathisers of the International Committee, especially those in North America and Latin America, underwent an experience with the Cuban revolution that was in many respects similar to the Fourth International's experience with the Algerian revolution.

In the International Committee, too, while the majority adopted positions converging with those of the majority of the International, there was a minority that was to hold differing and clearly opposed positions. This led to a split in the International Committee when the reunification took place. That committee's British and French groups, the Socialist Labour League (SLL) and the Organisation Communiste Internationaliste (OCI) respectively, while not holding identical positions on all questions, nevertheless agreed to reject the above-mentioned points of view and adopted ultra-left positions.

For them the colonial revolution does not exist. Colonial countries are capitalist countries -- which is true -- and consequently, without a really proletarian and revolutionary Marxist leadership, there can be no socialist revolution in these countries, only betrayal of the mass movements. The SLL (now the Workers Revolutionary Party) and the OCI have a limited understanding of the peasantry in these countries, identifying it with the relatively well-off peasantry in Western Europe. Although claiming to adhere to Trotskyism, they do not understand the permanent character of the revolution in these countries. When the revolution triumphed in Cuba, they refused to recognise it. A declaration of the National Committee of the SLL stated that in Cuba there had been 'a political revolution that has transferred power from the hands of one bourgeois class to another sector of that same class....Thus we have Kemal Ataturk, Chiang Kai-shek, Nasser, Nehru, Cardenas, Peron, Ben Bella -- and Castro'. 'Castro's regime has not created a new type of state', qualitatively different from the Batista regime. Even now, at this date, the WRP still considers Cuba a bourgeois state, and Castro a leader of the same stripe as Batista and Chiang Kai-shek !

As to de-Stalinisation, these groups almost completely deny the processes that have taken place in the Soviet Union since Stalin's death. They consider that acknowledging the existence of liberalisation measures is a 'capitulation' to Stalinism. They are incapable of differentiating between the 'liberalisation' that has taken place to a certain degree and 'democratisation' -- which does not exist at all.

In fact, in their eyes no profound changes have occurred in the world since 1938, when the Fourth International was founded and the *Transitional Programme* adopted. They hold on to every letter of it in an extremely rigid fashion, and denounce as capitulators those Trotskyists who have tried to understand the new conditions of our times and to define a revolutionary Marxist policy appropriate to these new conditions.

The International Reunited

A relatively prolonged period of crises and splits may prove to be a prelude to a period of reunification. All the great events of the epoch -- 'de-Stalinisation', the Sino-Soviet conflict, colonial revolutions -- had not only resulted in dividing the Trotskyists, they were to contribute to healing the most serious split, that of 1953-54.

The narrowing of the political differences between the majority of the Fourth International and the majority of the International Committee on such important questions as 'de-Stalinisation' and the colonial revolution; the similarity of experiences in Cuba and Algeria -- all this could not fail to raise the problem of reunification. At a time when a resurgence of Trotskyism was beginning to appear in the world, both sides were well aware that a divided movement would considerably diminish the prospects lying before the Fourth International. In 1961-62, contact was initiated. In the course of discussion, it became evident that the similarity of positions discernible in the respective publications was indeed substantial, and that there did not seem to be any major political obstacles in the way of reunification.

A Parity Commission between the Fourth International and the International Committee was established to prepare for reunification through a joint congress. In the Fourth International as well as in the International Committee, those who opposed reunification and who had opposing political orientations (the Pablo faction on one hand, the SLL and OCI on the other) wanted to subordinate the reunification discussion to a discussion of the 1953 split, of what caused the split and where the responsibility for it lay. The majority on both sides refused to accept such a proposal. No one dreamed of denying the value of such a discussion -- if it was placed in a context that could lead to positive results. If the split was based on questions of principle, these would continue to surface in one form or another in the 1960s, in connection with current political problems. If the split was essentially the product of conjunctural causes (errors of analysis or perspective) or organisational causes, as we thought, these should not constitute an obstacle to reunification. Study of the causes of the split and who was responsible for it should be of an educational nature; thus it was decided, by common accord, that this question would not be raised at the time of reunification and that it would be studied at a later time, when the reunification had been consolidated. The discussion could then take place without interfering with the organisation's activity and without necessarily following the lines of cleavage that existed during the split. It was clear to those who wanted reunification that lurking behind the demand of the minorities was, above all, their desire to use this discussion not to further reunification but once more to justify the split and, worse yet, to assure its perpetuation.

The Reunification Congress ('Dynamics of World Revolution Today')

At the same time that the International was preparing its Seventh Congress, and the International Committee a conference of its organisations, the Parity Commission worked on the reunification. The latter was to be effected at a joint congress held immediately after the two above-mentioned assemblies. The Parity Commission prepared the documents that served as the basis for what was to be jointly discussed.

Thus in June 1963, after the International's congress and the International Committee's conference, the Reunification Congress was held, with twenty-six countries represented. Invited to attend the Reunification Congress, the Posadas tendency did not reply, while the SLL and OCI refused to participate. Both assemblies were held, then a joint congress announced the reunification, formally adopted the documents that had been approved by the two assemblies, and elected the new, united leadership. The minority led by Pablo presented a counter-resolution on the international situation and the tasks of the Fourth International. This minority was given representation in the leadership bodies.

The congress decided to initiate a campaign to free Hugo Blanco, who had recently been arrested in Peru and was facing the death penalty.

This time the Ceylonese section was represented at the world congress, but we learned that the section was in bad shape and that its delegate represented only a minority in the leadership. What happened to this section will be described later.

The congress devoted an entire day to discussing the Algerian question, on which Pablo had presented a report. The congress was unanimous in seeing important possibilities for the development of the Algerian revolution towards a socialist revolution, as had happened in Cuba, and decided to do its utmost to mobilise the International and its sections in support of the Algerian revolution.

As a basis for reunification, the congress adopted a sixteen-point charter, compactly formulating the fundamental positions of Trotskyism. The charter had been adopted earlier by the US Socialist Workers Party, which wished in this way to show its complete support for reunification; the SWP could not participate in the reunification formally, on an organisational level, because of 'democratic' America's restrictive laws.

In addition to the resolution on the international political situation, the congress adopted two important political documents. One dealt with the Sino-Soviet conflict and the situation in the USSR and the other workers states; the other was devoted to the dynamics of the world revolution today.

The document on Stalinism gave an overall picture of the latter's decomposition. It dealt at length with the differences that came to the surface in the Sino-Soviet conflict, and offered a minutely detailed criticism of the positions of both sides. It also examined the differentiations that had appeared in the other Communist parties. The document analysed, among others, the Cuban leadership, stressing its generally progressive positions while noting that its perspectives were limited to Latin American problems. The text also included a detailed study of the situation in the workers states, where new contradictions -- as well as currents with oppositional potential -- were appearing. Yugoslavia was analysed as a special case: on important points the orientation had been more correct than in the other workers states, but decentralisation pushed to the extreme and acceptance of the free play of market laws brought serious dangers. Finally, the document reformulated the essential points of a programme of action for the workers states, enabling the Trotskyist movement to intervene in the crises of Stalinism and to find support inside the workers states.

The main document of the congress was devoted to 'Dynamics of World Revolution Today'. It embodied the conclusions reached by a very large majority of Trotskyists throughout the world in the wake of the gigantic upheavals of the post-war period.

This text began by pointing out the fact that the world revolution had extended from the Soviet Union towards the colonial countries and not, as had for a long time been expected, towards the economically developed capitalist countries. The document showed that this process, which had carried the revolution to the periphery first, before reaching the heart of the capitalist system, had in no way been an inevitable one: it was essentially a product of betrayal by the traditional working class leaderships, social-democratic and Stalinist.

The document then explained that in our era the world revolution was going forward on three fronts, each with its own distinct characteristics: the proletarian or classical revolution in the developed capitalist states; the colonial revolution in the underdeveloped capitalist countries, where it tended to become a permanent revolution; the political, anti-bureaucratic revolution in the workers states. The document emphasised that it was not a question of simply adding up the three sectors, since the world revolution constitutes a whole whose various parts have a reciprocal effect on each other. And most of the text was specifically devoted to a study of the characteristics of each of these sectors and their interaction with each other.

But the document was not limited to an examination of the 'objective' conditions of the world revolution; it dealt with the 'subjective' conditions in just as thorough a fashion. Reviewing the necessity for revolutionary leaderships (building such leaderships was the task the Fourth International had set itself from its very foundation), the document replied to a question raised by numerous militants who felt neither deliberate hostility towards the Fourth International nor hostility towards the necessity of a democratically centralised party. That question was: Why hasn't the Fourth International developed into a mass organisation? Why wasn't it able to do so after the period of ebb, which extended from 1923 to 1943, came to a close?

The document does not dodge this question. It points out how the defeat of Nazism, due in great part to the Soviet armies, had directly served to strengthen the Stalinist leaderships. The war of 1914-18 had been a war between imperialists, which mainly implicated the European workers. Organised then by the parties of the Second International, these workers came out of the war full of indignation against the betrayal by social-democracy; they responded *en masse* to the appeal of the October Revolution and the Communist International. Their feelings were unambiguous, although they were still in the grip of political confusion. The war of 1939-45, however, combined the previous war between imperialists with a war of defence of the Soviet Union against German imperialism and its allies.

Another element was added to this situation with the occupation of Europe by the armies of German imperialism. The European workers wanted to defend the Soviet Union and to fight Nazism in their own countries. Following the policies of Stalin and the CPs, they carried on their struggle not only in alliance with socialist and bourgeois organisations, but under the leadership of bourgeois governments 'allied' to the Soviet Union. For many of them, the military struggle had priority over everything else, in the hope that things would become clear with the coming victory. Besides, the programme of the Resistance also generated many illusions.

Thus the European workers, contrary to what occurred at the end of the First World War, came out of the war in 1945 with mixed feelings. In any case, they were very far from being hostile to the leaders of the CPs, who appeared to them as the representatives of the Soviet Union which had brought about victory through so many sacrifices. At the time the Trotskyist propaganda against the class collaboration of the CPs with the bourgeoisie of their country was not understood. These circumstances allowed the European bourgeoisie, with the help of the CPs, to contain the revolutionary upsurges which took place. The crisis of Stalinism began to appear and develop only after the beginning of the 'cold war' and during the period of prosperity dominated by the political apathy of the masses.

[?] of the CPs, to contain the revolutionary upsurges which took place. The crisis of Stalinism began to appear and develop only after the beginning of the 'cold war' and during the period of prosperity dominated by the political apathy of the masses.

'Dynamics of World Revolution Today' also showed how -- since the crisis of Stalinism developed under extremely complex conditions, while the countries with the greatest Marxist traditions were going through a stage of political apathy on the part of the working class -- the Fourth International had come up against numerous and substantial obstacles to progress. Nevertheless, these obstacles had not prevented the Fourth International from making more and more solid progress, as: the old leaderships suffered erosion. The document ended with an exceptionally forceful justification of the need, more imperative in today's world than ever before, for the Fourth International as it is today, in order to build the mass Fourth International of tomorrow. To our knowledge, no one has attempted to criticise this document, or even partially or indirectly answer it.

Attacks against the reunited International (the splitters)

The Reunification Congress had put an end to an organisational situation that had given momentum to the centrifugal forces operating on the International; but these forces had not disappeared with the reunification, nor had the difficulties in this area been overcome.

The majority of the organisations brought together in the reunited International encountered no difficulties, even of a minor order, amongst themselves. On the contrary, they had to defend the International against those who had not wanted to participate in the reunification, and for several months internally against the faction led by Pablo. For the latter groups, the reunification constituted a step that, in the long run, threatened their existence, and they had to try to break it up while it was still weak.

The congress had reunited a very large majority of the Trotskyist forces. The Posadas faction was soon to dwindle to a single group in Argentina of slight importance; everywhere else it was composed of individuals. When the Pablo faction publicly broke with the International, about a year after the congress, that faction, too, was numerically very weak. The only two groups of any size outside the International were the SLL in Great Britain and the OCI in France. But what could be clearly seen from inside the International was not so obvious to the world at large, since these groups made their existence known through publications that concentrated on attacking the International.

We have already presented the sectarian positions of the Healy and Lambert groups, and it is not necessary to take this up again at any length. Curiously enough, they intensified their attacks against the 'Pabloite' International even several years after Pablo's split, and their attacks were directed to a much lesser degree against Pablo himself, whom they ignored from the moment he broke with the International. It was not Pablo and his ideas that bothered them, but rather the very existence and activity of the International and its sections. The Healy and Lambert groups made a big fuss about holding an international conference of their 'Committee' in April 1966, aimed at 'reconstructing' the Fourth International; this conference was completely unsuccessful and wound up in a break with those who had attended as observers.

The Posadas group' had been especially harmful to the International in Latin America, where, to the Cubans in particular, it represented (wrongly) Trotskyism and the Fourth International. Castro's attack on the Fourth International -- as well as on other revolutionary tendencies -- at the Tricontinental Conference in Havana in January 1966 was partially based on the incorrect positions taken by the Posadas group. Without for one instant abating its activity in defence of the Cuban revolution, the Fourth International firmly but without exaggeration challenged Castro's anti-Trotskyist statements. We were able to ascertain the results obtained on this point when, the following year, on the anniversary of the Tricontinental Conference, Radio Havana re-broadcast Castro's speech without, however, including the part directed against the Fourth International and the other revolutionary tendencies.

The struggle that Pablo and his faction undertook, right after the congress, lasted several months, during which time they often went from one subject to another. With the defeat suffered by the French working class as a result of de Gaulle's coming to power, it was the development of the Algerian revolution, in the years preceding and immediately following its conquest of independence, that heavily influenced Pablo's thinking. He saw, and correctly so, analogies between the course of the Algerian revolution and the course of the Cuban revolution, and, consequently, hoped for a victorious socialist revolution in Algeria. There was no disagreement with Pablo on that point. But losing more and more contact with the Fourth International on one hand, and placing false hopes in his personal opportunities for intervening at the top levels of the Algerian movement on the other hand, he wound up not so much by elaborating an international political line, whether opportunistic or sectarian -- at that time he adopted positions in an impressionistic fashion and often changed them from top to bottom in a very short space of time[19] -- as by denying the need for an international organisation, functioning as at present on the basis of democratic centralism. He put forward a concept of the Fourth International that he had formerly vigorously denounced, i.e., a federation of factions independent of each other and acting in common only on questions on which they were in agreement. After the split, he devoted himself principally to commenting on events; thenceforth he favoured using mass movements as they are rather than building new revolutionary parties.

The degeneration of the Ceylonese section

One of the most painful questions facing the united leadership was that of the Ceylonese[20] section. This is the place to discuss the entire problem.

The Lanka Sama Samaja Party (LSSP) was a section of the Fourth International with very special characteristics in comparison with all the other sections, by reason of its origin, its composition, its functioning and its influence in its own country. To a large extent,

---

[19] To mention only a few examples of his most impressionistic positions: he counted on imperialism's rapid retreat from Vietnam early in 1965, which attested to his belief in 'peaceful co-existence'; he saw 'political revolution' in Yugoslavia when Rankovic was eliminated; he made an abrupt change on China, in favour of the Soviet leadership; he made a series of political zigzags on Ceylon, etc.
[20] Ceylon is now called Sri Lanka

this stemmed from certain characteristics of the political and social situation in Ceylon itself. This island had had no bourgeois movement for independence, unlike its neighbour India, whose Congress party even dared to organise an uprising against British colonialism during the Second World War, in British colonialism's most difficult days.

Ceylon's struggle for independence was launched by young intellectuals of bourgeois origin who, in the course of their stay in British universities during the 1930s, had been won over to communist ideas. Moreover, the most outstanding of these young people, moved by the defeat of the second Chinese revolution and seeking the reasons for that defeat, became aware of Trotsky's positions on China and adopted the theory of permanent revolution. Returning to Ceylon, they created the LSSP and began to organise the workers into trade unions. During the war, the LSSP got rid of the Ceylonese Stalinists who, because of the alliance between the Soviet Union and British imperialism, refused to wage a struggle against colonialism.

Imprisoned as a result of the repression, these young Trotskyists managed to escape and make their way to India, where they took part in that country's struggles and helped to found the Indian section of the Fourth International. Back in Ceylon after the war, their wartime attitude earned them enormous popularity among the working class masses. The Ceylonese bourgeoisie, more exactly its comprador part strongly attached to British capitalism, benefited from the latter's retreat and obtained independence in India's wake in 1948, without having to wage the slightest struggle for it. The political party of this comprador bourgeoisie, the UNP (United National Party), came to power. The LSSP then surged forward as the island's second party -- the party of the workers.

Thus this party, which had got rid of its Stalinist wing and had joined the Fourth International, did not arise out of crises within the working class movement and struggles against the old leaderships -- as did the other sections of the Fourth International. It was rather the fruit of courageous action by a team of young, revolutionary intellectuals who, the first to do so in Ceylon, had organised the working class and demanded the country's independence from British imperialism.

Heading the party was a team composed for the most part of people like Colvin R. de Silva, Leslie Goonawardene, Bernard Soysa, Doric de Souza, Edmund Samarakkody, people of great intellectual worth and great fighting spirit. There were also other elements in the leadership, such as N.M. Perera, far less interested in theoretical questions, opportunistic in character, whose authority stemmed from his systematic trade union work. These elements were held in check by the leading nucleus. The ranks of the party were composed of very militant workers, very devoted to their class.

But for objective reasons, there had from the start been quite a big gap between the political education of the leadership and that of the rank and file. The overwhelming majority of the workers do not know English. In the absence of adequate material in the Sinhalese or Tamil languages for their political education, the workers had only a rudimentary notion of Marxist principles and the theories of Trotsky and the Fourth International. In its mass, the LSSP was not really Trotskyist in origin.

The party also went through internal struggles, and bourgeois elements were fought and eliminated by the LSSP leadership, which for years acted as a true revolutionary leadership, working to advance its organisation towards Trotskyism. Its attitude on 12 August 1953, when a *hartal* (general strike) paralysed the country, was remarkable, and later it most courageously opposed the communalist currents which for a time set one of Ceylon's main nationalities against the other.

Nevertheless, despite their intellectual qualities, members of this leadership were not without weakness. The party did not have a real Bolshevik organisational structure; its congresses were actually general assemblies in which eloquent oratory often outweighed sound political argument. After a while, when the organisation had made electoral gains, political education was neglected in favour of superficial activism, and growing parliamentary tendencies in the party could be observed. While acknowledging these tendencies, the leadership did not fight against them hard enough, and eventually itself became infected.

Finally, while the party had a solid working class base, it barely had a toehold in the rural masses that constitute the majority of the island's population. The party hardly had a programme for them -- and this proved to be an important factor in leading to its political debacle. For a long time, the party had taken hold only among the Sinhalese workers (workers in the port city of Colombo, transport workers, clerical workers, etc.); only with difficulty did the party reach the biggest part of Ceylon's proletariat, the plantation workers made up of Indians 'imported' long ago by the British for the latter's needs. These workers still have no citizenship, neither Ceylonese nor Indian.

The International had frequently called the LSSP leadership's attention to these weaknesses and to the necessity for remedying them. But the International's efforts were limited to those members who could understand English, and under the circumstances, this meant the most advanced section, i.e., the leadership of the party. For many years, there had been only two opposing parties on the national level, the UNP and the LSSP. During the 1950s, however, the Sri Lanka Freedom Party (SLFP) arose out of a split in the UNP. To the surprise of the LSSP leaders, the new party's success in the 1956 election brought it to power. Instead of proceeding to a profound analysis of the causes for this electoral victory, the LSSP's leaders, who very correctly characterised the SLFP as a bourgeois party with a wider base than the UNP, judged that the new party, like the UNP, would rapidly wear out its credit and that the LSSP would then have a clear field.

It was with this perspective that the LSSP approached the March 1960 elections, in which it hoped to win a parliamentary majority. The tremendous effort the party put into these elections made its defeat all the more painful. From that time on, the LSSP's leadership found itself politically disoriented. It began to vacillate politically; the influence of N.M. Perera, who became more open in advancing reformist positions, began to spread. Right after these elections, N.M. Perera proposed that the LSSP enter a government coalition with the SLFP. This proposal was rejected, but the LSSP's parliamentary group practically gave the bourgeois government of the SLFP a vote of confidence. The Fourth International publicly disavowed that vote.

Later on, when the masses went into action against some of the new government's measures, the LSSP went over to the opposition, but without making a serious self-criticism of its previous attitude. The relative consolidation of the SLFP in the 1960 elections accentuated the vacillation of the LSSP leadership. It had to suffer the political consequences of neglecting the problems of the Ceylonese rural population. It did not understand that this new bourgeois party, unlike the comprador UNP, was based on the 'national bourgeoisie', and that this party had been able to win support among the rural masses neglected by the LSSP.

Nevertheless, there was another partial turn to the left by the party in 1962-63, when the masses again went into action. Together with the Ceylonese Communist Party and a small, radical-appearing bourgeois organisation, the Mahajana Eksath Peramuna (MEP), the LSSP formed what was called the United Left Front. This organisation was well received by the Ceylonese masses and could have, were it not for the inadequacy of its programme, constituted the point of departure of an extra-parliamentary struggle for power. But a half-fought fight paves the way for disaster.

THE LONG MARCH OF THE TROTSKYISTS

Inside the leadership, N.M. Perera, who for a long time had been held in check by the intellectual authority and political strength of the other members of the leadership, gained free rein as a result of the latter's vacillations. The leadership, disoriented and unsure, was divided: on one side, the main nucleus, including Colvin R. de Silva and Leslie Goonawardene, adopted a conciliatory position towards the SLFP; on the other, Edmund Samarakkody and Bala Tampoe defended correct, principled positions, but in a political form that the International considered sectarian and hardly likely to convince the rank and file to oppose the party's political concessions. In this troubled situation, N.M. Perera entered into negotiations with the prime minister, without the party's knowledge, and then demanded the immediate calling of a special congress of the party to answer the proposals for a government coalition that the prime minister had made to him. By then the Ceylonese organisation had reached an advanced stage of political degeneration. At the congress, about 25 per cent of the members rejected in principle any participation in the government, any participation in a bourgeois regime. The old Colvin R. de Silva-Leslie Goonawardene team, which for twenty-five years had led the party, received only 10 per cent of the votes on an amendment to the Perera resolution, and in the final vote only retained 4 to 5 per cent -- the remaining votes going to Perera, who became head of the organisation. With certain of his friends, he entered the government.

After the Sixth World Congress's condemnation of the LSSP's vote for the SLFP budget in 1960 -- a condemnation independently supported by the position publicly taken in *The Militant* by the US Socialist Workers Party -- the LSSP leadership still had not sufficiently rectified its orientation. Its oscillations continued. In numerous interventions, the International tried to change the LSSP's line in a more vigorous and thoroughgoing fashion. At the Seventh World Congress, which preceded the reunification of the International, Ceylon was represented by Comrade Samarakkody. At that time, the left wing to which he belonged had dissociated itself from the centrist majority of the leadership, but without deeming it necessary as yet to organise a faction for waging the struggle. The LSSP had just organised the United Left Front. The congress forwarded a long letter to the LSSP, in which it stressed the inadequacies of this policy on four fundamental points:
- Insufficient critical analysis of the 1960 error.
- Lack of clarity with respect to the extra-parliamentary nature of the potentialities of the United Left Front, in contrast with its parliamentary aspects.

- Failure to criticise publicly the opportunistic policy of its allies (the CP and the MEP).
- Failure to include the Tamil plantation workers' trade union organisations in the United Left Front.

Later, on 23 April 1964, when the United Secretariat of the Fourth International was informed of N.M. Perera's moves, it condemned them, declaring that accepting such a policy would be tantamount to betrayal. At the congress held in Colombo on 6-7 June of the same year, the Fourth International's delegate, Pierre Frank, denounced the policy of coalition from the speakers' platform. To all the Ceylonese people who were following the congress's proceedings, he publicly declared that if such a policy were adopted, it would cause a split between the LSSP and the International. Immediately after the vote, the break was effected by the United Secretariat.

Supporters of the Fourth International regrouped after the congress's vote for the purpose of re-establishing the Trotskyist organisation. Unfortunately, Trotskyism had suffered a severe blow in Ceylon and the Trotskyist movement in that country has yet to regain a firm foundation.

The campaigns of the International (The Second Congress after reunification)

Internal difficulties and attacks of hostile groups were, fortunately, not the only matters claiming the attention of the united leadership of the International. The entire Trotskyist movement was engaged in increasing its activities, consolidating the reunification and preparing for an expansion of the International.

The International undertook a campaign in defence of the imprisoned Polish revolutionists, two young leaders in particular, Modzelewsky and Kuron, who were spokespersons for left currents at the University of Warsaw. The International was responsible for publishing their 'Open Letter to the Polish Workers Party'" which was the first programmatic document of the anti-bureaucratic revolution to come out of a workers state since the days of Trotsky and the Left Opposition. The International also publicised the positions of Communists who criticised, from the left, the Yugoslav Communist League's policies. For the first time in many years, Marxist revolutionary thought was being formulated in places where Stalinism had exercised almost total domination, or where right-wing leaderships prevailed.

Moreover, the Fourth International was at various times able to publicise positions and documents coming from critical elements within the Soviet Union itself. It was also able to bring the positions of a left current in Czechoslovakia to the attention of world working class opinion.

The Fourth International intervened in various ways in the Sino-Soviet conflict. All the sections utilised the opportunities available to them for influencing the crisis in the Communist parties. As their differences became sharper, the two leaderships, Soviet and Chinese, each accused the other of playing into the Fourth International's hands.

We have already mentioned the defence of Cuba. On this subject, it should be pointed out that the activity of Latin American Trotskyists contributed a great deal towards clarifying the Cuban positions on Trotskyism. In accordance with the decision of the world congress mentioned above, an international campaign was launched for the defence of Hugo Blanco, a Trotskyist militant and leader of the Peruvian peasants. After a somewhat slow start, this campaign attained considerable proportions. Declarations of solidarity arrived from all over the world; more and more meetings and demonstrations were held in numerous cities everywhere. This campaign was so strong that it reached the reformist trade unions as well as organisations linked to the Communist parties. Never before had the International waged such a world campaign. Undoubtedly this campaign coincided with a development of the objective situation, first in Latin America and then in Vietnam, which assured it of a broader audience. At first this campaign resulted in several postponements of the trial -- a trial at which Hugo Blanco defended himself in masterful fashion. The campaign succeeded in averting the death penalty that the court would most certainly have pronounced, considering the charges against Hugo Blanco, if world opinion had not been alerted and mobilised.

Finally, from the beginning of 1965 -- immediately following the American escalation of the war in Vietnam -- the International alerted all its sections, the entire vanguard, to carry out actions in support of the Vietnamese revolution.

Less than two years after the reunification, the decision was made to call a world congress. Represented at this congress, held in December 1965 with over sixty persons present, were twenty-five countries. The congress demonstrated that the reunification had been effectively consolidated, the centrifugal forces having been largely overcome. The organisation was able to turn most of its forces outward and implement its policies under more normal conditions.

The congress gave top importance to the defence of Vietnam. On the heels of the serious defeats of the masses in Brazil and Indonesia, the congress forcefully proclaimed the need to counterpose a world strategy for socialist revolution to the global strategy of imperialism. It issued the following call for the defence of the Vietnamese revolution:

'Communists, worker-members of Communist parties, workers, youth, intellectuals of the workers states:
'Initiate and broaden your campaign to compel the Kremlin to end its shady and underhand dealings with the imperialist aggressor while it gives only miserly driblets of aid to the heroic masses of the Democratic Republic of Vietnam and the National Liberation Front of South Vietnam. By the millions raise the slogan, "Planes, guns for the Vietnamese people!"
'Workers, poor peasants, militant nationalists in the semicolonial countries:
'Rise up resolutely against imperialism, strike against it everywhere at the same time. Take advantage of the fact that imperialism has engaged its main forces in Vietnam. Open up many new fronts, and strike down imperialism's lackeys and toadies wherever conditions are favourable.
'Workers of the entire world:
'Compel the leaders of all mass organisations, the leaders of all workers states that claim to speak in the name of socialism, to form an unshakable anti-imperialist united front, under whose devastating blows imperialism will be forced to retreat.'

In addition to a political resolution dealing with several essential points, among others the crisis of leadership in the colonial revolution -- which had resulted in a series of grave defeats -- and the new oppositional currents that had appeared in the United States, several documents were discussed and adopted at this congress.

The development of West European capitalism and the tasks of revolutionary Marxists was the subject of one of these documents. This document, presented by I. Rivera, analysed in detail the development of the economic situation, which evinced different characteristics in different countries, and the contradictions of the Common Market. It stressed the trend toward a 'strong state' and the obstacles countering the trend. It took note of the appearance of reactionary currents and racist tendencies exploiting the immigration of foreign workers, often dark-skinned, in several countries. The document pointed out the thoroughgoing degeneration of the social-democratic and Stalinist leaderships and the danger of integration into the bourgeois state bearing down ever more heavily on the trade union organisations. It pointed out further that in countries where social-democracy dominated the working class movement, left tendencies made their appearance more often inside the trade union movement, because part of the trade union bureaucracy felt constrained to make a show of opposition in order not to lose all credibility with the workers. Finally, the document stated that, contrary to the thinking of numerous currents which maintained revolutionary positions theoretically but proved total sceptics concerning revolutionary possibilities in the present period, the contradictions of capitalism, even in the framework of neo-capitalism, were such that defensive economic struggles of the masses could at certain times lead to offensive struggles to win transitional demands, and to a revolutionary situation with the appearance of organs of dual power. Starting with these considerations and taking into account the international situation, a specific transitional programme for each country had to be formulated. The document on 'The Sino-Soviet Conflict and the Crisis in the International Communist Movement', presented by Livio Maitan, started off by examining a question that had frequently been raised in various places: was there a Stalinist phase in China (and, more generally, would there necessarily be such a phase in every backward workers state)? Replying in the negative, the document pointed out the differences between Maoism and Stalinism, and reaffirmed Trotsky's view that Stalinism was a form of bureaucratisation that would be unique, because it was due to a particular combination of circumstances -- a combination that would never again occur in history. This document then proceeded to a detailed examination of pro-Peking parties and groups, on the one hand, and pro-Moscow parties and groups, on the other. A section of the text was devoted to Castroism.

Another lengthy document dealt with 'Progress and Problems of the African Revolution'. About ten years had elapsed since the old African colonialism had largely given way to new structures. The document distinguished three major sectors in Africa: where colonialism and racism still exist; where there is a distinct neocolonial structure; and where revolutionary transformations have taken place.

The first sector was essentially confined to the southern part of Africa. It did not pose any special theoretical problems, the important matter being the problems raised by the struggle, which would become exceptionally intense there.

In the second sector were to be found countries like Morocco, Tunisia, Libya, most of the former French colonies in West Africa, the

Congo, Sierra Leone, Nigeria, Ethiopia, Somalia, etc. Nor did this sector pose any difficult theoretical problems. Its neo-colonialist nature was perfectly clear, and the tasks of revolutionists could easily be formulated.

The third sector comprised countries like Ghana, Zanzibar, Guinea, Mall, Egypt, Algeria. Generally speaking, these were countries where independence had been won by mass struggle, or countries which had adopted anti-imperialist, sometimes anti-capitalist, measures and which had been in the vanguard of the struggle against the colonial or neo-colonial systems. A goodly portion of the document was devoted to describing what had happened in these countries, their development, their class structure, measures taken, etc. The document dealt with the Algerian revolution at great length, with special attention to the Pen Bella experience and to the new situation that had been created just a few months before -- the *coup detat* of 19 June 1965, that had carried Boumedienne to power. In addition, the document pointed out the contradictions in these states and endeavoured to formulate the conditions that would assure a mass upsurge capable of transforming these countries into workers states.

The document ended with a section devoted to perspectives and tasks, as well as to several essential conclusions. It highlighted specific characteristics of the African revolution: the existence of very backward sectors; the confrontation between disintegrating tribal structures and the social perspectives of the Twentieth Century world; the extraordinary combined development that marks this continent. The document demonstrated that even where victory was assured by the presence of revolutionary Marxists, there would be no simple solutions to these problems without very substantial and unselfish assistance from the workers states. Such African countries would especially need the help of workers states created in the industrialised countries of Western Europe and North America. The document held it to be the duty of members of the International to help in the formation of African cadres capable of creating genuine revolutionary parties.

This document met with considerable discussion, especially the parts dealing with the Algerian revolution; characterisation of the Ben Bella government; characterisation of the regime in Egypt, etc. The document was adopted by the congress, although the latter felt that while the document could provide a good working basis, various questions needed further and more intensive study. It was therefore decided that discussion of this document should continue after the congress, and that the question of the African revolution would be placed on the agenda of a further world congress.

CONTRIBUTIONS TO THE HISTORY OF THE FOURTH INTERNATIONAL

Chapter 8: From 1968 to 1978. The Turn in the World Situation

The composition of the congress held in late December 1965 reflected the influx of youth that had revitalised the sections. The accentuation of this phenomenon in the following years was to pose a good many new problems. We have reached the point at which our history merges into current politics. It was the war in Vietnam that contributed, in the most conclusive and decisive fashion, to the turn in the world situation that had been ripening beneath the surface apathy, beneath Europe's political stagnation, beneath the reformism that followed 'de-Stalinisation' in the workers states. As Marx said, revolution, that old mole, was inexorably burrowing away, so that one fine day the ground, thus undermined, might cave in.

Other phenomena also operated in a direction equally favourable to the turn in the situation -- for example, China's 'cultural revolution', despite the extravagant forms that it often took. The announcement of the Ninth Congress of the Chinese CP showed that the 'cultural revolution' basically aimed at replacing a bureaucratically ossified apparatus by another apparatus, bureaucratic too, but more active. One of the ways this operation had been effected was through mass mobilisations against the old apparatus. But how many in the capitalist countries saw only these mobilisations and were thus encouraged to revolutionary action!

An international phenomenon, the activation of students in the capitalist countries, was a premonitory sign of this turn in the world situation. Up to then, only students in the under-developed countries participated in mass struggles; there was really nothing surprising about this in the colonial revolution, where students have always played a substantial role. But students entering the political arena in developed capitalist countries was a new phenomenon, whose extent had no comparable precedent in history not even in the bourgeois revolutions. Particular circumstances in each particular country played their part in this phenomenon; since the latter was international in scope, however, it had to have a common objective basis. For the first time -- and this in a by-and-large affluent period -- students, not in tiny minorities but in large masses, attacked university structures, then went on to attack the very social structures of capitalist society, independently of traditional working class leaderships. Various indications also pointed to an awakening of working class youth (even if this was, for the moment, less marked than that of the student youth), with the same tendency towards finding their own path outside the control of the traditional labour leaderships. Finally, an even more unexpected and novel phenomenon appeared -- a political awakening of adolescents in the schools. The International immediately grasped the unusual importance of these developments among the youth.

The sections very rapidly found themselves engaged in propaganda and agitation in favour of the Vietnamese revolution. The aim of this activity was to organise vigorous demonstrations which, in contra-distinction to the never-ending petitions and timid measures of the peace movement, would have real impact and would be really effective. This could be done only by clearly establishing the difference between the demand for 'negotiations' (which was formulated by this instrument of Moscow's peaceful co-existence policy) and a revolutionary policy whose aim was victory for the National Liberation Front, victory for Vietnam.

The policy followed by China and its supporters, confused as it may have been in many ways, also favoured this outflanking of the satellites of the Kremlin in aid to the Vietnamese revolution.

One of the most valuable contributions in furthering the revolutionary currents was Che Guevara's celebrated slogan, 'Two, three... many Vietnams'. He gave his life to make this slogan a reality, to engage the forces of imperialism on another front.

Trotskyists were always in the front ranks of the *ad hoc* groups organised in many countries, first in the United States and Japan, and then in several West European countries, for the purpose of bringing together into one broad, united front all who favoured mass actions on the Vietnam question. Trotskyists were behind the first demonstrations for Vietnam in West Europe (Liege, 15 October 1966; the October 1967 demonstrations at the time of Che Guevara's death; the Berlin demonstration of 21 February 1968). They were in the thick of the battle at Berkeley and in the forefront of all anti-war actions in the United States. It was they who maintained the unity of the movement conducting the campaign in Great Britain, which brought 100,000 demonstrators out in the streets of London on 27 October l968.[21]

---

[21] Never did the position of the Socialist Labour League sectarians appear more pitiful than when they refused to engage in joint actions with 'petty-bourgeois' groups. In the existing circumstances, this position reduced SLL activity to violent attacks against the Fourth International and its supporters,

On the heels of these actions for the defence of Vietnam, the Trotskyist organisations linked up with large layers of youth who, in their search for a revolutionary political programme, were beginning to learn the truth about the October Revolution, the ideas of Lenin and Trotsky, the Trotskyist movement. The Trotskyist organisations (especially those in the West European countries and in the United States, which had suffered long and difficult years of debilitation) were rejuvenated and reaped the benefits of a recruitment larger than they had ever before experienced. It was unavoidable that such a phenomenon would provoke sectarian criticism: students, not workers, are being recruited, etc. Vanguard organisations such as those of the Trotskyist movement have no reason to abstain from being active and recruiting among a social layer where valuable intellectual forces, indispensable for the working class movement, can be found. Aside from this fact, however, the generalised student radicalisation in the developed capitalist states merited analysis because it was specific to a new social situation, different from what had hitherto existed.

---

and to purely verbal denunciations of the reformist and Stalinist leaderships. It also led to the SLL's total isolation from the big mass demonstrations. Thus, after having sent several hundred British youth to Liège on 15 October 1966, in order to denounce the Fourth International, they abstained from participating in the 27 October 1968 demonstration in London, perhaps the greatest mass demonstration held in England since the end of the war -- the most spirited, at any rate. This anti-Vietnam war demonstration was also, in effect, a demonstration of the left against the Wilson government's general policy; the SLL characterised the demonstration as a petty-bourgeois assembly and a 'fraud'!

We do not care to act like scholastics, using and abusing quotations from on high; but with sectarians who follow the letter to better fight the spirit, it is often useful to let the classics take the floor. Let us hear what Lenin had to say in *'Left-wing' Communism: An Infantile Disorder:*

'...how is the discipline of the revolutionary party of the proletariat maintained?... First, by the class consciousness of the proletarian vanguard and by its devotion to the revolution, by its perseverance, self-sacrifice and heroism. Secondly, by its ability to link itself, to keep in close touch with, and to a certain extent, if you like, to merge itself with the broadest masses of the toilers -- primarily with the proletarian, but also with the *non-proletarian* toiling masses. Thirdly, by the correctness of the political leadership exercised by this vanguard....'(Emphasis in original).

Thus, merging to a certain extent with non-proletarian masses is placed above correctness of political line. It took the daring of a Lenin to express the thought. What would our sectarians have said if these lines had been written by us, poor sinners that we are?

THE LONG MARCH OF THE TROTSKYISTS

Technological progress, the needs of the economy, new developments in the sciences -- all this sparked a veritable explosion of the university population. So greatly increased was the size of the student body that it brought about a qualitative change in its social importance. At the same time, the position in society for which these students were being prepared was no longer what it had been. On entering the university -- and even earlier, at school -- they had become extremely concerned about the contradictions of capitalist society. They were even the first to be aware of the new contradictions in neo-capitalist society. This phenomenon assumed exceptionally large dimensions in the United States, but the same tendencies appeared elsewhere. Henceforth there would be about six million students in the fortress of imperialism -- a percentage of the population not very much lower than the percentage of farmers.

This student population is concentrated in university towns. Their studies are not preparing them -- as was formerly the case for most college students -- to fill their parents' shoes, to take their elders' places as bankers, industrialists, or petty-bourgeois professionals (doctors, lawyers, etc.). Gone is the hope that many technicians will be able to find important and high-paying positions in big industrial plants. The new students are destined to become people who work for a living, exploited either by the big corporations or by the state. Socially situated as middle layers, they are threatened with unemployment -- just as workers are. And the numerous social layers of this student population are particularly sensitive to the other multiple contradictions of society.

The use that capitalism makes of their higher education (whether in the natural sciences with, for example, utilisation of nuclear energy for military purposes; or in the social sciences for socially monstrous purposes), together with the criminal behaviour of capitalist society towards the most oppressed strata (colonial masses, blacks, etc.), forced students to go beyond a critique of an educational system that was being 'reformed' only to make it better able to fulfil its alienating functions. They moved on to criticise the underlying causes of the evils that were victimising students themselves, as well.

The International had barely begun preparations for a new world congress (at which, besides the general trend of the world situation, very important specific problems such as the Chinese 'cultural revolution' were to be examined) when a turn in the international situation took place -- the biggest turn, in fact, since the end of the Second World War.

The year 1968, which opened with the smashing defeat inflicted on the Americans by the Vietnamese Tet offensive, will assuredly be a

Landmark in the history of the socialist revolution. Two events stand out. First of all, May 1968 in France. Triggered off by a student revolution, a general strike of 10 million workers in its turn drew large sections of the petty bourgeoisie into an unprecedented challenge to the authority of the state, as well as to private ownership of the means of production and numerous other capitalist institutions. This was followed by a revolutionary upsurge in Czechoslovakia that, during the first week of Soviet military occupation, assumed a size and strength unprecedented in a workers state.

Several other events, smaller in scope but pointing in the same direction, should be added to these two, whose significance defies description:

- The crisis in US imperialism's two-party political system including a leadership crisis -- shown in the presidential election (Johnson's abdication and the general lack of enthusiasm for both Nixon and Humphrey, neither of whom had any political authority).
- The crisis in the international Communist movement, Moscow having definitively lost its authority as 'guide' in this long-time monolithic and extremely hierarchical outfit.
- The disgraceful bankruptcy of the British Labour Party government, the strongest party of the international social-democracy, which had strong hopes for it.
- The activation, after several years of relative passivity, of the Latin American urban masses. This included Mexico, a country considered by its bourgeoisie up to then as immune to Latin American-type revolutions.

These upheavals, the early outlines of which had been apparent for two years, particularly the entry into the lists of a new generation outside the control of the old bureaucracies, confronted the European sections of the Fourth International with the problem of changing their tactics. As soon as these phenomena appeared, the Trotskyist movement had undertaken certain tactical adjustments. This was particularly true in France at the time of the Algerian war, as a result of the working class parties' position on the latter, but they were only partial adjustments. The size and scope of these phenomena laid the groundwork for the formation of currents to the left of the Communist parties, currents strong enough to become factors on the political scene in several countries. Thus, beginning in 1967, the European sections opened a debate on tactics, with a view to revising the entryist tactic. The open discussion on this point was oriented towards a change in tactic. Entryism was the price that had to be paid because of the disproportion that existed between the hegemony of the old leaderships and the weakness of the vanguard, practically incapable of going beyond the stage of a propaganda group. The possibility now existed of organisations being formed that, while still largely in the minority, could nevertheless exercise enough strength in given sectors to acquire importance on a national scale. Moreover, the entryist tactic had been established almost fifteen years earlier on the perspective, based on the relationship of forces at the time, that the crisis would develop through the formation of left tendencies within those leaderships themselves. Because of the prolonged period of prosperity, leftists in the traditional organisations generally experienced the same slide to the right that the mass working class movement underwent as a whole. In only a few cases did the contrary occur. For us, those few cases nevertheless justified the tactic.

While those who kept denouncing 'entryism' ended up by withering away into sectarianism, it is sufficient for us, in view of May 1968, to point to the formation of the Jeunesse Communiste Revolutionnaire (Revolutionary Communist Youth) as a result of the application of this tactic within the Union des Etudiants Communistes (Communist Student Union). The JCR constituted Trotskyism's most valuable contribution to the French May.[22] Let us not forget, too, that the SDS in Germany (Sozialistischer Deutscher Studentenbund -- German Socialist Student Union) arose out of the Social Democracy, which is the mass organisation in that country.

The 1968 turning point marked the end of the period of apathy; the end of political stagnation in the advanced capitalist countries, which had begun shortly after the Second World War; the end of the period of reformism that had followed the first years of 'de-Stalinisation' in the workers states. This turning point marked the

---

[22] May 1968 in France also allowed for an evaluation of the policies of the Organisation Communiste Internationaliste. (This great opponent of entryism has followed a line similar to that of the British SLL on the question of Cuba and Vietnam). During the greatest event in the history of the European class struggle since the end of World War II, the daily denunciations of this group culminated in its abstaining from the confrontations with the bourgeois state. The OCI sounded the alarm each time and advocated retreat, in order not to be led into 'a slaughter'. On this I refer the reader to Daniel Bensaid and Henri Weber's *Mai 68, une repetition generale* (May 68: A Dress Rehearsal). The authors of this book illustrate, in excellent fashion, how and why the OCI's sectarianism changed into active opportunism at the decisive moments, only to change back into sectarianism when the upsurge receded -- an apt time for this group to indulge in denunciations.

end of the period in which the world revolution had been carried forward almost exclusively by the colonial revolution, a fact that distorted the world revolutionary process considerably and resulted in a proliferation of numerous theories, reformist or revolutionary, that had one point in common: the alleged incapacity of the proletariat, especially in the advanced capitalist countries, to play a revolutionary role. The activation of the working class masses in France and Czechoslovakia, as well as the demonstrations in the large Latin American cities, delivered a mortal blow to all these theories. The distortions that the world revolutionary process was prey to for almost twenty years were on their way out.

The changes in the international situation were also indirectly reflected even in the policy of the CPs. Since 1935 they have always put forward, especially in Western Europe, a policy of class collaboration with social-democracy and wings of the bourgeoisie under the name of 'Popular Front', 'national front', 'left union', etc. But the precise aims assigned to this policy have varied. Before the war, this policy had only the aim of 'stopping fascism'. Immediately after the war, it was a question of an 'advanced democracy' which would very gradually, during an indefinite period, lead on to socialism. At present, this 'advanced democracy' is increasingly often presented as a stage which would rapidly bring about socialism. Obviously a policy based on a peaceful and parliamentary road can lead only to defeats. But it is symptomatic that they are now compelled to speak of socialism in the short term in order to respond to the aspirations of their audience.

Under these new conditions, theoretically and politically so much more propitious, the International made preparations for its 1969 world congress. Ninety-eight section delegates, fraternal delegates, and observers, from thirty countries, were present at this congress, held in April 1969.

The main documents adopted by this congress were:
- Theses on the new rise of the world revolution and an introductory report on these theses by Comrade Ernest Mandel, passed unanimously except for two votes.
- Resolution on the perspectives of the Latin American revolution, presented by Comrade Roca and passed by a two-thirds majority.
- Resolution on the great 'cultural revolution' in China and the report of Comrade Livio Maitan, who presented the resolution to the congress, passed by a very large majority.
- A resolution orienting the International's work in the immediate future towards the radicalising youth and opening a discussion on

the problems posed by this orientation, with a document presented by Comrade Albert.

The congress also unanimously adopted the outgoing United Secretariat's report on activities, presented by Comrade Mandel; a report on the finances of the International; and resolutions dealing with the situation of the movement in Germany, Argentina, Ceylon, and Great Britain. In Great Britain, where there had been no official section, the congress recognised the International Marxist Group as the British section of the Fourth International.

The theses presented to the congress on the new rise of the world revolution summarised in six main points the turn in the world situation that took place in 1968:

1. The imperialist counter-offensive, unleashed by American imperialism following the victory of the Cuban revolution, after having met with some important temporary successes in Brazil, Indonesia, and in numerous African countries, had been stalemated by the heroic Vietnamese masses who recaptured the military initiative with the Tet offensive (1968).
2. The victorious resistance of the Vietnamese people coincided with a general slowing down in the economic growth of the imperialist countries, which sharpened the social contradictions and intensified the class struggle in most of these countries.
3. May 1968 in France had reactivated the revolutionary upsurge in Europe.
4. The victorious defence of the Vietnamese revolution and the reactivation of revolutionary struggle in several imperialist countries gave the colonial revolution the possibility of surmounting the obstacles of the preceding phase and again gathering momentum.
5. Stimulated by the Vietnamese revolution and by the revolutionary crisis in France, the ripening of conditions for the political revolution in the bureaucratically degenerated or deformed workers states has already led to large mobilisations in Czechoslovakia and Yugoslavia, and is at the doorstep of the USSR itself.
6. The appearance of a new, young vanguard on a world scale, largely outside the control of the traditional mass organisations, favours the solution of the central task of our era -- *creating a new, revolutionary leadership of the world proletariat.*

CONTRIBUTIONS TO THE HISTORY OF THE FOURTH INTERNATIONAL

The report on activities could justifiably record the important -- in many cases, decisive -- role played by the Fourth International's militants in the campaigns for the defence of the Vietnamese and Cuban revolutions; the defence of militants persecuted by the bourgeoisie (Hugo Blanco, the Peruvian revolutionists, the Mexican students) or by the bureaucracies of the workers states (the Polish comrades Kuron and Modzelewsky); the campaign for support of the socialist Arab revolution, etc. The activities report could also point to the considerable advances made by the Trotskyist newspapers and other publications throughout the world, and the extraordinary volume of editions and re-editions of Trotsky's works in many languages and in countries where they had never before appeared.

Most especially, the report had to evaluate the Trotskyist movement's participation in the May 1968 events in France. This participation had its climax at the world congress itself: the Ligue Communiste, ten times larger and with immeasurably greater influence than the pre-May 1968 Trotskyist organisation, became the new French section of the Fourth International.

Side by side with this striking advance, participants at the world congress reported on progress made practically everywhere. Leadership bodies of the International and its sections felt new blood coursing through their veins, supplied by young cadres expressing the high potential of the new generation in the ranks of the world socialist revolution.

The turn in the world situation was expressed not only in the composition and progress of the Trotskyist movement, but it was also examined very carefully in the course of in-depth analyses in the tradition of the Trotskyist movement itself. To the usual outline of general tasks, the discussions added an exceptionally strong note that emphasised the principal result of this turn, i.e., the necessity of raising the International's activity to a higher level, a level demanded by the new situation. The organisation would no longer content itself with participating in mass struggles by advancing its programme; it would now endeavour to intervene, at least in certain countries and on certain fronts of the struggle, with the object of playing a leading role in them. The question of the Trotskyist movement's making an eventual breakthrough on certain points, in and through action, thus constituted the guiding thread in the main discussions of the congress -- which were extremely lively.

During each of the discussions on the principal documents submitted to the world congress, it became apparent that the Trotskyist movement (after having tried for years to stem the Stalinist tide and then having participated in revolutionary upsurges that did not throw off the bureaucratic yoke) had for the first time in its history the possibility of making a breakthrough by effectively proving, on a few, still limited class struggle fronts, the validity of its programme -- no longer in a theoretical way, but in action. The world congress showed that it was very aware of this new situation, of its implications, of the perspectives it offered for constructing a revolutionary Marxist, mass International. It is obvious that such a turn cannot be taken just by voting at a congress, no matter how important that may be. The period after the Ninth World Congress demanded of the International, of its sections, of the organisations connected with it politically, persistent day-in, day-out work to make such a turn a reality -- as well as even closer ties among all the parties in the movement.

Shortly after the world congress, the Ligue Communiste showed the big gain made by the Trotskyist movement in France through the extraordinarily successful election campaign of Alain Krivine, the Ligue's presidential candidate. This campaign went far beyond the borders of France and made the International known to large sectors throughout Europe.

Most of the Fourth International's sections, as well as the Socialist Workers Party in the USA, grew considerably in the period following the Ninth World Congress -- in an uneven fashion from country to country, but very substantially nevertheless. At this time organisations were created in countries where the Fourth International had not been present before (Ireland, Luxembourg, Sweden); sections were rebuilt in countries where circumstances had reduced them considerably (Mexico, Switzerland, etc.) or had even forced them to disappear altogether (Spain, with the spectacular growth of the Liga Comunista Revolucionaria). This phenomenon extended also to countries like Japan, Australia, and New Zealand. More and more the Fourth International was committed in class struggles across the entire world.[23]

The progress made by the Fourth International could be seen concretely in two large demonstrations during 1970 and 1971. In November 1970, the International called a conference in Brussels, seat of the European Economic Community, at which it counterposed to the Europe of multinational trusts the slogan of a 'Red Europe', a

---

[23] The only serious setback for the Fourth International at this time took place in Argentina. Here the vast majority of the officially recognised section, the PRT *(El Combatiente)*, which was not of Trotskyist origin, laid more and more stress on the guerrilla activities of its military wing, the ERP, until it finally withdrew from the Fourth International under Cuban influence.

socialist Europe which alone can overcome the division between the Western and Eastern parts of the old continent. More than 3,500 enthusiastic people, most of them youth from all the countries of Europe, were present at the Brussels Conference.

The Fourth International issued an appeal for a demonstration to be held in Paris in May 1971 to celebrate the centennial of the Paris Commune by continuing its fight for a world commune, for the world socialist revolution. Over 30,000 people covered the Belleville and Menilmontant districts and filed past the Mur des Federes in the Père Lachaise cemetery, at the very place where the last fighters of the 1871 Commune met their death. An utterly astounded bourgeois press described the demonstration in terms such as 'composed mostly of young people', and 'vibrant with enthusiasm'. The press also had to acknowledge that of all the demonstrations organised for this anniversary (Socialist Party, PSU, etc.), this was -- except, of course, for the CP's demonstration, in which about 60,000 people participated -- by far the biggest.

The international situation since the Ninth World Congress has been marked by some very important events. On the one hand there has been a grave defeat for the Chilean masses with the overthrow of Allende's 'peaceful road' experiment by the generals headed by Pinochet. This in turn has encouraged a general strengthening of reaction in many Latin American countries: in Peru the 'reformist' interlude came to an end while in Argentina the Videla *coup* in 1976 ushered in a period of the most bloody repression in which the Trotskyists of the Partido Socialista de los Trabajadores (PST Socialist Workers Party) were among the major victims.

In contrast, the revolutionary upsurge of the European workers has won important successes, bringing down the Salazar-Caetano dictatorship in Portugal after half a century, ending the dictatorship of the Creek colonels, and enforcing a rapid liberalisation in Spain after the death of France. Despite subsequent setbacks (the Portuguese defeat of November 1975, the austerity policies imposed in Italy and Spain with the help of the CPs), the revolutionary process in Europe is clearly only marking time before the offensive is renewed in the coming years.

In Africa, too, imperialism has undergone important defeats. The struggle of the oppressed masses in Mozambique, Angola, and Guinea-Bissau not only achieved their liberation from Portuguese colonialism but also helped to stimulate the struggles in Africa south of the Zambezi. A growth in the guerrilla struggles in Namibia and Zimbabwe was followed by a mass upsurge in South Africa itself with the Soweto demonstrations in June 1976.

THE LONG MARCH OF THE TROTSKYISTS

Finally, and above all, the last period has seen the overwhelming victory of the people of Indochina. The capture of Saigon after a struggle lasting thirty years was an immense encouragement to the revolutionary movement in the whole of South-East Asia.

Meanwhile, the myth of the 'consumer society' in the advanced capitalist countries, of a so-called 'neo-capitalism' which would suppress the contradictions exposed by Marx, is dead for ever. The reality today is of an economic crisis, the first generalised recession since the Second World War, which has led to the unemployment of some 15 million men and women in Western Europe and the USA without at the same time being able to provide any permanent answer to the inflationary tendencies of this period.

The absolute hegemony of American capitalism since the end of the war seems to be over. This is expressed, for example, in the crisis of the international monetary system as its basic currency, the dollar, has steadily declined. This decline is watched with increasing anxiety by the capitalist powers of Western Europe and Japan, particularly as it is accompanied by a series of defeats and other incidents (Watergate) which testify to the disarray among the leadership of the world's most powerful capitalist country.

The progress of the Fourth International in this situation was expressed at its Tenth World Congress, held in the last week of February 1974. About 250 delegates and fraternal delegates participated, representing 48 sections and sympathising organisations from 41 countries. Compared to the previous congress the numerical strength of the Fourth International had increased some tenfold. This recruitment, although mainly of young people, was far from being confined to students or school students. It also included a substantial proportion of worker cadres who in some countries are now able to confront the ageing bureaucrats of the traditional organisations with growing success. This advance has also been reflected in the publications of the sections, as more and more are able to produce weekly papers along with theoretical reviews, pamphlets and books.

Apart from registering the progress of the movement, the Tenth World Congress was also important because of its work. A tendency struggle took place which was conducted in a very democratic fashion: more than 150 contributions to the discussion were distributed to the entire membership in every country; the discussion was conducted from the units at the base through regional and national congresses; tendencies and factions were established nationally or internationally; delegates were elected so that minorities were represented according to their proportion of the votes; finally the congress discussed and voted after having heard reports and counter-reports on the various questions at stake. The minorities were then represented on the leadership bodies elected by the congress, and the leadership of the International has subsequently published not only the documents adopted by the majority but also documents presenting the major minority positions, written by minority comrades. The importance of such democratic procedures for the life of the Fourth International cannot be over-estimated. Although every single one of our enemies predicted that a split between majority and minority was just around the corner, quite the reverse occurred: the differences were able to be resolved through the test of experience to the extent that by the end of 1977 the major factions and tendencies had been dissolved.

The debates of the Tenth World Congress took place on the following questions:

- The international situation, where the resolution presented by Ernest Mandel and adopted by the congress confirmed and updated the general orientation defined by the preceding congress on the new upsurge of the world revolution since May 1968.
- Aspects of the situation in Latin America (Bolivia, Argentina, problems of armed struggle on the continent). Most of the debate dealt with past positions, and it included an adjustment of the resolution on Latin America adopted by the Ninth World Congress.
- Problems of building revolutionary Marxist parties in Western Europe. The theses on this question were presented by Livio Maitan. The importance of this point on the agenda derived from the central place once again occupied by the working class movement of Western Europe in the world revolutionary upsurge, and the possibilities open to the sections of the Fourth International in this part of the world.

Among the organisational decisions of the congress, the main one concerned a substantial strengthening of the international centre. In collaboration with the US Socialist Workers Party, this has recently permitted the combination of previous journals into a single international weekly, *Intercontinental Press/Inprecor*, reflecting the views of the Fourth International.[24]

Since the Tenth World Congress the advance of the Fourth International has experienced very few interruptions: it has

---

[24] In 1982 the Fourth International launched *International Viewpoint*, a new magazine in English. In 1986 the SWP closed Intercontinental Press.

THE LONG MARCH OF THE TROTSKYISTS

penetrated various countries of the Middle East, several African countries, as well as further European countries such as Finland and Iceland -- not to mention Portugal, where the Liga Comunista Internacionalista (LCI -- Internationalist Communist League) has been built and stabilised almost from scratch since the fall of the dictatorship. Our publications in the languages of Eastern Europe (Russian, Polish, Czech) have increased as well; the Fourth International has now established a presence in some sixty countries.

The activity of the Fourth International has now reached a stage which it never attained in the past. Support for the Vietnamese revolution, solidarity with Chile, intervention in strike movements, in the struggle for women's liberation, in election campaigns, in anti-militarist work -- the sections of the Fourth International now intervene in all these areas, so that hardly a day now goes by without the mass media reporting some Trotskyist action, intervention or demonstration in this or that country.[25]

In relation to the years which have passed since its founding, the Fourth International has unquestionably made great progress. But we cannot stop here. We must turn our efforts to the ever greater demands made on us by the world situation.

---

[25] At the very time that the Fourth International is seriously growing, however, some observers -- either through ignorance or ill will -- talk about the existence of 'several' Fourth Internationals, owing to the fact that groups outside the Fourth International adopt this label in order to fight us. The Stalinists, of course, use this situation not to talk about 'several' Fourth Internationals but to amalgamate the positions of the Fourth International with those of these other groups. The present situation can be summarised as follows.
The main opponent of the Fourth International in this field was the 'International Committee', consisting of two quite important organisations, the OCI in France and the SLL in Britain, and a few insignificant groups in other countries. When these two organisations broke with each other, each created its own 'International Committee' proposing to 'build' or 'reconstruct' the international. We have mentioned already their political characteristics. We have also referred earlier to the impressionism which characterised the faction which broke with the Fourth International under the leadership of Pablo. This now concentrates its attention on the question of self-management, which it presents as a panacea for the working class movement. In line with this it has abandoned the 'Fourth International' label which it retained after the split and now poses a solution in terms of a united front composed of mass movements in some colonial countries, workers states, etc. As for the remaining handful of 'Posadists', a glance at any of their papers will show that their positions scarcely fall under the heading of political analysis.

CONTRIBUTIONS TO THE HISTORY OF THE FOURTH INTERNATIONAL

There is still a long way to go before the aims for which the Fourth International was founded are achieved, namely to create a mass, international, revolutionary Marxist leadership and mass revolutionary parties, capable of assuring the victory of the world socialist revolution. For a long time, Trotskyists pursued this aim on the sole basis of historical necessity, of their profound belief in the revolutionary capacities that the working class has evinced throughout history, and in the correctness of revolutionary Marxism and the analyses it enabled them to make. Their opportunities for mass-scale actions were then minimal. Today, the old leaderships continue to clutter the road, to poison working class consciousness; but from now on more than theoretical conviction underlies Trotskyist activity.

The new generation living under the contradictions of capitalism are seeking anti-capitalist solutions, and their vanguard is beginning to rediscover revolutionary Marxism in thought and action. The merging of the Trotskyist movement and this young vanguard is already beginning to take place.

Chapter 9: 1978. The 'Long March' of the Trotskyists

Conclusive statements cannot be made about the history of a movement that is engaged in so long a march, begun so long ago a movement which has undergone so many trials and tribulations and which, although a new and much more promising stage lies ahead for it, still has big obstacles to overcome before reaching its goal. Our few closing remarks will, first of all, answer the question raised by those attracted to Trotskyist ideas but surprised by the numerical weakness of the organisation that defends those ideas, a question that every Trotskyist as well has inevitably asked, in their heart of hearts, at certain times: *Is there a historical justification for the Fourth International?* Was Trotsky right to found the Fourth International and to say that the work he was doing for it was 'the most important' in his life, 'more important than 1917, more important than the period of the civil war', irreplaceable 'in the full sense of the word'?[26]

I do not think it necessary to answer those who attack the Fourth International by taking delight in stressing its difficulties; by

---

[26] From *Diary in Exile*. The third volume of Isaac Deutscher's remarkable biography of Trotsky, The Prophet Outcast (1929-40) (Oxford University Press, London), while factually correct, does not give an effective account of Trotsky's work and activity in this period, more especially for the last six years devoted principally to organising the International. Deutscher, who agreed in substance with Trotsky's ideas, felt that Trotsky should have devoted most of his time to writing works such as the *History of the Russian Revolution* rather than participating in the life, difficulties, and crises of the Trotskyist movement, which, for Deutscher, was really a waste of time. But like Marx, who for several years abandoned his theoretical work on economics in order to devote his time to the First International and its internal difficulties (often reminiscent of the Fourth International), Trotsky was first and foremost a revolutionary fighter. And above all, he had given profound thought to the error he had committed before 1917, in comparison with Lenin, on the question of the party. To struggle for the Fourth International was, for Trotsky, to continue Lenin's struggle for a Leninist party on a world scale.

failing to see its political strength, its vitality; by viewing its problems on a superficial level.

From the standpoint of historical perspective -- the only valid standpoint for a subject like this -- the long history of the Trotskyist movement, of the Fourth International, is in itself an objective verification of its historical justification. What has been the history of the international working class movement in the last fifty years -- a half-century that has seen the beginning of the disintegration of capitalist society and the advent of a socialist world? In every country where the working class movement had a long history, with Marxist traditions, one reality stands out: after several dozen years of wars, revolutions and counter-revolutions, fascism, and Stalinism, in the course of which numerous organisations claiming to be Marxist and claiming to stand for the working class came into existence -- after so many years, the only organisations that despite crises, splits, repression, alternating advances and retreats, have lasted are those connected with the Second International, or what was the Third International, or the Fourth International. A reality like this, which covers dozens of years (and what years!), can be attributed neither to chance nor to any specific militant qualities. All the organisations had dedicated and devoted militants with varied political and organisational talents, Such a phenomenon can only be explained by objective causes, profound historical causes. Here is really a case in which Hegel's thought can be applied correctly: *Was ist wirklich ist rationell, was ist rationell ist wirklich* (What is real is rational, what is rational is real). The underlying cause of this reality must extend throughout all these years and must have international validity, as we shall see.

At various times in the preceding pages, we have explained the difficulties that faced the Fourth International because of objective conditions. Above all, there was the eminently turbulent character of the world situation, with its sudden turns and its centrifugal forces -- a major difference from the earlier period of rising capitalism in the last third of the Nineteenth Century. The new world situation no longer permitted so gradual a building up of working class forces as had occurred in the earlier period, with the resultant formation of big parties organising the entire working class as well as the vanguard into vast networks. There was also the eruption of Stalinism, which destroyed the Bolshevik Party, pivot of the revolutionary International constructed around the October victory; the political convulsions and the cruelties of the Soviet bureaucracy more than once disoriented significant revolutionary forces and led them into blind alleys. The epoch of the gradual rise of capitalism had engendered the revisionism of Bernstein and the more insidious revisionism of Kautsky. The frightful history of the isolated first workers state engendered numerous 'revisionisms' (state capitalism in the USSR; the bureaucracy a new exploiting class) incapable of acknowledging the revolution disguised in so hideous a mask. Finally, there were the hundreds of millions of human beings in the colonial countries who stopped being pawns of history and tried to bridge the gap of centuries in a few leaps even in a single leap -- so that the revolution they made often assumed some strange aspects.

The arena of the workers movement, despite this situation or, more precisely, because of it, remained cluttered with the old formations -- because the working masses could not fall into disorganisation. There is no such thing in history as something born of nothing; it is only tremendous crises in the old organisations that will give birth to new revolutionary leaderships. If Marxism is history that becomes conscious of itself, under these conditions this consciousness could come about only with great difficulty, could be born only in hard labour. The organisations that could bridge all these years, all these trials, did it because they were strongly rooted in the deepest reality of the world of these fifty years.

On the one hand, the Second International's organisations are linked to the working class in the old European countries by the entire history of the class, when it sought successfully to organise itself on a mass scale to defend its day-to-day interests. On the other hand, these organisations are tied to capitalist society, which perpetuates itself as long as it has the means to accede to the workers' demands for reforms.[27]

---

[27] The question can be raised: If the existence of social-democracy is linked to the existence of capitalism, isn't its disappearance in the workers states to be explained independently of the Stalinist terror? Couldn't the 'single party' theory be justified in that way? This question would call for a thorough going, in-depth study, which is hardly within the scope of this book. Let it suffice here to say: (a) the revolutionary upsurge and victory of the revolution historically imply a considerable weakening, though not necessarily the disappearance, of the proletariat's reformist and centrist formations; (b) in the society in transition between capitalism and socialism, the working class will still remain differentiated for an entire period, to the extent that various layers retain differing views on the relationship between their everyday needs and their long-range interests. There will thus be room for different parties -- some more reformist, some more revolutionary -- in the transitional society. For a full discussion of this problem see *Socialist Democracy and the Dictatorship of the Proletariat,* theses adopted in 1985 by the world congress of the Fourth International (http://bit.ly/FISocDem).

The official Communist parties drew their basic strength from the fact that they were created around the October victory and the Soviet Union, and that they appeared to be an extension of these throughout the world. Because it was the first, and for a long time the only, workers state, the Soviet Union had been the pole of attraction for all who were awakening to the necessity of replacing capitalism with a new society. Trotskyists have frequently pointed out that for the broadest masses, particularly in the underdeveloped countries, the economic development of the Soviet Union had an infinitely greater significance than the total suppression of workers democracy under the bureaucratic regime, because these masses had no acquaintance whatsoever with the feeble advantages of bourgeois democracy. For the militants in those countries, the Soviet Union's material aid, no matter how slight, was indispensable and more tangible than the treacherous manoeuvres of Kremlin politics. In the capitalist countries, how many sincerely revolutionary militants remained members of the Communist Party for a long time, even though they had anxieties and fears about its policies, because during the ebb they could see no other organisation to belong to! It took the birth of other workers states and the rise of serious differences among them for layers broader than those of the extremely politicised militants to make a distinction between a workers state and its leadership of the moment, for these broader segments to understand the accommodations to world imperialism the Kremlin was seeking at the expense of the international socialist revolution -- so that, as a result, Moscow would no longer remain the 'guide', the pole of attraction; so that, this time, a mortal crisis would affect the Communist parties. Parties in the leadership of workers states are at the mercy of social crises in their countries. Reformist degeneration in the Communist parties of capitalist countries sooner or later will cause these parties to break up, their members having to choose between openly acknowledged reformism and the politics of rising new revolutionary formations.[28]

Obviously, the Fourth International has had no ties to capitalist society. At the hands of the first workers state, whose existence it never ceased to defend, both on the political plane against the capitalist world and on the theoretical plane against all the revisionist

---

[28] In the early days of Stalinism, Trotsky had pointed out that if it were not rejected, it would drag the Communist parties onto a path halfway between communism and reformism, and that such a position could not be held for any length of time. It has been held much longer than Trotsky foresaw, but he had discerned the basic tendency with a great deal of acuity.

tendencies -- Stalinism being one of the latter[29] -- the Fourth International suffered the most implacable persecution, often more murderous than that imposed by capitalism. The Fourth International has nevertheless been able to live and grow, because throughout all these years it alone represented the fundamental, historical interests of the world proletariat. There is no mysterious, esoteric reason for this. At its foundation, the Fourth International received, through Leon Trotsky and the Soviet Left Opposition, the heritage of direct descent from the Bolshevik Party and the Communist International. The Fourth International is their legitimate heir, taking up and continuing their traditions. The Communist parties that succumbed to Stalinism, and the Communist International itself, which Stalin had to debase and dissolve, are no longer anything but usurpers.

By the very fact of its existence as an International, the Fourth International continued to represent the interests of the proletariat. While not rejecting a single conquest of the proletariat, the Fourth International refused to grant special status to any one of them before the triumph of the revolution on a world scale. Every organisation that claimed to be socialist but had only national objectives, or was not an integral part of an international organisation, has in the course of these years seen itself condemned either to disappear or to stagger and fall under the impact of decisive political problems.

This international plane, on which history has passed its inexorable judgement, should never for a moment be overlooked by those who really want to assure the world victory of socialism; because the world today is incomparably more unified -- and in a more complex fashion -- than ever before. In a preface written for the ninetieth anniversary of the *Communist Manifesto,* taking up the passage in which Marx wrote, 'United action, of the leading civilised countries at least, is one of the first conditions for the emancipation of the proletariat', Trotsky added:

'The subsequent development of capitalism has so closely knit all sections of our planet, both "civilised" and "uncivilised", that the problem of the socialist revolution has completely and decisively

---

[29] Numerous works have been written, vainly attempting to prove that Stalinism was the legitimate offspring of Bolshevism. It is easy to show the theoretical affinities between Stalinism's political concepts and those of various left currents in Social Democracy immediately after the First World War: Menshevism, Austro-Marxism, Italian Maximalism, the Bracke-Zyromsky tendency in the SFIO, etc.

assumed a world character. The Soviet bureaucracy attempted to liquidate the *Manifesto* with respect to this fundamental question. The Bonapartist degeneration of the Soviet state is an overwhelming illustration of the falseness of the theory of socialism in one country.'

In the forty years that have passed since these lines were written, contrary to the opinions of supporters of socialism in one country' and then 'national roads' (which is an adaptation of the first theory, brought to the fore during the period of the isolated state, to conditions in the 'socialist camp'), the international character of the socialist revolution is even more obvious. The war in Vietnam has demonstrated, better than anything else, the necessity for the revolutionary movement to have a global strategy against imperialism. The invasion of Czechoslovakia has demonstrated, again better than anything else, how the term *socialism* can be besmirched by the nationalist interest of a bureaucracy.

To act truly as an internationalist, it is not enough to follow world politics in the press. An international political line has to be elaborated, and this can only be done by being organically connected with forces in struggle throughout the entire world. What has given the Fourth International incomparable political strength, despite its numerical weakness; what has made it feared by the leaders of powers like the Soviet Union and China, who have a very clear understanding of their bureaucratic interests and who certainly do not engage in tilting at windmills -- is that the Fourth International is a unity that, by the actions of its members, forges connecting links among the guerrilla fighters and the rebelling peasants of Latin America, the blacks of the United States, the fighters of South Africa, the peoples of Black Africa and North Africa, the revolutionary militants of the Middle East, the militants in many Asian countries, the vanguards in the workers states of Eastern Europe and the Soviet Union, the workers and the vanguard youth of Western Europe, etc. In both bourgeois and Stalinist counter-revolutionary campaigns against the Fourth International, a role is often attributed to it that it does not have, or a degree of influence is attributed to it that it does not possess. Nevertheless, no big struggle has taken place -- nor is taking place -- in which the militants of the Fourth International have not participated. The lessons drawn from these struggles by its militants become part of the political and theoretical analyses of the international movement. Since there can be no really valid knowledge unconnected with action, the Fourth International is today the only revolutionary organisation that integrates and unifies the lessons of the class struggle on all continents. That is why its analyses, the positions it takes on an international scale -- without any pretensions to infallibility -- have most often been superior to the analyses of individuals or groups, no matter how intelligent and sympathetic to the revolution and to socialism the latter may be.

On this subject, the Cuban leadership affords a striking example of what international limitations can do. The Cuban leadership distinguished itself from that of all the other workers states by proving itself truly internationalist when it tried to help organise the struggle for socialism throughout Latin America -- on a continental scale. Nevertheless, in 1968, it very much disappointed a number of its friends and supporters because of its silence on the French May and its position on the invasion of Czechoslovakia. Where do its political defaults come from, considering its good understanding of the problems of the colonial revolution? Its political deficiencies stem from the fact that its horizon has remained limited to Latin America and to the colonial countries. The problems of the European workers movements and the problems of the East European workers states and the Soviet Union escape it, because it is not connected internationally with formations that might enlarge its horizon and give it a profound, global grasp of these problems.

An argument that has been repeated many times since 1933 in connection with establishing the Fourth International maintains that we should start by building mass revolutionary parties on a national scale, that the founding of the International can only come about as a culmination of such a process. In other words, this question is posed as if we were building a house: first the walls (the national parties) must be raised before we can put the roof (the International) in place. This kind of thinking manifests a total misconception of the relationships between the International and its national sections in the Twentieth Century world. Let us recall that up to this day no specifically national organisation has acquired a programme that, in a truly complete fashion, answers the revolutionary needs of our epoch, including on a national scale. How, in an epoch characterised by constant wars, revolutions, and counter-revolutions, where everything which happens in the 'most remote' corners of the world has repercussions in the metropolitan countries, is it possible to envisage building a revolutionary party within national boundaries? Instead of allowing the revolutionary forces to prepare for the future, such a conception would return them to past periods whose possibilities have long been exhausted.

Because there is no such thing as 'socialism in one country', no such thing as 'national roads', the instrument of world revolution can only be a world party. It cannot be constructed evenly in all countries because of the uneven development of the revolution throughout the world. Creating a mass revolutionary International and creating revolutionary parties in each country do not constitute two tasks separate in time. It is a single process that takes place by constant interaction between the International and its national organisations. Finally, to understand the importance of this question, it is not without value to see to what point the bourgeoisie, throughout its history, has especially feared the existence of an International.

The question of the International was eclipsed during the years in which the world revolution resumed its momentum almost exclusively through the colonial revolution, while in Western and Eastern Europe the era was marked principally by reformism. It will not be long before the big turning point of 1968 makes the necessity of international coordination, on the level of a vanguard Marxist revolutionary organisation, the first item on the agenda. The idea of an International was born in Europe over a century ago. And it was in Europe that the idea became a reality several different times. A few decades of Stalinism have not destroyed this tradition. Moreover, Europe is the area of the world with the strongest concentration of productive forces. In Europe more than anywhere else these forces are coming into collision with the barriers of national states. The contradiction between the development of the productive forces and the superannuated national states in Europe was at the bottom of the two world wars. In the absence of victories for the socialist revolution, which would have created a socialist federation of European nations, for more than twenty years we have been witnessing the spectacle of a Europe cut in two, socially and geographically, by the division of Germany, accompanied by the establishing of two caricatures of 'unification' -- the European Economic Community on the one hand, and Comecon (Council for Mutual Economic Aid) on the other. The resumption of the revolutionary rise in Europe will not fail to place the socialist reunification of Europe on the agenda; as a consequence, the revolutionary International of the proletariat will also be placed on the order of the day.

Will the international revolutionary organisation of the future be simply an enlargement of the cadre organisation that constitutes the present Fourth International, or will it be achieved by other means? To pose the question in this fashion, like it or not, is to duck the problem as it exists today. No one can maintain that mass revolutionary Marxist organisations are going to spring up all of a sudden, like Athena from the head of Zeus, and miraculously create a mass revolutionary International. The organisations are what they are today, and to be able to change the situation, our struggle must use existing conditions as its point of departure.

We are the very first to regret the Fourth International's incapacity for so many years to mobilise and lead mass movements. Without denying the errors that have been committed, we think that these did not bear on the essential problems, so that even if these errors had been avoided, changes of a qualitative nature in the relationships between the Fourth International and the mass workers movement would not have resulted. It is difficult to imagine that during fifty years, had there been objective possibilities for so doing, a team capable of solving the problem of a mass revolutionary Marxist leadership could not have been found what with all the numerous attempts that were made. None of the Fourth International's manifold critics have demonstrated how to do better -- and none have done better. On the contrary, when the socialist revolution made a new advance in the European countries, it was the Fourth International that was to be found in the forefront of the battle, and it was the members of the Fourth International who began to activate the mass movements in many of these countries.

The Fourth International is not one of a number of sects. Its history is that of the international revolutionary Marxist party in the most tumultuous epoch of the socialist revolution. The expansion of the working class movement over and beyond organisations struggling in the framework of capitalist society -- as a result of the creation of states rejecting the capitalist system -- has given rise to an extraordinary phenomenon of combined development. Actually this expansion of the working class movement has for years been combined with a considerable setback on the organisational level for the revolutionary Marxist vanguard. We have had to lose ground as far as political action is concerned. But not for one moment has the Fourth International yielded an inch as far as theory is concerned. In addition, it has made available to new generations a rich theoretical and political contribution on numerous questions: bureaucracies in working class organisations and bureaucracies in workers states; Stalinism; political revolution; permanent development in the colonial revolution; theories relating to fascism and the Bonapartist strong state, etc. Those who have participated in the Fourth International have a legitimate right to be proud of its history. The theoretical and political conquests of the Fourth International as an organisation of vanguard cadres will enable it to go beyond the stage it has had to traverse for so long.

Joining the Fourth International today means becoming part of the battle being fought in many countries, on every continent; it means developing a global strategy against capitalism, along with the other militants of the Fourth International, and applying that strategy wherever possible; it means, across the years, raising aloft the banner of October, of Bolshevism, of the Communist International, and bearing it to victory in the battle of today.

Chapter 10:
Those Who Died So That the International Might Live

We have intentionally devoted this work, above all, to the Trotskyist movement's activity in the area of theory, politics, and organisation relative to half a century of great events -- and to the problems these events have raised in the course of constructing a revolutionary Marxist leadership and revolutionary Marxist parties in every country. We have seen how difficult it is to make progress on the theoretical and political level, how this is possible only at the price of incessant internal debate and discussion, of analysis and re-analysis. But ideas, programmes, and organisations are created by people and kept alive by people. Only in passing have we mentioned the names of the Trotskyist movement's militants.

What books could be written on such a subject! Conditions have been far harsher for Trotskyists than for any other working class tendency -- bourgeois repression being generally a stimulus, while the repression exercised against Trotskyists within their own class, very often by sincerely revolutionary workers misled by bureaucrats who were backed by a powerful workers state, has pushed many able revolutionists into situations where they could not give the best of themselves.

Trotsky's name, to which is inseparably linked that of his companion Natalia, towers over the names of all those who joined the movement he created, and is again beginning to be as celebrated as it was in the heroic days of the revolution. But how many others are there whose names remain stained in the eyes of the workers by the Stalinist slanders, or who remain unknown to the new generations! The Trotskyist movement itself has generally not been very forthcoming about those who fought for the victory of its programme. History will little by little, internationally and in every country, give them their due.

Another result of Stalinism's implacable persecution of the Trotskyists was the confusion and intimidation it sowed in many people over a long period. This drastically reduced the movement's periphery of friends and sympathisers -- a periphery that all vanguard movements need. Thus we also pay homage to those who were our friends in such adversity, as well as to the revolutionary leaders who came out of the Communist International and its parties who, although they did not march with us all the way, or had differences with us, remained faithful to the cause of world revolution to the end of their days.

Among them are:

Alfred and Marguerite Rosmer, in whose home the founding congress of the Fourth International was held.

Maurice Spector, founder of the Canadian Trotskyist movement.

Isaac Deutscher, historian and essayist. He joined the Polish Communist Party in 1926, but was expelled in 1932 for his activities as leader and spokesperson of the anti-Stalinists. In 1939 he came to Britain, where he lived until his death in 1967. Although he opposed the foundation of the Fourth International in 1938, his writings, especially his trilogy on the life of Trotsky -- *The Prophet Armed, The Prophet Unarmed*, and *The Prophet Outcast* -- have had an incalculable effect in drawing people to the basic ideas of our movement.

H. Stockfisch (Hersch Mendel), fighter in the 1905 and 1917 Russian revolutions, who founded the Polish Trotskyist movement, to which he won Isaac Deutscher.

Andres Nin, assassinated by the GPU during the Spanish revolution.

Paul Frölich, Arkadi Maslow, Hugo Urbahns, former leaders of the German Communist Party.

André Marty, who established fraternal contacts with us after his expulsion from the French Communist Party.

John Baird, Labour Party MP, who was always on our side.

Roman Rosdolsky, the eminent Ukrainian Marxist.

Elsa Reiss, barely escaped Stalin's assassins in 1937 when they had orders to kill her and her son as well as her companion Ignace (see below). Her book *Our Own People* (published under the name Elisabeth K. Poretsky) relives the drama of that terrible period of the 'Yezhov terror', during which Stalin exterminated more revolutionary militants than did the capitalist world, including Hitler.

Louis Polk, member of the Central Committee of the Belgian Communist Party, who participated in founding the Opposition in Belgium and who died in the Neuengamme concentration camp.

Tan Malakka who in 1914 was, with Sneevliet, a founder of the revolutionary socialist movement in Indonesia, missing in action during the guerrilla fighting following the war.

THE LONG MARCH OF THE TROTSKYISTS

Mario Roberro Santucho, leader of the Argentinian PRT/ERP, murdered by security forces in 1976. A genuine revolutionary internationalist, he joined the Fourth International in 1967 through fusion of his group with the section; our failure to convince him of the correctness of the Trotskyist programme, leading to his break with the International in 1973, was a real defeat for our movement.

Sara (Weber) Jacobs, who served as Trotsky's secretary for almost three years from 1931, and again in 1939.

There follows a very incomplete list of those who carried aloft the banner of Trotskyism, and who died in battle:

Nicola di Bartolomeo (Fosco), Italian Communist worker, in exile in France during the fascist regime, participated in the war in Spain. On his return to France, he was turned over to the Italian authorities, who deported him to a concentration camp. Liberated at the end of the war, he rebuilt the Trotskyist organisation in Italy. He died in 1946, at the age of forty-four.

Angel Amado Bengochea (1926- 1964), a leader of the first student revolts in Argentina in the 1940s, leader of the Socialist Youth. A student at the Faculty of Law in La Plata, he organised a Marxist opposition in the Socialist Party, and joined the Trotskyist movement in 1946. In the 1950s he worked in a factory and became a leader in the Peronist unions. Imprisoned for six months in 1957. Linked to the struggle in other Latin American countries, in 1963 he formed a political-military group and was killed during an explosion.

Edith Beauvais, joined the Trotskyist movement in Canada in the early 1960s, then moved to France. Active in building the JCR and the Ligue Communists; but her most important work was in strengthening the international commissions of the Fourth International. She died in a car accident in 1972.

Fernando Bravo, leader of the Bolivian teachers, representative of the Bolivian FOR (Partido Obrero Revolucionario) to congresses of the International, died in the line of duty.

Antoinette Bucholz-Konikow (1869-1946), became a revolutionary socialist at the age of seventeen and joined Russia's first Marxist organisation, the Emancipation of Labour group, led by Plekhanov. Exiled to the USA, she worked in the Socialist Labour Party and later helped to found the Socialist Party with Debs and others, becoming a member of its Women's Commission. She was a founder of the Second International but broke with it after its capitulation to chauvinism in 1914, helping to launch the Communist Party and the Third International. Among the first to rebel against the rise of the Stalinist bureaucracy, she participated in the ten years of activity that culminated in 1938 with the founding of the US

Socialist Workers Party and the Fourth International. She was also an early advocate of birth control; as a doctor, she wrote two handbooks on the subject, and in 1928 was arrested for exhibiting contraceptives.

James P. Cannon (1890-1974), joined the Industrial Workers of the World (IWW) in 1910. As a supporter of the October Revolution, he joined the Socialist Party in 1918 and was a founder of the CP in 1919. Sent as its president to Moscow in 1922, he participated for eight months in the work of the Executive Committee of the Comintern. At this time he played a leading role in the International Labour Defence, notably in the campaign to save Sacco and Vanzetti.

A delegate to the Sixth Congress of the Comintern, and made a member of its programme commission, he came to hear of the exiled Trotsky's criticisms of the congress programme presented by Bukharin. Won to Trotsky's arguments, Cannon and Maurice Spector (a member of the Canadian delegation) secretly took his text back to North America and published it. Following his expulsion from the CP for Trotskyism, Cannon -- together with Max Shachtman and Martin Abern -- founded the Communist League (Opposition) in May 1929. He was to remain the central leader of the American Trotskyist movement until ill-health reduced him to an advisory capacity in the 1960s.

In 1934 he played a prominent role in the famous Teamster strikes in Minneapolis. Then in the next years he was instrumental in an important expansion of the American Trotskyist forces, first through a fusion with the Workers Party and then through a short spell of entry into the Socialist Party in 1936-37. The expulsion of the Trotskyists from the SP led to the formation of the Socialist Workers Party. In 1938 Cannon participated in the founding congress of the Fourth International, and in 1939-40 he collaborated with Trotsky in the famous struggle against the petty-bourgeois opposition in the SWP led by Shachtman and Burnham. During the Second World War he was imprisoned for sixteen months along with other members of the SWP under the Smith Act.

Cannon was a prolific writer, particularly for the party press (some of his best articles are collected in *Notebook of an Agitator*). He also wrote several books. Indeed, as a propagandist and agitator he was perhaps the most prominent figure of the American labour movement in the generation which followed Eugene Debs and Bill Haywood.

Tomas Chambi, member of the Central Committee of the FOR in Bolivia, imprisoned during the Barrientos-Ovando dictatorship, freed when the dictatorship ended; he fell in combat in 1971 while leading a column of poor peasants from the La Pat region in the battle against the Banter coup d'etat. On his body was found a note written in his own hand, a kind of testament by this militant whose sole possession was his revolutionary conviction:'I am a member of the Partido Obrero Revolucionario, which taught me to be brave and to fight for a just cause. For national liberation, and forward to the final victory!'

Emile Decoux (1910-1970), Belgian miner and exemplary militant for thirty-seven years. Joined the Jeune Garde Socialiste (Socialist Young Guard) in 1934, then the Belgian section of the Fourth International. Fulfilled important functions during the period of clandestinity.

Vincent Raymond Dunne (1889-1970), joined the Industrial Workers of the World (IWW) at the age of 17; a founder of the US Communist Party in 1919 and, in 1928, participated in the founding of the US Trotskyist movement. At the head of the great Minneapolis Teamster strikes in 1934, which were a forerunner of the mighty trade union upsurge of the following years. In 1938 participated in discussions with Trotsky preparatory to the founding congress of the Fourth International. Imprisoned in 1941 for sixteen months.

Heinz Epe (Waiter Held), joined the German Left Opposition in 1931 as a student. Forced into exile in March 1933, he organised the first German publication in the emigration, *Unser Wort*. In 1934 he was one of the secretaries -- along with Willy Brandt -- of the 'International Bureau of Revolutionary Youth Organisations', until the Trotskyists were expelled at Brandt's instigation. In 1934 he organised Trotsky's arrival and stay in Norway. Moving to Sweden after the occupation of Norway, he tried to travel to the US via the Soviet Union in 1941 but disappeared with his wife and child.

Ezio Ferrero (Ettore Salvini) (1938-1976), joined the Italian CP and went to Moscow in 1956 to attend the university. As a result of his stay he developed positions critical of the bureaucracy, and joined the Fourth International in 1962. He was a member of the national leadership of the Italian section, the Gruppi Comunisti Rivoluzionari (GCR), and a delegate to the Eighth World Congress; but was best known as a frequent contributor to our press, especially on the Soviet economy and Italian political and economic problems.

Josef Frey (1882-1957), prior to 1914 journalist on the Vienna *Arbeiterzeitung*, president of the Vienna Council of Soldiers in the 1918 revolution, broke with Otto Bauer and Fritz Adler to join the CP, expelled from the latter in 1927 as a Trotskyist.

José Aguirre Gainsborg, Bolivian revolutionist in exile, leading member of the Chilean CP. Founder of the Bolivian FOR in 1934 --

which he armed theoretically. For many years lived in exile and in prison; died at the age of thirty-four.

Renzo Gambino (1922-1972), a member of the Socialist Party when fascism was overthrown, joined the Italian section of the Fourth International in 1949 and was a member of its national leadership until his death. He was a delegate to many world congresses and for a long time a member of the International Control Commission, becoming its secretary in 1969.

Peter Graham (1945-1971), young Irish revolutionary, started out as a member of the Connolly Youth, rapidly developed towards Trotskyism, became a member of the Irish Workers Group, and then participated in founding the League for a Workers Republic and the Young Socialists in Dublin. He came to London where he joined the International Marxist Group (IMG -- British section of the Fourth International) and was a member of the editorial staff of *The Red Mole*. Barely returned to Dublin for the purpose of building an Irish section, he was assassinated under circumstances that have never been clarified. The IRA and all the militant organisations of the Irish socialist movement paid homage to his memory.

Arturo Gomes, joined the Trotskyist movement in Argentina as a student leader in the midst of the mass mobilisations in 1958-59. Played a central role in winning a base for Trotskyism in the La Plata region. A member of the Executive Committee and Secretariat of the Partido Socialista de los Trabajadores (PST), and a delegate to the Tenth World Congress of the International, he was elected to the IEC with consultative status. Died of a heart attack in 1976 as he was preparing the underground struggle after the military coup.

Jules Henin (1882-1964), miner, member of the Parti Ouvrier Belge (Belgian Workers Party) from 1905. One of the first Belgian Communists in 1919, founder of the Trotskyist organisation in 1927, one of the leaders of the Charleroi miners' strike (1932), as a result of which he was imprisoned. Conducted underground activity during the war. Member of the Control Commission of the Fourth International for many years.

Marcel Hic, joined the French Trotskyist movement (POI and Jeunesses Léninistes) in 1933 at the age of eighteen. He rebuilt the French organisation and published *La Vérité* starting in August 1940. Secretary of the French section during the occupation, he participated in the founding of the European Secretariat of the Fourth International. Arrested in 1943, he was distinguished by his courageous attitude in the Dora concentration camp, where he died.

Joseph Jakobovic (1915-1943), leader of the Austrian group 'Gegen den Strom' (Against the Stream) during the Hitler occupation.

He was tried in October 1943 for high treason and for encouraging disaffection in the armed forces, condemned to death and executed.

Georg Jungclas (1902-1975), joined at the age of fourteen the Socialist Youth of Altona (near Hamburg), which opposed the war and the betrayals of the Social Democracy. Became a member of the Spartakusbund and then of the German Communist Party (KPD), and participated in the revolutionary struggles, notably the Hamburg insurrection in October 1923. A supporter of the left in the KPD, he was expelled in 1928, becoming a member of the Leninbund founded by Urbahns. However he defended Trotsky's positions against Urbahns and in 1930 participated in the creation of the German Left Opposition.

He moved to Denmark after Hitler's rise to power, and participated in the Danish Resistance until his arrest by the Gestapo in 1944. Saved from death only by the collapse of the Nazis, he struggled almost alone after the war to rebuild the German section in the choking atmosphere of the Federal Republic. From 1948 he participated in all the world congresses of the International and was elected to its International Executive Committee and its Secretariat. Among the first to begin organising the immigrant workers in Germany, he was also at the centre of activity in support of the Algerian revolution.

Zavis Kalandra, communist historian, denounced the Moscow trials in 1936; secretary of the Czechoslovakian section of the Fourth International, he was arrested and executed in 1950 by the Stalinists as a 'spy'; was rehabilitated during the 'Prague Spring'.

Rose Karsner (1890-1968), joined the US Socialist Party at the age of eighteen. In 1909 she became secretary of the magazine *The Masses*. She participated in the founding congress of the unified US Communist Party in 1921, and devoted herself to the defence and aid of the victims of repression (notably the Sacco-Vanzetti case). In 1928 she participated in founding the Trotskyist organisation in the United States, to which she was completely committed until the end of her life.

Franz Kascha (1909-1943), leader of the Austrian group 'Gegen den Strom' during the Hitler occupation. He was tried in October 1943 for high treason and for encouraging disaffection in the armed forces, condemned to death and executed.

Rudolf Klement, young German Trotskyist, secretary to Trotsky, assassinated in France by the GPU in 1938 on the eve of the founding congress of the Fourth International, to the preparation of which he had devoted himself.

CONTRIBUTIONS TO THE HISTORY OF THE FOURTH INTERNATIONAL

Robert Langston (1933-1977), a true internationalist and revolutionary intellectual, won to our movement from the chauvinist American Socialist Party on the question of Cuba. After joining the SWP he worked as a staff writer for *The Militant* from 1968-70 and also devoted himself to the education of cadres. His unstinting financial contribution was an invaluable aid to our work.

Rafael Lasala (Nestor), participated in the student struggles in Argentina in 1958-59, joined the Trotskyist movement in 1967. In 1971 he helped to form the Grupo Obrero Revolucionario (GOR), a sympathising group of the International, and was its representative at the Tenth World Congress. Arrested in August 1974, he was tortured and finally murdered in cold blood at the La Plata prison in August 1976.

Abraham Leon (1918- 1944), born in Warsaw, broke with Zionism and wrote *The Jewish Question: A Marxist Interpretation*. At the beginning of the war he joined the Belgian Trotskyist organisation, of which he became the main organiser, and participated in founding the European Secretariat. Arrested in June 1944, he died in the Auschwitz concentration camp in September 1944.

Leon Lesoil (11(92-1942), soldier in the Belgian Mission in Russia during the First World War, he came out for the October Revolution and was one of the founders of the Belgian Communist Party. He became a member of its Central Committee in 1923, and then was prosecuted for 'plotting against the security of the state'. He was a founder of the Belgian Trotskyist organisation in 1927; leader of the miners' strike in the Charleroi Basin in 1932; and delegate to the founding congress of the Fourth International. Arrested in 1941, he died in the Neuengamme concentration camp in 1942.

Cesar Lora, leader of the Bolivian miners at the Siglo XX mine; was assassinated on 19 July 1965 by Barrientos's troops.

Sherry Mangan (Patrice), American author and journalist, was a Trotskyist from 1934. He participated in the activity of the French Trotskyist organisation under the occupation and though expelled from France by Petain he maintained liaison among the underground groups during the war. Reduced to very difficult living conditions by McCarthyism, he again participated in clandestine work in France to help the Algerian revolution. A member of the International's leadership for many years, he died in 1961 at the age of 57.

Charles Marie (1915-1971), railroad worker, joined the Trotskyist movement shortly after the end of the war. Impassioned and indefatigable militant, for a long time he was practically alone in defending Trotskyism in Rouen. During the Algerian war, in legal and extra-legal activities, he began to build a resurgence of the movement, recruited young people who, in the aftermath of May 1968, were to make Rouen the largest provincial branch of the Ligue Communiste. A cell of railroad workers in Rouen bears his name. He was named honorary chairman of the second national congress of the Ligue Communiste, held in Rouen.

Jean Meichler, was one of the founders of La Vérité in 1929. Editor of Unser Wort, organ of the German Trotskyists in exile, he was arrested for this and held hostage at the time that France was occupied. He was one of the first hostages executed, dying at the age of 45.

Fernando Lozano Menendez, a 22-year-old student and member of the national leadership of the Frente de Izquierda Revolucionaria (FIR), murdered by the Peruvian police in November 1976.

Luiz Eduardo Merlino (Nicolau) (1947-1971), Brazilian journalist assassinated in July 1971 by the repressive forces in his country. Began his activity as a militant in the student organisations in Santos, then in newspaper circles in Sao Paulo, constantly filling the role of inspirer and leader. In 1968 joined the Partido Operario Comunista (POC -- Communist Workers Party), in which he rapidly rose to a leading position. His experiences led him to the positions of the Fourth International. He organised an opposition for which he wrote theses on national and international questions. Shortly after his clandestine return to Sao Paulo from a visit of several months in France, he was arrested, tortured, and murdered.

Chitta Mitra (1929-1976), a leading member of our Indian section, chiefly responsible for establishing a Trotskyist press in Bengali. He also translated a number of Trotsky's works, and wrote a biography of Trotsky, *Tomader Trotsky* (Your Trotsky), for young people in very simple Bengali.

Henri Molinier (More Laurent) (1898-1944), was an engineer who participated in the founding of *La Vérité* and carried out many missions with great discretion. In charge of military matters for the PCI during the war, he was killed by a shell in the course of the fighting for the liberation of Paris.

Georg Moltved (1881-1971), Danish doctor. At the turn of the century he belonged to a petty-bourgeois party, but developed towards Marxism, contributing to intellectual periodicals. After 1933, he aided the German anti-fascist refugees in his country. In 1943, under the occupation, he was one of the main leaders of the illegal CP for the region north of Copenhagen. After the war, he was opposed to the CP's acceptance of ministerial posts in the government and to the

CP's reformist policy. Expelled in 1950, he joined the Fourth International in 1955. He translated *The Revolution Betrayed* into Danish, wrote biographies of Lenin and Trotsky, and often presented Trotskyist viewpoints on the radio. Recognised in his country as an eminent person, Moltved was a man of great intellectual capacity.

Martin Monat (Paul Widelin) (1913-1944), was originally a leader of the Socialist Zionist movement and a sympathiser of the German CP before 1933, but then moved towards Trotskyism and broke with Zionism. He emigrated to Belgium in 1939, where he joined the Trotskyist section. During the war he was responsible for organising fraternisation inside the German army in France, publishing the paper *Arbeiter und Soldat* (Worker and Soldier). He created a cell of German soldiers in Brest, many of whom were arrested and shot. Arrested by the French police and handed over to the Gestapo, he was shot and left for dead in the forest of Vincennes, but managed with help to reach a hospital. Here however, he was recaptured and killed by the Gestapo.

Moulin, German Trotskyist, killed by the GPU during the civil war in Spain.

Jabra Nicola (Abu Said) (1912-1974), was born in Haifa and joined the Palestinian CP before he was 20. As a member of its leadership, he was given responsibility for its organ in Arabic, *At Ittihad*, but the party split in 1939 along nationalist lines and he refused to join either wing. He was imprisoned under the British occupation from 1940-42. In 1942 he joined a group of Trotskyists, many of them refugees from Europe, but the dislocation of the Trotskyist organisation in the Middle East after the war led him to rejoin the CP, and he was once again given the editorship of its paper in Arabic. In 1956, however, the CP leadership suspended him from his functions because of political disagreements, and in 1962 he joined with others who had left the CP to form the Matzpen group, from which the Israel section of the Fourth International was to develop. Placed under house arrest after the Six Day War in 1967, he left Israel for London in 1970, where he died.

Jabra Nicola was a member of the IEC of the Fourth International from its Seventh World Congress (1963). A brilliant journalist, he wrote numerous articles and pamphlets and also translated some of the classics of Marxism into Arabic. His contribution, both theoretically and politically, to the Fourth International on the problems of the Arab East and the question of Israel within it was unparalleled.

Pantelis Pouliopoulos, prosecuted for his activity in the Creek army in 1922. He translated *Das Kapital* into Greek. A delegate of the

Creek CP to the Fifth Congress of the Communist International, he became secretary of the CP in 1925, but was expelled as a Trotskyist in 1927. Secretary of the Creek Trotskyist organisation, he went underground following the Metaxas coup d'etat in 1936, but was arrested in 1939. He was shot as a hostage by the Italians in 1943 at the age of 43, making a speech to the Italian soldiers while facing the firing squad.

Art Preis (1911-1964), American Trotskyist, while a student at the University of Ohio founded the *Free Voice*, which was later banned. In 1933 he organised the unemployed in Toledo, then organised employed workers into trade unions and was a member of the Toledo CIO Council. From 1940 on, he was labour editor of *The Militant*. Author of *Labor's Giant Step. Twenty Years of the CIO*, a history of the American trade union movement from 1929 to 1955.

Luis Pujals (1942-1971), young Argentinian revolutionist, joined the Palabra Obrera group in 1961. A founding member of the PRT in 1964, he was elected a member of its Central Committee at its Second Congress and later elected to its Executive Committee. He was in charge of political and military affairs for the Buenos Aires region. Arrested on 17 September 1971, he was sent by the authorities to Rosario and brought back to Buenos Aires on 22 September, at the very moment the authorities were denying that he was in custody. According to all indications, he died under torture.

B. Mallikarjun Rao, participated in the revolutionary movement as a student in Andhra and then in Bombay, and became active in the trade union movement. One of the founders in 1941 of the Mazdoor Trotskyist Party of India, in 1942 he participated in the uprising against British imperialism, went underground, was arrested in 1944 and sentenced to two years in prison. In 1947-48 he took part in the guerrilla movement against the Nizam of Hyderabad until this principality was integrated into the Indian Union. He was elected to a trade union post in 1949; and arrested anew in 1959 for his role in the civil service strike in Andhra Pradesh. In 1965 he was a member of the organising committee of the Socialist Workers Party (Indian section of the Fourth International). He died in 1966 after more than thirty years of militant activism.

Ignace Reiss (Ludwig), Polish communist, hero of the civil war during the Russian Revolution, was one of the principal leaders of the Soviet Union's special services. In 1937, following the first Moscow trial, he broke with Stalinism and returned his medals, declaring,'I am joining Trotsky and the Fourth International'. He was assassinated by the GPU a few weeks later near Lausanne.

CONTRIBUTIONS TO THE HISTORY OF THE FOURTH INTERNATIONAL

Alfonso Peralta Reyes (1939-1977), lecturer and member of the Political Bureau of the Mexican Partido Revolucionario de los Trabajadores (PRT), assassinated by the 'Liga Comunista 23 de Septiembre' guerrilla group in May 1977 while leading a struggle by the university trade unions against the government's austerity measures.

German Rodriguez Sainz, joined the Trotskyist movement in Spain in 1971 and played a prominent part in the fusion between the LCR and ETA(VI), the revolutionary wing of the Basque nationalist movement. He was an active member of the Workers Commissions and a central leader of the 1973 Pamplona general strike, for which he was jailed for two and a half years. Over 30,000 attended his funeral after he had been murdered by police during a Basque nationalist protest in Pamplona in July 1978.

Wolfgang Salus, young Czechoslovakian communist, participated in founding that country's Trotskyist movement in 1929 at the age of 18. He died in exile after having contributed to the reorganisation of the Czechoslovakian movement after the war.

Leon Sedov (1905-1938), Trotsky's son, was expelled from the CPSU in 1927 and from that time on devoted his life to helping Trotsky in the latter's work. Was a defendant along with Trotsky in all the Moscow trials, in which he was sentenced to death. He died mysteriously in Paris, most assuredly assassinated by the GPU.

Henricus Sneevliet (1883-1942), Dutch working class leader, founder of the Indonesian socialist movement in 1914, then of the Indonesian CP in 1920. He was its delegate to the Second Congress of the Communist International, and representative of the Communist International to the Chinese CP, but broke with Stalinism. A leader of the Dutch trade union confederation NAS, he was imprisoned in 1932 for his support of a sailors' mutiny. A founder of the RSAP, he was arrested during the war, and shot by the Nazis on 13 April 1942. His heroic death has been held up as an example in his country.

Shuji Sugawara (1949-1978), national secretary of the Japan Communist Youth (Trotskyist youth group) and a national organiser for the struggle against the opening of Narita airport, died of a brain haemorrhage.

Chen Tu-hsiu (1879-1942), professor at the University of Peking, was one of the leaders of the democratic revolution of 1911. A founder of the Chinese CP, of which he was secretary from 1920 to 1927, but then joined the Trotskyist Opposition. He was seized by the Kuomintang in 1932 and sentenced to thirteen years in prison. Freed on parole in 1937, he died in 1942. His memory is still slandered today by the leadership of the Chinese CP.

THE LONG MARCH OF THE TROTSKYISTS

Ta Thu Thau, founder of the Vietnamese Trotskyist movement, leader of the Saigon workers in the years preceding the war and imprisoned during the war. Freed in 1946, he disappeared mysteriously shortly thereafter, probably assassinated by the Stalinists.

Pierre Tresso (Blasco) (1893-1943), member of the Central Committee and the Political Bureau of the Italian CP from 1925, party delegate to congresses of the Communist International. Expelled as a Trotskyist in 1930, he was active as an exile in France; participated in the leadership of the Ligue Communiste, in the Copenhagen Conference in 1932, and in the founding congress of the Fourth International. Condemned to ten years of forced labour during the war by the Marseilles military court, and placed in the Puy prison, he was liberated along with all the others by the Resistance forces, shortly thereafter, as was the case with other Trotskyists, he disappeared while with the Resistance forces, in all likelihood assassinated by the Stalinists.

Humberto Valenzuela (1908-1977), born in the nitrate-mining area of northern Chile, recording secretary of the nitrate miners union in Huara at the age of fourteen. Joined the Chilean CP soon after its foundation, but left after the Trotskyists were expelled to join the Izquierda Comunista (Communist Left), formed in 1931. A leader of the United Construction Union, he also helped in the formation of peasant unions. In 1942 he ran as Trotskyist candidate for the presidency. In 1969, he devoted himself to the foundation of a new Chilean section, the Partido Socialista Revolucionario (PSR); he also worked with the MIR to build organs of popular power and was elected a national leader of the Revolutionary Workers Front. After the coup he continued to work underground, organising resistance committees and Marxist education classes.

Joseph Vanzler (John G. Wright), student in chemistry at Harvard University, joined the American Trotskyist organisation in 1929, translated numerous works by Trotsky, died in 1956 at the age of 52.

Libero Villone (1913-1970), became active in the Italian CP under the fascist regime, when it was illegal. He was expelled from the CP in 1938 for having criticised the Moscow trials. Arrested in 1943, he was freed when Mussolini fell. Readmitted to the CP, he was soon expelled for criticising the policy of class collaboration. He joined the Trotskyist movement in 1945. A teacher, he held various positions in the teachers' union. He was editor of *Bandiera Rossa* for several years.

CONTRIBUTIONS TO THE HISTORY OF THE FOURTH INTERNATIONAL

Neil Williamson, Scottish militant of the International Marxist Group, who played the key role in leading the IMG to understand the new prominence of the national question in Scotland. His funeral after his death at the age of 26 in a car crash in October 1978 was attended by representatives of every significant section of the labour movement, testifying to the enormous respect he had won in ten years of unceasing political activity.

Erwin Wolf (N. Braun), Trotskyist of Czechoslovakian origin, Trotsky's secretary in Norway, was assassinated by the GPU during the civil war in Spain.

Niiyama Yukio (1954-1978), member of the Japan Revolutionary Communist League, died of injuries received during the struggle against the opening of the Narita international airport at Sanrizuka.

Joseph Hansen (1910-1979), a central leader of the American Socialist Workers Party and the international Trotskyist movement, died as this book was going to press. From 1937 he spent much time with Trotsky in Mexico, assisting in the preparation of the founding congress of the Fourth International. He was present when Trotsky was assassinated, and prevented his killer from fleeing. A very talented journalist, he was editor of *The Militant* for several years after 1940. He played a decisive role in reunification of the Fourth International in 1962-63 and was subsequently a regular observer at its congresses and plenums. In the last years of his life his political activity mainly centred on the editing of the weekly *Intercontinental Press/Inprecor*, which he had helped to launch as *World Outlook* in the wake of the 1963 reunification.

* * *

In ending this most incomplete list at this point, with the observation that the losses of the Trotskyists, relative to their number, are probably greater than those of all other tendencies in the working class movement, let us remember once again the exceptional pleiad of revolutionists who originated the movement, the Soviet Trotskyists, who stood up against all persecution until the day that Stalin decided on their total extermination. The story of their struggle at Vorkuta, of (among others) the great hunger strike conducted by more than a thousand prisoners for 132 days (from October 1936 to March 1937), in the course of which many perished, has come down to us through eyewitnesses returned from the camps. Alexander Solzhenitsyn in *The First Circle* has given their heroic end a suitable place in the great literature of the world. To their memory, and to the memory of all those who died fighting for the Fourth International, I dedicate this book.

Appendix: 2010 World Congress.
Role & Tasks of the Fourth International
Fourth International

1. We are in a context marked by an unprecedented combination of a global economic crisis and a worldwide ecological crisis, a multidimensional crisis without precedent, that puts capitalist and patriarchal civilisation into crisis. This is a major turning point. This dual crisis shows the failure of the capitalist system and puts on the agenda the reorganisation and reconstruction of an anti-capitalist workers' movement.

The social and economic attacks and neoliberal counter reforms against the popular classes are going to increase. These attacks will particularly affect women, given that their situation is worse to start with (much higher rates of poverty, unemployment and casualisation than men) and they will have to compensate for the cuts in public services and social allowances increasing their unpaid work within the family. There will be more wars and conflicts.

Religious fundamentalism will be increasingly used as the ideological underpinning both for attacks on the popular classes, targeting notably women's control of their own bodies, and wars and conflicts between nations and ethnic groups. A non-Eurocentric approach to sexual oppression and emancipation is important to opposing both Islamic fundamentalism in particular and the Islamophobic ideology of 'clash of civilizations' that helps fuel it. Ecological catastrophes will hit millions of people particularly in the poorer regions making the situation of women who are heads of family disproportionately worse.

A new historical period is on the horizon. New relationships of forces between imperialist powers on world economy and politics are taking shape, with the emergence of new capitalist forces like China, Russia, India and Brazil. The combination of the weakening of US hegemony and the sharpening of inter-capitalist competition between Europe, Russia, Asia and the USA also has geo-strategic effects in new political and military configurations, with an increased role for Nato, and new international tensions. In recent years, American imperialism has compensated for its economic weakening by redeploying its military hegemony in the four corners of the world. The social and economic contradictions have led even in the USA to the discredit of the Republican team around G.W. Bush. The election of Obama is a response to this discrediting as an alternative solution for US imperialism, even if his election also responds to a desire for change on the part of a section of US society which will be disappointed but is real.

In conclusion, the crisis makes obvious the failure of neoliberal ideology although the relationship of forces remains favourable to capital. As an ideology, it shows itself incapable of offering a solution, which is why the G-20 proposals are a return to the past that blew up with the crisis, wrote an end to the Washington Consensus, but placed the IMF in the decision-making center with its clearly neoliberal priorities. All the contradictions inherent to this social system are going to are going to come under stress without social democracy and the centre left being able to offer an adequate response. Even neo-Keynesian measures, which have not been adopted anyway, would not be enough to resolve the crisis. In this way the gap between the discourse, the pretensions of the class of the ruling class and the reality of the suffering and catastrophes which are inflicted on the peoples and workers, the building up of pressure on them, create the conditions for exacerbated social tensions and political crisis.

The crisis has a particularly harsh impact on women and on sexual minorities that are excluded from the family (or choose not to live in it) and are thus cut off from its resources. The crisis is driving many of the most marginalized people, such as transgenders, into even deeper poverty. This is true especially in dependent countries where a welfare state is weak or non-existent.

2. Social fightbacks are continuing to rise on a world scale but in a very unequal fashion and remain on the defensive. The global justice movement lost its dynamic that it had had up to 2004. The Belem WSF shows, nevertheless, the need and the possibility for international convergences, but in a framework where struggles are more fragmented and dispersed. In Europe the success of the mobilisations against the G20 and NATO give an indication of a renewal of the global justice movement. The Istanbul ESF could be another important occasion. The World March of Women proposes a new occasion of common initiative in 2010 which could become a step in rebuilding and strengthening this international feminist movement.

- In certain European countries – France, Greece, Germany, Poland, Italy – social struggles have a central impact on the political scene, but these struggles are not sufficient to block or turn around the underlying trends in the capitalist offensive and the effects of the crisis. They have not succeeded in overcoming the process of division and fragmentation of workers. These struggles remain defensive.

THE LONG MARCH OF THE TROTSKYISTS

They have not yet found an expression in terms of anti-capitalist consciousness. In this framework, in the absence of an anti-capitalist left reactionary, even xenophobic and racist alternatives and trends can get stronger.

- In the Middle East, peoples are continuing to resist Western and Israeli occupation and aggression, in Palestine, in Iraq and in Lebanon. The murderous aggression waged by the Zionist government in Gaza, two years after that in Lebanon, has not been able to defeat the resistance. Although Hamas and Hezbollah are now the main political references in this resistance. Outside these organisations there are left currents that act not only with a perspective for national liberation but also for social liberation, which reject human exploitation and which reject categorically the segregation of women. This is the position that we want to strengthen.

- Latin America continues to be the centre of resistance to neoliberalism and the continent with the most explosive situations, even though these are uneven from one country to another. Venezuela, Bolivia and Ecuador experience the most radical processes, with partial breaks from imperialism that have meant some important advances at the levels of government and/or social movements. There are others where the prognosis is unclear, like Paraguay, and all these find in Cuba a point of reference. Some others maintain versions of neoliberal policies, with neo-developmentalism in Argentina, or social liberalism in Uruguay and Brazil. The latter, in spite of its sharp contradictions with the US, especially over defence policy, its membership of Unasur and its agreements with Venezuela, nonetheless collaborates with fundamental policies of Washington and aims to achieve regional leadership. For their part, Colombia, Peru, Chile and Mexico remain clearly neo-liberal.

Nonetheless, a new political situation is emerging, with the renewed imperialist threat in the region, with the presence of the Fourth US Fleet, the coup in Honduras, seven new US military bases in Colombia, the direct intervention of the US embassy in the most important trade union conflict in Argentina for years, the political and military interference in Haiti. All these aim to roll back the political advances and develop an international response.

This means that the class struggle will intensify in Latin America in the coming period. The governments of Venezuela and Ecuador are moving back from their most radical proposals, showing two aspects in particular that cause concern: the orientation towards the extractaction of natural resources and the limited democratic participation of social sectors. In Bolivia, there is a radicalisation of the processes of change, which rests directly on the social movements.

Although these processes are in dispute, with advances and retreats, they run the risk, in the course of their evolution, of not advancing to anti-capitalist positions, unless there is a strengthening of the self-activity of wage earners, indigenous peoples and other oppressed social sectors, and greater pressure from these sectors on the governments of Venezuela, Bolivia and Ecuador.

At the same time, the radicalization of social movements, especially the struggle of indigenous and peasant movements, is putting pressure on these governments and at the same time posing an clear anti-capitalist perspective, in defence of natural resources – land, water, biodiversity, etc. – and a change in the development model, as was expressed in the Declaration of the Assembly of Social Movements at the Belem WSF, and the recent assembly of Alba TCP, which in its final statement denounced capitalism and called for its overthrow. The national, regional and international meetings of the social movements demonstrate the radical potential contained in the southern part of Latin America.

One urgent political task for the organisations is to stimulate the self-activity of the masses, generalising workers' control and the creation of bodies of popular power; otherwise, in Venezuela, Bolivia and Ecuador, there is a risk of a definitive reverse and a consolidation of capitalism in these countries, where it is currently challenged.

The activity of the sections and groups of the Fourth International in Latin America need to take into account these tendencies – the national question in the region and the connections between anti-imperialism and anti-capitalism – and define a tactic for intervention in a process characterized by the inter-relation between the states that make up the ALBA and social movements with strong histories of self-organization and self-management. These two forces sometimes converge and sometimes enter into contradiction. This implies promoting demands for unitary struggles in defence of the rights of indigenous peoples, against the criminalization of protest, privatizations, extractivism of natural resources, machismo and the economic and ecological crisis, thereby stimulating the strategic political debate about power and hegemony in our societies.

- In a series of what are usually called emerging capitalist countries or those resulting from capitalist restoration, – China, Russia or the former eastern bloc – the whirlwind of globalisation is tending to proletarianise hundreds of millions of human beings. But this new social power, which can play a key role in the coming years, has not yet formed mass independent organizations – trade unions, associations, and political organisations capable of facing the challenge of this global reorganisation.

- The pillaging of resources in Africa to the benefit of big capitalist multinationals is increasing with the complicity of the existing governments. The continued growth of GDP in recent years in sub-Saharan Africa does not benefit the population, only social inequality in increasing. Faces with the deterioration in living conditions, there have been major struggles, such as the general strikes in Guinea, the demonstrations in Togo, the general strike in the public sector in South Africa. The food crisis at the end of 2008 sparked many demonstrations. However, the absence of a political alternative is a heavy obstacle to the success of these struggles, such as in Guinea or in the Cameroons. They are either diverted to wards bourgeois political formations as in Madagascar or they lose themselves in religious dead-ends as in Nigeria or Congo (DRC) or worse in ethnic or racist ones like in Kenya or South Africa.

The building of democratic peoples' and workers' organisations' remains an absolute necessity for the success of struggles.

- In Asia, the ongoing fast development of capitalism in China and in India and in most of South-Asian countries raises crucial political questions. Around half of the global working class lives in Asia and the necessity to create or strengthen revolutionary parties in this part of the world is critical. The situation is very different from one country to another:

• China is of the outmost importance. Decades of repression explain why the creation of a revolutionary party in China has to start from scratch. Bringing the experience and tradition of the international labour movement to China will be necessary to stimulate the creation of a revolutionary party as well as international solidarity. The Fourth International will have to pay special attention to the social and political developments that the present international crisis could bring about in the near future.

• In India, whose population will supersede the Chinese one by 2050, and where faster industrialisation has increased the number of workers and the rural crisis is deepening, the political situation and our tasks are different. The labour movement is very well developed and organised but dominated by Stalinist or Maoist political parties. The construction of a revolutionary party defending our program cannot just ignore them.

• In South-East Asia, the situation is very uneven. In some countries like Thailand and Burma, the labour movement is very weak. In these countries there is neither social democracy nor radical left parties. In these countries our task is to establish stronger links with the social movements that are active in the defence of farmers, women and workers when trade unions exist. Indonesia and Malaysia are in an intermediary situation. There are some small revolutionary parties with whom we can engage a constructive political debate and collaboration.

• In the Philippines and Pakistan, the Fourth International has strong organisations which can be a basis of our political activity throughout Asia.

In these countries we are confronted with Islamic fundamentalism. We oppose the Taliban in Afghanistan and the Muslims extremists in the Philippines like the Abou Sayaf because they are reactionary forces. We cannot make any agreement with them in the name of anti imperialism. In other countries like Indonesia or Malaysia, we also could be confronted to Islamic fundamentalism and the FI has to strengthen its analysis.

• In Sri Lanka, after several decades of war, the government has defeated the LTTE militarily but the root cause of the Tamil question has not yet been addressed. Besides, the Rajapaksa government uses open and brutal repression to silent his opponents and the media. The FI should be part of the international campaign of solidarity with the Tamil people. In all Asia, the FI defends the rights of ethnic groups and indigenous peoples and support their struggle for self determination.

• In Japan, the process of fusion of the two organisations linked to the FI is underway. Since September, they are jointly publishing a common newspaper.

In South Korea too, where the labour movement is strong, there is also a convergence of different forces toward the creation of a new anticapitalist party. Because this country has a strong tradition in the working class struggle, the Fourth International has to follow this event closely. Besides, the FI should organise solidarity campaigns to support the militants of revolutionary parties who are now repressed by the State.

3. The dynamic of capitalist globalisation and the current crisis have also changed the framework of evolution and development of the traditional left. Reformist bureaucracies have seen their leeway considerably reduced. From reformism without reforms to reformism with counter-reforms, social democracy and equivalent forces in a series of dominated or developing countries are experiencing an evolution towards social-liberalism; that is these forces are directly underwriting neo-liberal or neo-conservative policies. All the forces politically or institutionally linked to social-liberalism or to the centre

left - including the women's movement, notably in the institutionalised forms of NGOs, women's aid associations, etc, - are, to varying degrees, being dragged into these qualitative changes in the workers' movement and are incapable of formulating a plan for getting out of the crisis. What is more, we are seeing policies - such as that of the Lula government in Brazil - which are making the ecological crisis worse. The clash with these parties is more difficult since they maintain their control, particularly electorally, of part of the workers movement, and it is therefore necessary to build a real, credible political alternative.

The traditional communist parties are continuing their long decline. They try to break this decline by grabbing onto the coat tails of the leading forces in the liberal left and the institutional apparatuses or falling back on their nostalgic and self-affirming positions. While there are sectors or currents who wish to build the social movements with anticapitalist forces, such as Synaspismos in Greece, they are doomed to have contradictions and divisions because of their reformist nature. In effect, the decision to build anti-capitalist parties does not mean we are not cognizant of the existence of radical, anti-liberal, left reformist currents that play a role and have electoral credibility. Therefore, they continue to be competitors and-or politcal adversaries. Their position can be reinforced by occasional tactical shifts - generally electoralist - to the left, by social-liberalism, often to reestablish its consensus among the working class and popular sectors. This poses the challenge for us of implementing a united front offensive capable of responding to the needs of men and women wage earners. At the same time, when on the basis of clear political conditions we decide to intervene inside anti-liberal, reformist left parties (such as in the case of Die Linke), we do it with no illusions about the nature of these parties, and we build anti-capitalist tendencies linked to social movements, that fight electoralism, institutionalism, and any attempt to compromise with capitalism.

4. We want to get involved in this reorganisation to create a new left that is capable of meeting the challenge of this century and rebuilding the workers' movement, its structures, its class consciousness, its independence from the bourgeoisies at the political and cultural level.

• An anti-capitalist, internationalist, ecologist and feminist left;
• A left that is clearly alternative to social democracy and its governments;
• a left which fights for a socialism of the 21st century, self-managed and democratic and which has a coherent programme for getting there;

• a left that is conscious that for this goal it has to break with capitalism and its logic and thus that is cannot govern with the political representation with which it wants to break;

• a pluralistic left rooted in the social movements and the workplaces which integrates the combativity of the workers, the struggles for women's and LGBT liberation and emancipation and ecologist struggles;

• a non-institutional left which bases its strategy on the self-organisation of the proletariat and the oppressed on the principle that emancipations of the workers is the task of the workers themselves;

• A left that promotes all forms of self-organisation by workers and by the popular classes that encourages thinking, deciding, and doing things for itself and on the basis of its own decisions;

• a left which integrates new social sectors, new themes such as those expressed by the World Social Forum in Belem, and above all the new generations because you cannot make new things with old material;

• an internationalist and anti-imperialist left which fights against domination and war and the self-determination of the people and which lays out the framework for a mass democratic international;

• a left able to link the precious heritage of critical and revolutionary Marxism with developments of feminism, ecosocialism and the indigenous movements of Latin America;

• an independent and class-struggle left which fights for the broadest united action against the crisis and for the rights, the gains and the aspirations of the workers and all the oppressed.

These are the criteria and the general content of our orientation for building new useful anti-capitalist instruments for fighting the current system.

5. This is the aspiration in which the problems of building the Fourth International and new anti-capitalist parties and new international currents are posed. We expressed it in our own way, from 1992 onwards, so in the last two world congresses, with the triptych "New period, new programme, new party", developed in documents of the International. We confirm the essential of our choices at the last World Congress in 2003 concerning the building of broad anticapitalist parties. The Fourth International is confronted, in an overall way, with a new phase. Revolutionary Marxist militants, nuclei, currents and organizations must pose the problem of the construction of anti-capitalist, revolutionary political formations, with the perspective of establishing a new independent political representation of the working class that takes into account the

diversity of the working class – in gender, race, residence status, age, sexual orientation - in defending a resolutely class-based programme.

Building broad anti-capitalist parties is the current response we offer to the crisis in the workers and left movement and the need for its reconstruction. This project is based on mass struggles, bringing mass movements to the forefront and the emergence of a new generation. Of course, this does not eliminate our revolutionary Marxist, ecologist, feminist internationalist identity and our basic aim of defeating capitalism to create a new ruling order based on democracy and direct participation: that is, a real socialist democracy.

That is true on the level of each country and at an international level. On the basis of the experience of the class struggle, the development of the global justice movement, defensive struggles and anti-war mobilizations over the last ten years, and in particular the lessons drawn from the evolution of the Brazilian PT and of Communist Refoundation in Italy and from the debates of the French anti-liberal left, revolutionary Marxists have engaged in recent years in the building of the PSOL in Brazil, of Sinistra Critica in Italy, of the new anti-capitalist party in France, Respect in England. In this perspective we have continued to build the experiences of the Bloco de Esquerda in Portugal and the Red Green Alliance in Denmark.

The common goal, via different paths, is that of broad anti-capitalist parties. It is not a question of taking up the old formulas of regroupment or revolutionary currents alone. The ambition is to bring together forces beyond simply revolutionary ones. These can be a support in the process of brining forces together as long as they are clearly for building anti-capitalist parties. Although there is no model, since each process of coming together takes account of national specificities and relationships of forces, our goal must thus be to seek to build broad anti-capitalist political forces, independent of social democracy and the centre left, formations which reject any policy of participation or support to class-collaborationist governments, today in government with social-democracy and the centre left, forces which understand that winning victories on women's rights, like in the abortion referendum in Portugal, strengthen the radical anti-capitalist forces.

It is on the basis of such a perspective that we must be oriented. What we know of the experiences of differentiation and reorganization in Africa and Asia point in the same direction. Nevertheless in the countries of Latin America the construction of broad anti-capitalist parties should integrate from its beginnings a clear stand for socialism. It is through this complex and diverse process that we can make new advances.

Where we are working inside such broad political forces, it is important to fight for the right of self-organization within these parties by women and LGBTs, and on this self-organization's being reflected in the parties' programmes and practice. This self-organization is a means of resisting pressures towards electoralism and institutionalization. In new radical political formations in several Latin American countries, the right to self-organization is important to fighting for a 21st-century socialism from below that rejects authoritarian tendencies and the temptation to repeat 20th-century errors. In general within such broad forces, we start from an understanding, as an indissoluble part of our socialism, of the necessity for a collective and resolute response to all manifestations of prejudice including sexism, racism, Islamophobia, anti-Semitism, homophobia and transphobia. We also fight for specific attention to organizing by youth; for the integration of black, immigrant, women's and LGBT issues into the party's public statements and daily interventions; and for representation of specially oppressed comrades in the party leadership and among its spokespeople and candidates for office.

6. This is the framework in which we must approach the question of the relationship between the building of the Fourth International and a policy of anti-capitalist coming together at the national, continental and international levels. We must discuss how to strengthen and transform the Fourth International in order to make it an effective tool in the perspective of a new international grouping. We already have started, with limited results it has to be admitted, conferences of the anti-capitalist left and other international conferences. On the international level, we have initiated, on this political basis, many conferences and initiatives of international convergence and coming together: the constitution of the European Anti-capitalist Left (EACL), with the Portuguese Left Bloc, the Danish Red-Green Alliance and the Scottish Socialist Party. We worked with organizations like the English SWP. Other parties - even left reformists of who had at one time or another a political evolution "to the left", like Communist Refoundation in Italy, tor Synaspismos, also took part in these conferences. We also held international conferences of revolutionary and anti-capitalist organizations, on the occasion of the World Social Forums at Mumbai in India and Porto Alegre in Brazil. On this level, we created bonds of solidarity with the Brazilian PSOL in its break with Lula's PT. We have supported the efforts of our Italian comrades to build an anti-

capitalist alternative to the policies of Communist Refoundation in Italy. These few elements show the type of orientation that we want to implement. The different conferences this year such as those in Paris or Belem show the necessity and the possibility of joint action and discussion by a large number of organizations and currents of the anti-capitalist left in Europe. It is now necessary to continue a policy of open meetings and conferences on topics of strategic and programmatic thinking and joint action through campaigns and initiatives of international mobilization.

7. The Fourth International and its sections have played and still play a vital road in defending, promoting and implementing a programme of demands that are both immediate and transitional towards socialism; a united-front policy that aims for mass mobilization of workers and their organizations; a policy of working-class unity and independence against any type of strategic alliance with the national bourgeoisie; opposition to any participation in governments that merely manage the State and the capitalist economy having abandoned allinternationalism or fight for an end to inequality and discrimination on gender, racial, ethnic, religious or sexual orientation grounds.

The Fourth International has played and still plays a functional role to keep alive the history of the revolutionary Marxist current, "to understand the world", to confront the analyses and the experiences of revolutionary militants, currents and organizations and to bring together organizations, currents and militants who share the same strategic vision and the same choice of broad convergences on revolutionary bases. The existence of an international framework that makes it possible "to think about politics" is an indispensable asset for the intervention of revolutionaries. Consistent internationalism must pose the question of an international framework. But for historical reasons that it has itself analyzed, the Fourth International does not have the legitimacy to represent in and of itself the new mass International that we need. So when it is a question of taking a step forward in the bringing together of anti-capitalist forces, these new organizations, in particular in Europe and Latin America, cannot relate to and join this or that current identified with the Fourth International, and this is true whatever the reference point – the various Morenoites, the Lambertists, the SWP or other variants of Trotskyism.

Let us note, nevertheless, that a major difference between the FI and all these tendencies, over and above political positions, which is to the credit of the International, is that it is based on a democratic coordination of sections and militants, whereas the other international tendencies are "international-factions" or coordinations based on "party-factions" which do not respect rules of democratic functioning, in particular the right of tendency. The historical limits of these international "Trotskyist" currents ", like other ex-Maoist or ex-Communist currents, prevent us today from advancing in the crystallization of new international convergences. Chavez's call to found a Fifth International poses other questions about its origins, its framework, that is to say, its viability. The Fourth International declares that it is willing to participate in the debates and preparatory meetings that may be organized. We will contribute our historic gains and our vision about what a new international and its programatic foundations could be. A genuine new international can only be born if its members share a programme, an ability to intervene in society, a democratic, pluralist form of functioning, as well as clear independence from governments in order to break with capitalism.

In the present relationship of forces, the policy for advancing towards a mass International must rather take the road of open and periodic conferences on central political questions – activity, specific themes or discussions - which make possible the convergence and the emergence of anti-capitalist and revolutionary poles. In this sense, the Fourth International is in favor of the proposals from revolutionary Marxist currents and/or groups who share with us a common understanding of the international situation and our aspirations for building new international frameworks.

In the new anti-capitalist parties which may be formed in the years to come, and which express the current stage of combativeness, experience and consciousness of the sectors that are the most committed to the search for an anti-capitalist alternative, the question of a new International is and will be posed. We act and we will continue to act so that it is not posed in terms of ideological or historical choices, which are likely to lead to divisions and splits. It must be posed on a double level, on the one hand real political convergence on tasks of international intervention, on the other pluralism of the new formations, which must bring together currents of various origins: Trotskyists of different kinds, libertarians, revolutionary syndicalists, revolutionary nationalists, left reformists. So in general, when there have been concrete steps towards new parties, we have proposed that the new broad anti-capitalist party functions with the right of tendency or currents, and that the supporters of the Fourth International in these new parties organize themselves in ways to be decided, according to the specific situation of each party. Our Portuguese comrades in the Left Bloc, our Danish comrades in the Red-Green Alliance, our Brazilian comrades in the

PSOL, are organized, in particular forms, as a Fourth International current or in class struggle currents with other political tendencies.

8. In this movement we are confronted with desynchronizations between the building of parties on a national level and the construction of new international groupings. There can be, in the present situation or in the next years, new anti-capitalist parties in a series of countries, but the emergence of a new international force, and all the more so, of a new International, is not, at this stage, foreseeable. A new International will only be the result of a prolonged period of joint action and common understanding of events and tasks for overthrowing capitalism. While we affirm a policy of international convergence, this confirms the particular responsibilities of the FI, and thus the need for its reinforcement. We can and we seek to represent an organizational framework that is attractive and, democratic, for revolutionary organizations which share the same political projects as ours. It is in this dynamic that the Filipino comrades are situated, the Pakistani comrades and the Russian comrades are situated, and that can be the case tomorrow of, for example, the Polish or Malian comrades.

9. We have, in fact, a particular role that is recognized by a series of political currents. We may be the only ones who can make political forces of various origins converge. This is for example, what in Latin America the Venezuelans comrades of left currents of the Bolivarian process say to us. It is also the case in Europe, in the framework of the relations of the EACL and of other currents. So, the next world congress must be an important step for the meeting of all these forces. This Congress will be a congress of the FI and there will be no organisational growing over at this stage. But we want the FI to play the role of a "facilitator" of convergences in the perspective of new international groupings.

10. As a result, in order to strengthen ourselves and play this role all the bodies of the FI must be reinforced: regular Bureau meetings, International Committees, specific working commissions, travel, exchanges between the sections. It is necessary to reinforce the activity that the International has deployed over the last few years in regularising and strengthening EPBs meetings and the efforts of coordination between the Latin American sections. The meetings of the International Committeee (IC) which are held every year representing about 30 organisations must ensure the organisational continuity of our international current.

Lack of resources as well as the decline in the presence of women, notably in our leading bodies, in the last period (result of the decline in activity of a strong autonomous women's movement which has had an impact on our national organisations and thus the International), have meant that we have not sustained an active women's commission and a corresponding network of regional meetings and international schools. Three women's seminars have been held since 2000 as well as meetings of the women comrades present at each IC. These have maintained a limited and fragile but neverthless real feminist internationalist perspective. In the next period, given the centrality of our understanding of women's oppression and the strategic nature of the fight against it and the struggle to build the autonomous women's movement in an anticapitalist perspective, we must find the necessary resources to ensure that this question is developed as a central element of the anticapitalist perspective we propose. In this framework we must at the same time strengthen our internal commission and be on the offensive in proposing discussions to our partners, including participation in seminars and schools in our Institute. This process must also find a reflection at national level.

At the same time we must ensure that the women in our organisations – and in the new parties we are building – find their full place and that the simple adoption of parity or quotas for leadership bodies or electoral lists is not considered a sufficient answer to the obstacles to women's full participation in the political process. The range of measures constituting a postive action plan were presented in the 1991 World Congress resolution on positive action.

The youth camp which is held every year with around 500 comrades must have a central place for the youth work of our European sections, in the perspective of forming young internationalist cadres. As more and more of our organisations in Europe are within broader anti-capitalist formations we continue to encourage our comrades to invite youth from the broader organisations to the camp, and to participate in the preparatory seminar held in Amsterdam every Easter. The camp is also an important occasion for young comrades from Europe to meet comrades from other continents and the efforts made by organisations outside Europe to send comrades to participate in the camp is very important. As the only regular public initiative of the FI, the camp also plays a role as a place to which younger people from organisations with which we are building relations can be invited, as was the case with camp in Greece in 2009 with the presence of small delegations from Russia, Ukraine, Belarus, Poland and Croatia

The Amsterdam educational institute has taken on a fresh impetus. We now have to ensure that the schools and seminars are held and ensure the equilibrium of its management and its organisation. The FI must also open up its meetings and its Institute. The Institute occupies a central place, not only to educate the cadres of the section but also to contribute to the exchanges between currents and to various international experiences. The seminar on climate change open to a series of international experts is a good example. Like other meetings it indicates the necessity and the possibility that we are a crucible for programmatic elaboration of essential questions that anti-capitalist and revolutionary currents are tackling.

The existence of an international school in the Philippines is a tool of great importance to form new generations of revolutionary militants coming from all parts of Asia and to share their experiences. In the near future, there will be a new school in Islamabad in Pakistan which enlarge our capacity to form militants and organise political debates in South Asia. The FI has to give full support to the IIRE in Manila and in Islamabad.

Our schools have always been an occasion for inviting participation from organisations with which we are building relations. This role must be strengthened and broadened in the coming period throughout the IIRE network.

To sum up, in the coming period, and on an orientation aimed at building a new international force or a new International, the FI as an internal framework, represents an essential asset for revolutionary Marxists.

Appendix: 2008.
From the LCR to the NPA
Members of the LCR

by H. Adam, D. Bensaïd, F. Coustal, L. Crémieux,
J. Guillotin, S. Johsua, A. Krivine, O. Martin, C. Poupin,
P. Rousset, F. Sabado, and R. Vachetta

For 20, 30 or 40 years now, we have built the LCR. Today, we are fully part of the constituent process leading to the launch of the NPA. We approach this new enterprise with confidence thanks to – and not in spite of – what the LCR has accomplished over these past few decades. This is a momentous development; the LCR's decision to dissolve itself in order to take up a broader challenge is a rather exceptional event in the history of the French working-class movement.[30]

We are able to take this gamble because we are not beginning from scratch. It is no accident that – of all the groups within the French and even international revolutionary Left – it is the LCR that has taken such an initiative. We are the product of a particular history of the revolutionary movement – the fusion of a current of Trotskyism with the youth radicalization of the 1960s. We are a non-dogmatic current of revolutionary Marxism that has been able to preserve fundamental elements of continuity in the history of the working-class movement, particularly in relation to Social Democracy and Stalinism. These include the defence of a program of demands that are both immediate and transitional towards socialism; a united-front policy that aims for mass mobilization of workers and their organizations; a policy of working-class unity and independence against any type of strategic alliance with the national bourgeoisie; opposition to any participation in governments in the advanced-capitalist countries that merely manage the State and the capitalist economy; and unfailing internationalism.

---

[30] This contribution was written as part of preparations for the January 2009 congress of the Revolutionary Communist League (LCR), the French section of the Fourth International. The congress agenda included the political "self-dissolution" of the LCR, to set the stage for the new challenge of the New Anti-Capitalist Party (NPA). The authors of this piece belong to the generation of activists from the 1960s and 1970s. The translation is by Raghu Krishnan.

THE LONG MARCH OF THE TROTSKYISTS

Unlike other currents, we have endeavoured to incorporate a wide range of new factors into our political tradition: the post-war evolution of capitalism; active solidarity with the anti-colonial revolutions and with the anti-bureaucratic movements in the Eastern bloc; an analysis of the new social movements such as the women's movement and, today, growing eco-socialist awareness in the face of the ecological crisis; and, above all, ongoing examination and enrichment of one of the key points of our program, socialist democracy.

This is a trademark of the LCR. The LCR has been able to ensure the continuity of the Left Opposition's struggle against Stalinism. What is more, unlike most currents of the revolutionary Left in France and in a whole host of countries, it has also upheld the principles and practical application of democratic and pluralistic organization and functioning. Throughout its history, taken together, our sensitivity to this question and our democratic and pluralistic internal functioning have enabled the LCR to provide a home for a series of currents and organizations with different origins and political cultures. And it has meant that the LCR is now in a position to build something with other forces and to embrace the new challenge of the NPA.

The NPA is the result of the political work of recent years, especially of our contribution to the renewal of the social movements and of the success of the presidential campaigns of 2002 and 2007 around Olivier Besancenot. But the idea goes back much further than that.

Beginning in the early 1990s, the collapse of the USSR and of the Eastern-bloc countries, combined with neo-liberal capitalist globalization, brought one historical cycle to a close and opened another. "New epoch, new program, new party": this was a three-pronged approach towards thinking about the new historical period. Political action would be framed by a new set of parameters. It would henceforth be possible to overcome the divisions that had separated the many revolutionary and anti-capitalist currents born in the 19th and 20th centuries.

Of course, we were uncertain about the new organizational forms, characteristics, limits and dynamics. But the question was posed, on both the international and national level. Internationally, we took initiatives through international conferences and went through a number of experiences, each with its own specificities: the PSOL in Brazil, after the experience of the PT; Sinistra Critica in Italy, after the experience of Rifondazione Comunista; Respect in Britain and the Scottish SSP, before the splits in these two organizations; the Left Bloc in Portugal; and the Red-Green Alliance in Denmark.

In each one of these processes, some questions were settled – especially around the matter of the relationship with political power and participation or not in centre-Left and social-liberal governments. These questions led to the split of PSOL from the PT and Sinistra Critica from Rifondazione Comunista. They also underlie our differences with the leadership of Die Linke in Germany, which has declared its support for parliamentary and governmental alliances with Social Democracy.

The NPA will be clearly defined politically. Its preliminary documents set out some unmistakable terms: class struggle and support for all the struggles of the exploited and oppressed; unity in action of workers and their organizations; a break with the capitalist system; an eco-socialist project; opposition to any policy of managing the capitalist economy and the central executive powers of capitalist institutions; the struggle for a workers' government; the revolutionary transformation of society; socialist democracy; and an internationalist program and practice. To be sure, a number of questions will remain open: the nature of revolutions in the 21st century; problems of the transition to socialism; and a whole range of other questions having to do with the reformulation of the socialist and communist project. But we are not beginning from scratch; and the NPA will collectively determine its own positions on the basis of new common experiences.

It is therefore not a matter of building a revamped LCR. We don't only want to build a broader party; we want to build a party that is a new social and political reality. It will be pluralistic. It will take the best of all the revolutionary traditions of the working-class movement and of other movements such as eco-socialism. Its goal is to bring all anti-capitalists under one roof.

The NPA will be an internationalist organization, in charge of its own policies on international matters. It will not be a section of the Fourth International (which is a specific international political current). As a pluralistic party, the NPA cannot join the Fourth International (FI) as such. The process of building a new International – which has always been and remains our goal – will be long and complicated. The building of anti-capitalist formations in individual countries will not take place in synch with the building of a new international grouping. As allowed for by its statutes, we remain members of the FI, with ties to the LCR comrades elected to its leadership bodies. Given the role the LCR plays within the

International, we have proposed that the NPA continue to shoulder a number of tasks for which the LCR was responsible within the FI.

We are also proud to have passed on to a new generation not only a part of our political heritage but also the full range of leadership responsibilities – without the turmoil and crises of succession that most parties experience. Credit for this goes equally to the older generation, the youth and those somewhere in between. As the LCR dissolves into the NPA, though, we make a specific appeal to the sense of responsibility of LCR members. Their experience and training are vital to the building of the NPA. They are among the preconditions for the new party's success, and for the successful synthesis of new and old. Everyone should get fully involved, as we have decided to do ourselves. Without a doubt, this will be a remarkable exercise in learning to speak with broader sectors, in paying special attention to the vocabulary we use, in learning to listen to and respect others, and in learning from them without underestimating what we bring to them ourselves. After the NPA founding conference, every comrade from the LCR should get involved in building this new project, for which we have fought for so many decades.

15 December 2008

Appendix: From 1979 to 2007. Trotskyisms: What I know
Daniel Bensaïd

Changing times

With the capitalist counter-offensive, the Reagan administration's new arms race, the American "low intensity" war in Central America, and Britain's expeditionary force to the Malvinas-Falklands Islands (foreshadowing a new round of imperialist intervention), the beginning of the 1980s signalled a radical change over the previous decade.[31] The Soviet Union had sunk into the deep stagnation of the Brezhnev period. The international working-class movement was being thrown onto the defensive on nearly every front. This reversal opened the way for major social-movement defeats – such as the defeat of the British miners' strike in 1984, the failure of the Italian movement in defence of wage indexation in 1985, and trade-union defeats in the USA and Japan during the same period. In France, the austerity turn sealed the Socialist Party's conversion to social-liberalism.

Still, despite this right-wing counter-offensive, signs of renewal were appearing – especially in Brazil with the foundation in 1979 of the Workers Party (PT), which would become one of the country's main political organizations within a decade; and in South Korea, with the huge student mobilizations and formation of new trade unions. Nevertheless, the Nicaraguan revolution – which had fired hopes for a revival of the Latin American revolution – failed to spread to El Salvador and Guatemala. It had been contained by the strategy of counter-insurgency implemented with Israeli and Taiwanese assistance, and by the so-called "low intensity" war waged by the Americans. In the Southern Cone, the transition away from dictatorship was relatively well handled by the ruling classes of Brazil, Argentina, Uruguay and Chile, where social movements were still reeling from the blows endured under the military heel. The last major Bolivian miners' strike (in 1985) brought to a close the period inaugurated by the Bolivian revolution of 1952. The fraudulent

---

[31] This appendix is reprinted from "Strategies of Resistance", issue 42-43 of the Notebooks for Study and Research. The translation is by Nathan Rao.

victory of Salinas de Gortari against Cuauhtémoc Cárdenas in the Mexican elections of 1988 was a highly symbolic event; it cleared the way for the dismantling of the populist welfare state and initiated a wave of major neoliberal reforms: privatization, agrarian counter-reform, and the signing of a free-trade agreement with the USA and Canada.

At the beginning of the 1980s, a rejuvenated and highly internationalized Fourth International collective leadership team – from the USA, Mexico, Spain, Sweden, Japan, Belgium, Italy, Switzerland, Australia, Britain and France – initiated a wide range of organizational projects. These included the establishment of a permanent international leadership school, an overhaul of the press, support for the creation of youth organizations, and the setting up of continental coordinating bodies. However, differences reignited by the revolution in Central America showed that the FI was running out of steam.

A product of the December 1980 Open World Conference, the International Committee lasted only a few short months. Its unity had been based on opposition to the "United Secretariat liquidationists" and lacked a solid foundation. True to his brand of pragmatic manoeuvring, Lambert steered clear of core political debates – at a time when the Nicaraguan revolution was reviving old debates regarding the characterization of the Chinese, Yugoslav and Cuban revolutions and their political leadership. For his part, Moreno settled the matter by declaring that the October Revolution had been the only authentic social revolution and that the post-war period had only experienced "February revolutions" with no genuine self-organization among the masses; these revolutions had nonetheless been "categorically socialist", he argued, inasmuch as they had dismantled the existing state apparatus. Moreno presented these theoretical gymnastics in a more systematic way in a book that appeared under the pen name Dariush Karim. The book differentiated a stage of confrontation with imperialism from a stage of socialist construction strictly speaking. This approach sacrificed principles of socialist democracy to *realpolitik* and ultimately diminished the importance of the fight against bureaucracy during the anti-imperialist stage.

Behind the outward show of unity at the Eleventh Congress against the split orchestrated by Moreno and Lambert, cracks began to form within the International majority. The disagreements concerned controversial questions such as the unity of the Trotskyist movement and the "turn to industry", but also unresolved debates reignited by developments in Central America and Poland.

Differences revolved yet again around the lag between the revolutionary act of seizing power and the transformation of the relations of production. As 1979 drew to a close, new differences appeared following the entry of Soviet troops into Afghanistan purportedly to defend the secular government against reactionary tribal and religious forces supported by the Pakistani dictatorship. Besieged by the Cold War mood of the Reagan era, the American SWP opted to support the Soviet intervention. Adopting a more cautious stance, the United Secretariat majority condemned the intervention as being guided primarily by the geostrategic interests of the bureaucracy; but it did not demand the withdrawal of Soviet troops, arguing that the internationalization of the conflict had set secular progressive forces supported by the Soviet Union against reactionary religious forces supported and armed by the United States. A minority around Tariq Ali, Gilbert Achcar and Michel Lequenne took the soundest position – arguing that the Soviet intervention would only cloud the meaning of anti-imperialist struggle and bolster the most reactionary religious and nationalist forces. They demanded the immediate withdrawal of Soviet troops and advocated support for the most progressive elements of the Afghan resistance. In 1982, the International adopted a self-critical resolution along the lines of this position. This fumbling approach was an example of the difficulty the FI was having in relation to new armed confrontations – such as the Malvinas/Falklands conflict and the war between Iran and Iraq – that highlighted the centrifugal dynamics of the new world situation.

And yet, on the eve of the 1980s, developments such as Solidarność's anti-bureaucratic struggle in Poland and the rise of the revolution in Central America seemed to lend themselves to a reading of the world situation using updated models of political revolution and permanent revolution. This became the focus of debates leading up to the Twelfth World Congress in 1985. The American SWP and Australian SWP deepened their rapprochement with the Castro leadership in Cuba and revised their traditionally orthodox outlook in harmony with this new orientation. In a 1983 essay entitled "Their Trotsky and Ours", Jack Barnes left no room for doubt: "The change I am proposing is one of the most important ones since the founding of our movement." He argued that the theory of permanent revolution was "an obstacle to reviving the tradition of Marx, Lenin and the first congresses of the Communist International." Trotsky's return to the ultraleft demons of his youth, he added, had cut the Fourth International off from the real historical movement. This was a selective embrace of a brand of Trotskyism purged of the struggle against Stalinism; it enabled Barnes to erase references to the anti-bureaucratic revolution and, on the sly, go back to the position of promoting the reform path in the countries of the Soviet bloc. When the SWP relegated support to the Polish uprising to the background – on the pretext that it might weaken the socialist camp just as Reagan was embarking on a new Cold War – it confirmed the organization's new turn. The Barnes essay focussed unilaterally on the fact that defence of the Soviet workers' state had proven "vital to the extension of the world socialist revolution." He conveniently ignored the cost of the Soviet policy of peaceful coexistence for colonial peoples and the workers of Western Europe; and said nothing about the Greek, Spanish, Indonesian and Chilean tragedies – let alone the price paid by the Chinese, Cubans and Vietnamese for the conditional assistance of their Soviet big brother.

The SWP comrades had always claimed to be the standard-bearers of Trotskyist orthodoxy. That they should find themselves so far adrift was a sure sign of demoralization and the replacement of the class struggle by the struggle between camps and states. The SWP turn seemed all the more unfounded in that – from the OLAS conference onwards – experiences in Latin America and elsewhere had actually prompted a critical review of the stagist strategies of the Stalinist period and called attention to the dissenting strategic lineage shared by such figures as José Carlos Mariátegui from Peru, Antonio Mella from Cuba, Farabundo Martí from El Salvador, and Augusto César Sandino and Carlos Fonseca Amador from Nicaragua. Similarly, the demands of the Polish movement and the Solidarność congress of 1980 – captured in the slogan "Give us back our factories!" – actually provided a striking defence and illustration of the strategy of political revolution in the Soviet bloc.

The Australian SWP were more interested in engaging with political developments in their country and weren't as concerned as the leaders of the American section with matters of programmatic heritage. Australian delegates to the Thirteenth World Congress candidly told the gathering that permanent revolution was a "useless fetish" that had led to the sectarian degeneration of the International and to "an overestimation of the role of the political revolution against the castes in power in the bureaucratic socialist states." The Australian delegates were so candid, in fact, that they went so far as to justify the Stalinist repression against Vietnamese Trotskyists – granting only the belated self-criticism of the Vietnamese Communist Party itself, according to which the (anti-Trotskyist) violence had been "excessive relative to the situation."

CONTRIBUTIONS TO THE HISTORY OF THE FOURTH INTERNATIONAL

The majority resolutions for the Twelfth World Congress stressed that the crisis of the international revolutionary leadership could no longer be posed in the same terms as in the 1930s. It was no longer a matter of providing alternative leadership to an international working-class movement bathed in the revolutionary culture of the period opened up by the Russian Revolution. A lot of water had flown under the bridge since that time. That tradition had been destroyed during the long night of Stalinism and by Social Democracy's embrace of the capitalist order. A worldwide renewal of trade-unionism and working-class politics was now on the agenda. It was therefore a matter of plunging into the uneven and prolonged process of rebuilding. The Fourth International could play an irreplaceable role in this process – on the condition that it not see itself as the mythical "World Party" of socialist revolution. "Failing world-shaking events powerful enough to upset the relationship of forces between the classes and cause a general realignment of political forces, the recomposition of the international workers movement will remain slow, uneven and extremely differentiated [...] The time now is neither to abstractly proclaim a mass International nor to search out shortcuts towards that end. We stand now merely at the beginning of profound and lasting transformations in the workers movement. We should approach them by a combination of building the Fourth International as it is and collaborating with the vanguard forces evolving in the different countries and continents." This was an open-ended approach that, however, did not make a clean slate of history; there was no question of scrapping the movement's programmatic heritage – whether around the struggle against bureaucratic totalitarianism or the logic of permanent revolution.

The anticipated major events were not a long time coming – with the overthrow of bureaucratic regimes in 1989, German reunification, and the disintegration of the Soviet Union in 1991. This brought an end to what historians came to call "the short twentieth century" – extending from the First World War and the Russian Revolution through to the collapse of bureaucratic totalitarianism. Far from giving rise to renewed hope and a new project, these events were rather more in the nature of creative destruction – a necessary process of negation and decomposition rather than of recomposition. Following the turning point of 1989-1991, the dynamic of capitalist restoration won the day in the East, with little in the way of popular mobilization in defence of the supposedly workers' states. There were no signs of political revolution tending towards workers self-management, and not even the emergence of significant currents advocating a revival of the revolutionary tradition. Meanwhile, the

THE LONG MARCH OF THE TROTSKYISTS

Brazilian PT came close to winning the 1989 presidential elections, the Sandinistas lost the 1990 elections in Nicaragua, and in El Salvador the FMLN laid down its arms after leading a number of failed insurrections. In Cuba, the 1989 trial and execution of General Arnaldo Ochoa – in a Moscow-style show trial – revealed the scale of bureaucratic decay within the country's increasingly dictatorial regime.

For a minority within the FI, however, the fall of Stalinist despotism and the good news brought in by the East wind were a cause for celebration with copious amounts of champagne. The FI majority responded along Spinozian lines: neither laughing nor crying, but trying to understand. There was nothing to lament – on the contrary – about the fall of these regimes. Their function since the 1930s had been to preserve a world order created through negotiation with the imperialist powers, and to smother working-class movements in their own countries. Their collapse was the epilogue of a bureaucratic counter-revolution completed long before. In the context of the 1980s, though, their fall did not benefit the people but rather the rulers, the rich and bureaucrats transformed into mafia-style capitalists. Champagne? Sure, but with a strong dose of Alka Seltzer as a chaser. The bureaucratic dictatorships had indeed fallen under the pressure of popular movements and velvet revolutions in East Germany, Czechoslovakia, Poland and Romania; but they had also fallen under the pressure of the world market and the imperialist-initiated arms race. The iron grip of the bureaucracy had lasted more than 50 years in these countries; it had shattered political traditions, atomized the proletariat, destroyed public life and demolished civil society. Aspirations for reform and political revolution had indeed appeared at the time of the 1956 uprisings in Hungary and Poland, during the Czechoslovak spring of 1968, and in the working-class struggles of 1976 and 1980 in Poland. But the appearance of Solidarność marked the end of an old cycle rather than the beginning of a new one. Far removed from Khrushchev's promise to catch up and overtake capitalism, the Soviet Union had been sinking into a deep stagnation from the mid-1970s onwards. The Soviet regime was going senile, life expectancy was beginning to decrease, and the economy was suffocating under the controls and waste of a petrified bureaucracy. Unlike what had occurred in the 1960s, the working-class movement in the West – thrown on to the defensive by neoliberal reforms – was unable to exert even the slightest attraction on the protest movements in the East. Russian, Polish and East German workers dreamed of a Swedish standard of living. In reality, the implacable law of uneven and combined development condemned them to a subordinate role in the world market, to a massive decline in their living conditions, and to political instability – hovering between truncated democratization and authoritarian backsliding, bearing a greater resemblance to countries of the Third World than to "Western democracies".

These momentous developments obviously called into question the very raison d'être of organizations with roots in Trotskyism. In their own way, the leaders of the American SWP had anticipated the events in Eastern Europe – opting to quietly leave the International with the prospect of "merging with the Castroist current." The Australian SWP had preceded them along this path with its attempts to link up with new forms of radicalization, particularly in Asia and Oceania. Conversely, a minority of the French section claimed that the fall of the bureaucratic dictatorships heralded an imminent political revolution. The Thirteenth World Congress met in January 1991, on the eve of the Gulf War and the implosion of the Soviet Union. The majority resolution focussed on the contradiction between this euphoric outlook and the fact that the orthodox Trotskyism championed by this current was, by its own admission, holed up and under siege in a few residual holy places such as Paris and San Francisco. If the situation was as wonderful as they claimed, why did they represent such a small minority within organizations that were themselves rather marginal? The position was untenable; and the minority was hit hard by the disillusionment that soon followed. Most of the French supporters of the Congress minority position promptly joined the Socialist Party, led by Gérard Filoche and Daniel Assouline. This confirmed the old rule that the most ostentatious displays of orthodoxy sometimes set the stage for the most spectacular capitulations. With some time lag, the French minority was following the move to the Socialist Party initiated at the beginning of the 1980s by Julien Dray, Henri Weber, Harlem Désir and Pierre Moscovici from the LCR; and by Jean-Luc Mélanchon, Jean-Christophe Cambadélis and 400 other members of the Lambertist OCI. This embrace of the Socialist Party reflected the May 68 generation's newfound appetite for administrative realism and positions of power – which Mitterrand exploited masterfully through his paternalistic sponsorship of the anti-racist campaigning group SOS Racisme. This return to the old Socialist homestead – of which Léon Blum had declared himself caretaker at the Tours Congress in 1920 – was also a way of bidding farewell to the proletariat and the lyrical illusions of the post-68 period. Lionel Jospin's silent transformation was part of this overall redeployment.

The new century

As the "short twentieth century" drew to a close, so too did a cycle in the history of the working-class movement. A new chapter is just now beginning. Trotskyists were the first to fight Stalinism, in the name of revolutionary Marxism. But does the history of Trotskyism now end, along with that of Stalinism? Will some of the currents that come out of this experience successfully redeploy their experience and memory in a new context whose contours are just beginning to take shape? Will they be able to harness their experience to enrich the re-emerging social movements? Will they be able to provide a bridge between the lessons of the past and the challenges of the future? The answer cannot be known beforehand; it depends on future struggles.

Of the different branches that grew out of Trotskyism's origins, the Fourth International and the International Socialist Tendency (the British SWP's international current) are the most significant – given their presence in certain key countries and their actual international weight. Their groups and sections are generally very active in the international movement against capitalist globalization and imperialist war, and in the renewal of social movements. They are often involved in national regroupments with currents from the Communist Party tradition, radical ecology and revolutionary feminism. The Moreno and Lambert tendencies have been weakened and by and large only exert influence on a national or regional level. The Militant tendency from Britain has split into various groupings. In France, Lutte Ouvrière (LO) received more than five percent of votes in the 1995 presidential elections and often rates better in opinion polls than the Communist Party candidate; but LO is a phenomenon specific to France, where taken together the far-Left of Trotskyist extraction gets between 5.5 percent and 12 percent (in some municipalities) of votes cast, depending on the type of election.

How can Trotskyists enter the new century without renouncing their past or slipping into sectarianism? They will have to update their theory and practice – and challenge a vision of history linked to the teratological vocabulary of "degeneration" and other "monstrosities" that presupposes a standard, unilinear course of historical progress.

This essay stops on the threshold of the 21st century. But the march of world events itself does not. The times are more convulsive and violent than ever before. It is no longer merely a crisis of growth, but a full-blown crisis of a civilization in its twilight years. The social relations of human beings between themselves – and the human relationship with the natural conditions of our species' reproduction

– cannot be reduced to the short-sighted arbitrations of the markets and the generalized poverty of market measurements. When they declare that "the world is not for sale," demonstrators against imperialist globalization in Seattle and Genoa – but also in Porto Alegre (the symbolic city where the Trotskyist leftwing of the Workers Party has played a decisive role over the last 20 years) – raise the question of what we want for humanity and what kind of world we wish to live in. If the world should not be a commodity, what should it be? And what exactly are our plans for this world?

The collapse of "actually non-existent socialism" has freed the new generation from anti-models that paralyzed the imagination and compromised the very idea of communism. But the alternative to Capital's barbarism will not take shape without a thoroughgoing balance sheet of the terrible century that has just ended. In this sense, at least, a certain type of Trotskyism – or a certain spirit of Trotskyism in all its variants – is not outmoded. Its instruction-deficient legacy is certainly insufficient; but it is nonetheless necessary for those who wish to unravel the association between Stalinism and communism, to free the living from the weight of the dead, and to turn the page on the disillusions of the past.

The start of a new chapter

France's April 2002 presidential elections saw the socialist candidate eliminated in the first round. The second round was a mug's game between outgoing president Jacques Chirac and far-Right candidate Jean-Marie Le Pen. The trauma caused by this unexpected turn of events somewhat overshadowed another major feature of the election results: for the first time, two candidates associated with Trotskyism – Arlette Laguiller from Lutte Ouvrière and Olivier Besancenot from the LCR – came out ahead of the Communist Party (PCF) candidate. Together they received 10 percent of the vote, as opposed to 3.5 percent for the PCF. This peculiarity of the French scene did not fail to attract the attention of journalists and political analysts.

And yet France is not an exception. Some thought that political currents from the historical tradition of Trotskyism were doomed to wither and fade away. After all, the argument went, their role as critics of Stalinism had evaporated following the collapse of the Berlin Wall and the implosion of the Soviet Union. But these currents have survived. Of course, they have transformed themselves – but they have done so without abandoning their heritage. The end of the twentieth century also marked the end of the historical cycle

THE LONG MARCH OF THE TROTSKYISTS

inaugurated by the First World War and the Russian Revolution. However, the new century which began under the ashes of the Twin Towers of New York has not started from zero; nor can we make a clean sweep of the past. We always start again in the middle, as Gilles Deleuze would say. Following the failure of "real socialism", Louis Althusser mourned the destruction of "a world of thought". In our case, our world of thought requires critical examination, but it has neither been buried under the rubble of the Berlin Wall nor swallowed up by the Gulag. It survives as a thread of understanding essential for deciphering the riddles of the present.

Re-energized by the emergence of the global justice movement in 1999, Trotskyism (or at least some of its currents) has survived the bureaucratic debacle. It has even made new progress in new geographic areas – particularly in Asia, and more modestly in Africa and the Arab world. It has also made a fragile comeback in Russia, Ukraine and Eastern Europe.

This resurgence can be explained easily enough.

For one thing, neo-liberal globalization has generated a need not only for international solidarity but also for a common understanding of the events and requirements of the present context – whether in response to global environmental challenges, in opposition to the global war without end, or in the fight against multinationals and social dumping. But now there are effectively no remaining "socialist motherlands" in a position to provide logistical support (usually on unfavourable terms) and serve as a base for these movements. The demise of the Soviet Union, and China's conversion to capitalism, has freed the currents of revolutionary Marxism from the orthodoxies that held them in their grip for so long. Likewise, a new form of active internationalism has been freed from the stranglehold of state and diplomatic interests.

For another, today's new revolutionaries feel a pressing need to gain a thorough understanding of the failures of the past and the lessons for the future – not out of academic curiosity, but to find their bearings in these sombre times. Having failed to understand the difference between the Russian Revolution and the bureaucratic counter-revolution, and between Bolshevism and Stalinism, many erstwhile doctrinaire "communists" have become zealous Social Democrats – while others have even become soldiers in the West's anti-totalitarian crusade.

Lastly, while Trotskyists have experienced the defeats of the broader working-class movement and suffered their consequences, they have not experienced the political and moral bankruptcy of the big Left parties. That is why they have at least earned the right to start again and to continue on – in the manner of those social revolutions which Marx said *"criticize themselves constantly, interrupt themselves continually in their course, come back to the apparently accomplished in order to begin it afresh, deride with unmerciful thoroughness the inadequacies, weaknesses and paltriness of their first attempts."* While Trotskyists are not in a position to single-handedly fill the vacuum created by the collapse of the Stalinist parties and the conversion of Social Democrats into moderate neoliberals, they can enrich new generations of activists with the wealth of their experience.

Indeed, it is now that the "baggage of exodus" – lugged for many long years around a "planet without a visa"– has proven to be invaluable.

There has been an uneven but real upturn in social struggle since the beginning of the new century; the Bolivarian revolution in Latin America faces a number of challenges; and the illusion that the new social movements are all that is required to meet the challenges of capitalist globalization has been discredited. Such developments have placed the strategic question of power back on the agenda, resurrecting it from the dark and dusty corners where it had languished since the end of the 1970s. The forces involved in the anti-globalization movement and social forums are at a crossroads. For starters, the most politically aware among them must make the leap from ideological condemnation of neo-liberalism to political anti-capitalism. Failing this, they are doomed to embrace the illusory *realpolitik* of participation in neoliberal governments such as the ones led by Lula in Brazil and Prodi in Italy. The link between social movement and political representation must be firmly established; when it is not, the example of Rifondazione Comunista in Italy has shown how short the path can be from spouting radical social-movement rhetoric to occupying an utterly servile position within a governmental alliance.

On a symbolic level, it says a great deal about our political ethics that two of our comrades have been sacrificed by their parties on the altar of class collaboration. Senator Heloisa Helena was expelled from the Brazilian Workers Party (PT) in 2003 for refusing to support a neo-liberal reform of the pension system. In striking this stance, she was merely sticking to the positions adopted at the PT's most recent party congress. In Italy, Senator Franco Turigliatto was expelled from Rifondazione Comunista in 2006 for refusing to vote in favour of an imperial military expedition to Afghanistan. These comrades were worthy of their elders who, in the far more tragic circumstances of the Stalinist show trials, were virtually alone in refusing to "confess". In their memoirs, Leopold Trepper and David Rousset say that this was because the Trotskyists did not renounce their political positions and knew exactly what they were being accused of. In the life of a revolutionary, some principles are worth a great deal more than a seat in parliament.

By avidly participating in the methodical demolition of the welfare state, European Social Democracy has helped to saw off the branch on which it was perched. Blairite and won over to social-liberalism, its strategy now consists of forming centre-Left coalitions and dutifully managing capitalist globalization with an inhuman face. The communist parties that had tied their fate to the Soviet bureaucracy have almost all been swept away by its downfall. Having long ago ceased to be revolutionary, they have been doomed to playing a second-tier supportive role to Social Democracy; and to being subjected to pressure on their left from the newly resurgent forces of the revolutionary Left.

The renewal of social struggle has opened up a space to the left of the traditional governing parties of the Left. But it isn't an empty space that one can simply occupy. It's a force field, criss-crossed by projects that while sometimes in their infancy are often contradictory with one another. In the 2007 French presidential elections, the LCR's Olivier Besancenot was the only one among the candidates of the non-social democratic Left to better his 2002 results – with more than four percent (1.5 million) of votes. This was not only because he is a talented representative of a generation of rebellious young workers, but also because he placed the dire socio-economic situation at the heart of his campaign, advocated unity in struggle while asserting intransigent independence in relation to the Socialist Party (PS) and prospects of a PS-led government coalition, and framed the day-to-day struggle within a medium-term historical perspective.

Whether in England with Respect, in Portugal with the Left Bloc, in Italy with Sinistra Critica, in Denmark with the Red Green Alliance, or in Turkey with the ÖDP, organizations and activists from the Trotskyist tradition are participating in a non-sectarian way – but with all their convictions intact – to the recomposition now underway. They are also part of the revival of the revolutionary Left in Spain, Germany and Eastern Europe.

One chapter has ended. A new one is just beginning.

Filling the pages of this new chapter will require clarity, courage and a great deal of hurried patience.

Appendix: 1963.
'For Early Reunification of the World Trotskyist Movement'
Socialist Workers Party resolution

The world Trotskyist movement has been split since 1954. Various efforts in the past to heal the rupture proved unsuccessful. On both sides, however, it has been felt for some time that a new and more vigorous effort for reunification should be made in view of encouraging opportunities that now exist to further the growth and influence of the Fourth International, the World Party of Socialist Revolution.[32]

The Socialist Workers Party has stressed that a principled basis exists for uniting the main currents of the world Trotskyist movement. During the past year the International Secretariat took the initiative in urging the necessity and practicality of ending the split. For its side the International Committee proposed that a Parity Committee be set up. Although some of the comrades in the IC viewed this as involving no more than a practical step to facilitate common discussion and united work in areas of mutual interest, the majority, it appears clear, welcomed the formation of the committee as an important step towards early reunification.

While substantial differences still remain, especially over the causes of the 1954 split, the area of disagreement appears of secondary importance in view of the common basic programme and common analysis of major current events in world developments which unite the two sides. With good will it should be possible to contain the recognised remaining differences within a united organisation, subject to further discussion and clarification, thus making possible the great advantages that would come through combining the forces, skills, and resources of all those now adhering to one side or the other.

The main fact is that the majority on both sides are now in solid agreement on the fundamental positions of the world Trotskyist

---

[32] The following resolution, adopted by the US Socialist Workers Party on 1 March 1963, provided the political basis for the reunification of the Fourth International later that year.

movement. As briefly as possible we will indicate the points of common outlook:

1. The present agonising world crisis reflects at bottom a prolonged crisis in revolutionary leadership. The development of the productive forces on a global scale has made the world overripe for socialism. Only a socialist planned world economy can rapidly overcome the economic under-development of the colonial and semi-colonial countries, deliver mankind from the threat of nuclear extinction, and assure a world society of enduring peace, of boundless plenty, the unlimited expansion of culture and the achievement of full freedom for all. Without the international victory of socialism, decaying capitalism will continue to waste enormous resources, to hold two-thirds of the earth's population in abject poverty, to maintain social and racial inequality, and to support dictatorial regimes. To complete this grim perspective of hunger, insecurity, inequality and oppressive rule, capitalism offers the permanent threat of nuclear destruction.

2. The delay of the world socialist revolution beyond the expectations of all the great Marxists before our time is due basically to the lack of capacity of the traditional leaderships of the working class movement and to their cynical service as labour lieutenants of the capitalist class or the Kremlin bureaucracy. They are responsible for preventing the main revolutionary post-war crises of 1918-23 and of 1943-47, as well as the lesser crisis of 1932-37, from ending as they should have ended with the proletariat coming to power in the advanced capitalist countries.

3. Only by building new revolutionary Marxist mass parties capable of leading the working class and working farmers to power can the world crisis be met successfully and a third world war prevented. To build such parties is the aim and purpose of the world Trotskyist movement. A programme of transitional slogans and measures plays a key role in party-building work inasmuch as the principal problem in overcoming the crisis of leadership is to bridge the gap between the present consciousness of the masses which is centred around immediate problems and preoccupations -and the level of consciousness required to meet the objective necessity of overthrowing capitalism and building workers states based upon democratically elected and democratically functioning councils of the working people. Leninist methods must be used to construct revolutionary socialist parties. These include patient, persistent recruitment of workers to the nuclei of revolutionary socialist parties already established; but also, where necessity or opportunity dictates, flexible advances towards various tendencies in mass organisations

which may eventually be brought to the programme of revolutionary Marxism. Individual recruitment and tactical moves of wide scope are complementary ways of party construction, but each carries its own problems and special dangers. In the one instance a tendency towards sectarianism can arise out of converting enforced isolation into a virtue; in the other, adaptation to a reformist environment can lead to rightist opportunism. In the tactic known as 'entryism', where unusually difficult and complicated situations can occur, it should be the norm for those engaging in it to maintain a sector of public work, including their own Trotskyist publication. Departure from this norm must be weighed with full consciousness of the heavy risks involved.

4. The Fourth International as an international organisation, and its sections as national parties, must adhere to the principles of democratic centralism. Both theory and historic experience have demonstrated the correctness of these principles. Democratic centralism corresponds to the need for quick, disciplined action in meeting revolutionary tasks while at the same time assuring the freedom of discussion and the right to form tendencies without which genuine political life is denied to the ranks. In its adherence to internal democracy, the world Trotskyist movement stands at the opposite pole from the stifling regimes imposed on working class organisations controlled by bureaucrats trained in the schools of Stalinism, social-democracy or reformist unionism.

5. The bureaucratic reformist and Stalinist machines do not use the organised strength of the working class to overthrow capitalism where this is possible. They are primarily interested in their own privileges and power instead of the long-range interests of the working class. Because of inertia, an anti-socialist outlook, or recognition that an upsurge can sweep over their heads, they undertake struggles in the interests of the proletariat only with great reluctance and under great pressure. While condemning and opposing the twin evils of reformism and Stalinism, Trotskyists refuse to identify the genuinely socialist or communist workers of these mass organisations with their treacherous leaderships. The Trotskyist movement recognises that the main task is not simply to wage literary war on reformism and Stalinism, but actually to win these socialist- and communist-minded workers to the programme and organisation of revolutionary Marxism. Under the pressure of long years of prosperity in the advanced capitalist countries and in reaction to the crimes of Stalinism, petty-bourgeois intellectuals have opened a wide assault on the fundamentals of Marxism. It is necessary to wage a firm ideological struggle against this revisionist current.

6. The Soviet Union is still a workers state despite the usurpation of power by a privileged bureaucracy. The mode of production is non-capitalist, having emerged from the destruction of capitalism by the socialist October Revolution; and, whatever its deficiencies, lapses and even evils, it is progressive compared to capitalism. The tremendous expansion of Soviet productive forces through a colossal industrial and cultural revolution transformed a backward peasant country into the second industrial power of the world, actually challenging imperialism's lead in many fields of technology. This great new fact of world history bears witness to the mighty force inherent in planned economy and demonstrates the correctness of the Trotskyist position of unconditional defence of the degenerated workers state against imperialism.

7. In the wake of World War II, the Soviet bureaucracy was able to extend its power and its parasitism into the so-called 'people's democracies' of Eastern Europe and North Korea. But to maintain its position of special privilege, it had to destroy capitalism in these countries, doing so by bureaucratic-military means. That such means could succeed was due to the abnormal circumstances of temporary collapse of the local capitalist-landlord rule coupled with extreme weakness of the working class following the carnage of war and occupation. In this way deformed workers states came into existence. These are defended by the Trotskyist movement against imperialist attempts to reintroduce capitalism.

8. In the workers states where proletarian democracy was smashed by Stalinism, or where it never came into existence because of Stalinist influence, it is necessary to struggle for its restoration or construction, for democratic administration of the state and of the planned economy by the toiling masses. Through a political counter-revolution, Stalin destroyed the proletarian democracy of the time of Lenin and Trotsky. The Leninist forces are therefore faced with the need to organise revolutionary Marxist parties to provide leadership for the working class in exercising its right to overthrow the dictatorial rule of the bureaucratic caste and to replace it with forms of proletarian democracy. This signifies a political revolution. With the rebirth of proletarian democracy on a higher level, the workers states -- the Soviet Union above all -- will regain the attractive power enjoyed before the days of Stalin, and this will give fresh impetus to the struggle for socialism in the advanced capitalist countries.

9. The appearance of a workers state in Cuba -- the exact form of which is yet to be settled -- is of special interest since the revolution there was carried out under a leadership completely independent from the school of Stalinism. In its evolution towards revolutionary

Marxism, the July 26 Movement set a pattern that now stands as an example for a number of other countries.

10. As a result of the new upsurge of the world revolution, above all the tremendous victory in China which changed the relationship of class forces on an international scale, the Soviet proletariat already strengthened and made self-confident through the victory over German imperialism in World War II and the great economic, technological and cultural progress of the Soviet Union -- has exerted increasingly strong pressure on the bureaucratic dictatorship, especially since Stalin's death. In hope of easing this pressure, the ruling caste has granted concessions of considerable scope, abolishing the extreme forms of police dictatorship (dissolution of the forced labour camps and modification of Stalin's brutal labour code, destroying the cult of Stalin, rehabilitating many victims of Stalin's purges, granting a significant rise in the standard of living of the people, even easing the strictures against freedom of thought and discussion in various fields). The Khrushchev regime has no intention of dismantling the bureaucratic dictatorship a piece at a time; its aim is not 'self-reform' but maintenance of the rule of the caste in face of mounting popular pressures. But the masses accept the concessions as partial payment on what is due and seek to convert the gains into new points of support in pressing for the ultimate objective of restoring democratic proletarian controls over the economy and the state. This slow but solid strengthening of the position of the proletariat in the European workers states is one of the basic causes of the world crisis of Stalinism.

11. The differences which finally shattered the monolithic structure of Stalinism began in a spectacular way with ideological and political conflict between the Yugoslav and Soviet Communist party leaderships. This conflict was widened by the attempted political revolution undertaken by the Hungarian workers. The Cuban Revolution deepened the crisis still further. With the Chinese-Soviet rift it has become one of the most important questions of world politics. While expressing in an immediate sense the conflict of interests among the various national bureaucratic groups, and between the Soviet bureaucracy and the working classes of countries under its influence, the crisis reflects fundamentally the incompatibility of Stalinism with living victorious revolutions in which the militant vanguard seeks a return to the doctrines of Lenin. The crisis is thus highly progressive in character, marking an important stage in the rebuilding of a revolutionary Marxist world mass movement.

12. In conjunction with the world crisis of Stalinism, the colonial revolution is now playing a key role in the world revolutionary process. Within little more than a decade, it has forced imperialism to abolish direct colonial rule almost completely and to turn to indirect rule as a substitute; i.e., form a new 'partnership' with the colonial bourgeoisie, even though this bourgeoisie in some places may be only embryonic. But this attempt to prevent the countries awakened by the colonial revolution from breaking out of the world capitalist system runs into an insuperable obstacle. It is impossible in these countries to solve the historic problems of social, economic, and cultural liberation and development without overthrowing capitalism as well as breaking the grip of imperialism. The colonial revolution therefore tends to flow into the channel of permanent revolution, beginning with a radical agrarian reform and heading towards the expropriation of imperialist holdings and 'national' capitalist property, the establishment of a workers state and a planned economy.

13. Along the road of a revolution beginning with simple democratic demands and ending in the rupture of capitalist property relations, guerrilla warfare conducted by landless peasant and semi-proletarian forces, under a leadership that becomes committed to carrying the revolution through to a conclusion, can play a decisive role in undermining and precipitating the downfall of a colonial or semi-colonial power. This is one of the main lessons to be drawn from experience since the Second World War. It must be consciously incorporated into the strategy of building revolutionary Marxist parties in colonial countries.

14. Capitalism succeeded in winning temporary stability again in Western Europe after the Second World War. This setback for the working class was due primarily to the treacherous role played by the Stalinist and social-democratic leaderships, which prevented the masses from taking the road of socialist revolution during the big post-war revolutionary crisis. However, this temporary stabilisation of capitalism and the subsequent upsurge of productive forces gave rise to more extensive, and ultimately more explosive, contradictions. These involve the other imperialist powers, above all the USA and Japan. They include sharpening competition in a geographically contracting world market; increasing incompatibility between the need to fight inflation and the need to transform potential major economic crises into more limited recessions; mounting conflict between the desirability of maintaining 'social peace' and the necessity to attack the workers' standard of living, job conditions, and employment opportunities in order to strengthen competitive efficiency. These contradictions point to increasingly fierce class

battles which could become lifted from the economic to the political level in acute form and, under favourable conditions of leadership, arouse the labour movement to a new upsurge in the imperialist countries, challenging capitalism in its last citadels.

15. Socialist victory in the advanced capitalist countries constitutes the only certain guarantee of enduring peace. Since the close of World War II, imperialism has methodically prepared for another conflict, one in which the capitalist world as a whole would be mobilised against the workers states, with the Soviet Union as the main target. Rearmament has become the principal permanent prop of capitalist economy today, an economic necessity that dovetails with the political aims of the American capitalist class at the head of the world alliance of capitalism. American imperialism has stationed counter-revolutionary forces in a vast perimeter around China and the Soviet Union. Its first reaction to new liberating struggles is to seek to drown them in blood. Its armed interventions have become increasingly dangerous. In the crisis over Cuba's efforts to strengthen its military defence, the billionaire capitalist families who rule America demonstrated that they were prepared to launch a nuclear attack against the Soviet Union and even risk the very existence of civilisation and of mankind. This unimaginable destructive power can be torn from the madmen of Wall Street only by the American working class. The European socialist revolution will play a decisive role in helping to bring the American proletariat up to the level of the great historic task which it faces -- responsibility for the final and decisive victory of world socialism.

16. While participating wholeheartedly in all popular mass movements for unilateral nuclear disarmament, while fighting for an immediate end to all nuclear tests, the world Trotskyist movement everywhere clearly emphasises the fundamental dilemma facing humanity: world socialism or nuclear annihilation. A clear understanding of this dilemma does not demoralise the masses. On the contrary, it constitutes the strongest incentive to end capitalism and build socialism. It is a suicidal illusion to believe that peace can be assured through 'peaceful coexistence' without ending capitalism. Above all in America. The best way to fight against the threat of nuclear war is to fight for socialism through class-struggle means.

In view of the agreement on these basic positions, the world Trotskyist movement is duty bound to press for reunification. It is unprincipled to seek to maintain the split. Reunification has also become an urgent practical question. On all sides, opportunities for growth are opening up for the revolutionary movement. The Cuban Revolution dealt a blow to the class-collaborationist policy of

THE LONG MARCH OF THE TROTSKYISTS

Stalinism in Latin America and other colonial countries. New currents, developing under the influence of the victory in Cuba, are groping their way to revolutionary socialism and seeking to apply the main lessons of the colonial revolution to their own situation. The Algerian Revolution has had a similar effect on the vanguard of the African revolutionary nationalist movement. To meet these leftward-moving currents, to work with them, even to combine with them without giving up any principles, has become an imperious necessity. Reunification will greatly facilitate success in this task by strengthening our own forces and bringing the attractiveness of Trotskyism into sharp organisational focus. The immediate corollaries will be increased effectiveness of our defence of the colonial revolutions within the imperialist countries and the added weight which the principled programme of Trotskyism will gain among all serious revolutionists who seek the fundamental economic, social and political transformation of their countries. On the other hand, it is self-evident that the continued division of the world Trotskyist movement in factions wrangling over obscure issues will vitiate its capacity to attract these new forces on a considerable scale.

Similarly, the crisis of Stalinism, which has led to the great differentiation visible in the Chinese-Soviet rift, has unlocked tremendous forces within the Communist parties throughout the world. Attracted by our Leninist programme and traditions, by the vindication of our decades of struggle against Stalinism, and by our insistence on internal democracy, many militants are puzzled and repelled by our lack of unity, by our seeming incapacity to mobilise our forces into a single cohesive organisation. The reunification of the world Trotskyist movement would contribute powerfully towards re-educating Communist militants in the genuine spirit of Leninism, its real tradition of international solidarity and proletarian democracy. Obviously a united world Trotskyist movement would prove much more attractive to all those forces within the world Communist movement who are increasingly critical of Stalinism and its offshoots, and who are ready to examine the views of a movement which appears serious not only in its theory but in its organisational capacity.

Finally, we should consider with utmost attentiveness the problem of appealing to the youth, both workers and students, who are playing an increasingly decisive role in demonstrations, uprisings, and the leadership of revolutionary upheavals. The Cuban Revolution was essentially fought by the youth. Similar young people overthrew the corrupt dictatorial regimes of Menderes in Turkey and Syngman Rhee in South Korea. In the struggle for Negro equality in the USA, for solidarity with the Algerian Revolution in France, against rearmament in Japan and Western Germany and against unemployment in Britain, the shock forces are provided by the youth. Youth stand in the forefront of the fight to deepen and extend de-Stalinisation in the USSR and the East European workers states. Throughout the world they are the banner bearers of the struggles for unilateral nuclear disarmament. We can attract the best layers of this new generation of rebels by our bold programme, our fighting spirit and militant activity; we can only repel them by refusing to close ranks because of differences over past disputes of little interest to young revolutionists of action, who are primarily concerned about the great political issues and burning problems of today.

Early reunification, in short, has become a necessity for the world Trotskyist movement. Naturally, difficult problems will remain in various countries where the faction fight has been long and bitter. But these problems, too, can best be worked out under the conditions of general international reunification, so that it is possible for the outstanding leaders of both sides to begin the job of establishing a new comradely atmosphere and of removing fears which have no real basis in the situation in the world Trotskyist movement today. After a period of common fraternal activity in an Increasing number of areas, we are convinced that what may appear at the outset to be insuperable local problems will be solved by the comrades themselves through democratic means.

We think that it should also be possible for a reunified organisation to bring in recommendations for subsequent consideration and adoption which, without breaching the centralist side of democratic centralism, would remove any doubts that might still remain as to the guarantee of democratic rights contained in the statutes.

Our movement is faced with a responsibility as great and grave as the one it faced at the founding of the Fourth International in 1938. We ask both sides to decide at their international gatherings in the next months that the time has come to reunify the world Trotskyist movement, and that they will do this at a World Congress of Reunification to be held as rapidly as possible after these gatherings.

1 March 1963

Appendix: 1940-1944. Trotskyists and the Resistance
Ernest Mandel

I want to go into the question of the resistance movement in Europe between 1940 and 1944 in detail. I want to do so especially because some comrades for whom I have respect, and whom I hope to see back in the Fourth International, the comrades of the Lutte Ouvrière group in France, have made it their special point of honour to raise this question against the Fourth International.[33]

From the foundation of the Communist International, communists were educated in a principled rejection of the idea of 'national defence' or 'defence of the fatherland' in the imperialist countries. This meant a total refusal to have anything to do with imperialist wars. The Trotskyist movement was educated in the same spirit. This was all the more necessary with the right-wing turn of the Comintern and the Stalin-Laval pact in 1935, which turned the Stalinists in the West European countries, and in some colonial countries, into the worst advocates of pro-imperialist chauvinism.

In India, for instance, this led to the disastrous betrayal by the Stalinists of the national uprising in 1942. When the uprising took place, the British colonialists opened the jails for the leaders of the Indian Communist Party in order to transform them into agitators against the uprising and for the imperialist war. This tremendous betrayal laid the basis for the continuous mass influence of the bourgeois nationalist Congress Party in the following decades.

Our movement was inoculated against nationalism in imperialist countries, against the idea of supporting imperialist war efforts in any form whatsoever. That was a good education, and I do not propose to revise that tradition. But what it left out of account were elements of the much more complex Leninist position in the First World War. It is simply not true that Lenin's position then can be reduced to the formula: 'This is a reactionary imperialist war. We have nothing to do with it.' Lenin's position was much more

---

[33] The following is excerpted from the transcript of a school in London on the history of the Fourth International organised by the British section of the FI in 1976.

sophisticated. He said: 'There are at least two wars, and we want to introduce a third one.' (The third one was the proletarian civil war against the bourgeoisie which in actual fact came out of the war in Russia.)

Lenin fought a determined struggle against sectarian currents inside the internationalist tendency who did not recognise the distinction between these two wars. He pointed out: 'There is an inter-imperialist war. With that war we have nothing to do. But there are also wars of national uprising by oppressed nationalities. The Irish uprising is 100 per cent justified. Even if German imperialism tries to profit from it, even if leaders of the national movement link up with German submarines, this does not change the just nature of the Irish war of independence against British imperialism. The same thing is true for the national movement in the colonies and the semi-colonies, the Indian movement, the Turkish movement, the Persian movement.' And he added: 'The same thing is true for the oppressed nationalities in Russia and Austro-Hungary. The Polish national movement is a just movement, the Czech national movement is a just movement. A movement by any oppressed nationality against the imperialist oppressor is a just movement. And the fact that the leadership of these movements could betray by linking these movements politically and organisationally to imperialism is a reason to denounce these leaders, not a reason to condemn these movements.'

Now if we look at the problem of World War II from that more dialectical, more correct Leninist point of view, we have to say that it was a very complicated business indeed. I would say, at the risk of putting it a bit too strongly, that the Second World War was in reality a combination of five different wars. That may seem an outrageous proposition at first sight, but I think closer examination will bear it out.

First, there was an inter-imperialist war, a war between the Nazi, Italian, and Japanese imperialists on the one hand, and the Anglo-American-French imperialists on the other hand. That was a reactionary war, a war between different groups of imperialist powers. We had nothing to do with that war, we were totally against it.

Second, there was a just war of self-defence by the people of China, an oppressed semi-colonial country, against Japanese imperialism. At no moment was Chiang Kai-shek's alliance with American imperialism a justification for any revolutionary to change their judgement on the nature of the Chinese war. It was a war of national liberation against a robber gang, the Japanese imperialists, who wanted to enslave the Chinese people. Trotsky was absolutely clear and unambiguous on this. That war of independence started before the Second World War, in 1937; in a certain sense, it started in 1931 with the Japanese Manchurian adventure. It became intertwined with the Second World War, but it remained a separate and autonomous ingredient of it.

Third, there was a just war of national defence of the Soviet Union, a workers state, against an imperialist power. The fact that the Soviet leadership allied itself not only in a military way which was absolutely justified -- but also politically with the Western imperialists in no way changed the just nature of that war. The war of the Soviet workers and peasants, of the Soviet peoples and the Soviet state, to defend the Soviet Union against German imperialism was a just war from any Marxist-Leninist point of view. In that war we were 100 per cent for the victory of one camp, without any reservations or question marks. We were for absolute victory of the Soviet people against the murderous robbers of German imperialism.

Fourth, there was a just war of national liberation of the oppressed colonial peoples of Africa and Asia (in Latin America there was no such war), launched by the masses against British and French imperialism, sometimes against Japanese imperialism, and sometimes against both in succession, one after the other. Again, these were absolutely justified wars of national liberation, regardless of the particular character of the imperialist power. We were just as much for the victory of the Indian people's uprising against British imperialism, and the small beginnings of the uprising in Ceylon, as we were in favour of the victory of the Burmese, Indochinese, and Indonesian guerrillas against Japanese, French, and Dutch imperialism successively. In the Philippines the situation was even more complex. I do not want to go into all the details, but the basic point is that all these wars of national liberation were just wars, regardless of the nature of their political leadership. You do not have to place any political confidence in or give any political support to the leaders of a particular struggle in order to recognise the justness of that struggle. When a strike is led by treacherous trade union bureaucrats you do not put any trust in them -- but nor do you stop supporting the strike.

Now I come to the fifth war, which is the most complex. I would not say that it was going on in the whole of Europe occupied by Nazi imperialism, but more especially in two countries, Yugoslavia and Greece, to a great extent in Poland, and incipiently in France and Italy. That was a war of liberation by the oppressed workers, peasants, and urban petty bourgeoisie against the German Nazi imperialists and their stooges. To deny the autonomous nature of that war means saying in reality that the workers and peasants of Western Europe had no right to fight against those who were enslaving them at that moment unless their minds were set clearly against bringing in other enslavers in place of the existing ones. That is an unacceptable position.

It is true that if the leadership of that mass resistance remained in the hands of bourgeois nationalists, of Stalinists or social-democrats, it could eventually be sold out to the Western imperialists. It was the duty of the revolutionaries to prevent this from happening by trying to oust these fakers from the leadership of the movement. But it was impossible to prevent such a betrayal by abstaining from participating in that movement.

What lay behind that fifth war? It was the inhuman conditions which existed in the occupied countries. How can anyone doubt that? How can anyone tell us that the real reason for the uprising was some ideological framework -- such as the chauvinism of the French people or of the CP leadership? Such an explanation is nonsense. People did not fight because they were chauvinists. People were fighting because they were hungry, because they were over-exploited, because there were mass deportations of slave labour to Germany, because there was mass slaughter, because there were concentration camps, because there was no right to strike, because unions were banned, because communists, socialists and trade unionists were being put in prison.

That's why people were rising, and not because they were chauvinists. They were often chauvinists too, but that was not the main reason. The main reason was their inhuman material living conditions, their social, political, and national oppression, which was so intolerable that it pushed millions onto the road of struggle. And you have to answer the question: was it a just struggle, or was it wrong to rise against this over-exploitation and oppression? Who can seriously argue that the working class of Western or Eastern Europe should have abstained or remained passive towards the horrors of Nazi oppression and Nazi occupation? That position is indefensible.

So the only correct position was to say that there was a fifth war which was also an autonomous aspect of what was going on between 1939 and 1945. The correct revolutionary Marxist position (I say this with a certain apologetic tendency, because it was the one defended from the beginning by the Belgian Trotskyists against what I would call both the right wing and the ultra-left wing of the European Trotskyist movement at that time) should have been as follows: to support fully all mass struggles and uprisings, whether armed or unarmed, against Nazi imperialism in occupied Europe, in order to fight to transform them into a victorious socialist revolution -- that is, to fight to oust from the leadership of the struggles those who were linking them up with the Western imperialists, and who wanted in reality to maintain capitalism at the end of the war, as in fact happened.

We have to understand that what started in Europe in 1941 was a genuine new variant of a process of permanent revolution, which could transform that resistance movement into a socialist revolution. I say 'could', but in at least one example that was what actually happened. It happened in Yugoslavia. That's exactly what the Yugoslav Communists did.

Whatever our criticisms of the bureaucratic way in which they did it, the crimes they committed in the course of it, or the political and ideological deviations which accompanied that process, fundamentally that is what they did. We have no intention of being apologists for Tito, but we have to understand what he did. It was an amazing thing. At the start of the uprising in 1941 the Yugoslav CP had a mere 5,000 active participants. Yet in 1945 they took power at the head of an army of half a million workers and peasants. That was no small feat. They saw the possibility and the opportunity. They behaved as revolutionaries -- bureaucratic-centrist revolutionaries of Stalinist origin, if you like, but you cannot call that counter-revolutionary. They destroyed capitalism. It was not the Soviet army, it was not Stalin, as a result of the 'cold war', who destroyed capitalism in Yugoslavia. It was the Yugoslav CP which led this struggle, accompanied by a big fight against Stalin.

All the proofs are there -- all the letters sent by the Communist Party of the Soviet Union to the Yugoslavs, saying: 'Do not attack private property. Do not push the Americans into hostility to the Soviet Union by attacking private property.' And Tito and the leaders of the Communist Party did not give a damn about what Stalin told them to do or not to do. They led a genuine process of permanent revolution in the historical sense of the word, transformed a mass uprising against foreign imperialist occupation an uprising which started on an inter-class basis, but under a bureaucratic proletarian leadership -- into a genuine socialist revolution.

At the end of 1945, Yugoslavia became a workers state. There was a tremendous mass uprising in 1944-45, the workers took over the factories, the land was taken over by the peasants (and later by the state, in an exaggerated and over-centralised manner). Private property was largely destroyed. Nobody can really deny that the Yugoslav Communist Party destroyed capitalism, even if it was through its own bureaucratic methods, repressing workers democracy, even shooting some people whom it accused of being Trotskyists (which was not true -- there was no Trotskyist section in Yugoslavia then or at any time previously). And it did not destroy capitalism through some bureaucratic moves with a foreign army, as in Eastern Europe, but through a genuine popular revolution, a huge mass mobilisation, one of the hugest ever seen in Europe. You should study the history of what happened in Yugoslavia -- how, as bourgeois writers say, in every single village there was a civil war. That's the truth of it. The only comparison you can make is with Vietnam.

So I think that revolutionaries should basically have tried to do in the other occupied countries what the Yugoslav Communists did in Yugoslavia -- of course with better methods and better results, leading to workers democracy and workers power directly exercised by workers councils, and not by a bureaucratised workers party and a privileged bureaucracy.

That is not to say at all that it was our fault if the proletarian revolution failed in Europe in 1945, because we did not apply the correct line in the resistance movement. That would be ridiculous. Even with the best of lines, the relationship of forces was such that we would not have succeeded. The relationship of forces between the Communist parties and us, the prestige of the CPs, the links of the CPs with the Soviet Union, the low level of working class consciousness as a result of a long period of defeats -- all that made it impossible for the Trotskyists really to compete with the Stalinists for the leadership of the mass movement. So the mistakes which were made, both in a right-wing sense and in an ultra-left sense, actually had very little effect on history. They are simply lessons from which we have to draw a political conclusion in order not to repeat these mistakes in future. We cannot say that we failed to influence history as a result of these mistakes.

These lessons were of a dual nature. The leading comrades of one of the two French Trotskyist organisations, the POI (which was the official section), made right-wing mistakes in 1940-41. There is no doubt about that. They started from a correct line essentially, the one I have just outlined, but they took it one step too far. In the implementation of that line they included temporary blocs with what they called the 'national bourgeoisie'.

I should add they were able to use one sentence by Trotsky in support of their position. Remember that before arriving too hastily at a judgement on these questions. This sentence came at the beginning of one of Trotsky's last articles: 'France is being transformed into an oppressed nation.' In an oppressed nation there is no principled reason to reject temporary, tactical agreements with the 'national bourgeoisie' against imperialism. There are conditions: we do not make a political bloc with the bourgeoisie. But purely tactical agreements with the national bourgeoisie are acceptable. We should, for instance, have made such an agreement in the 1942 uprising in India. It is a question of tactics, not of principle.

What was wrong in the position of the POI leadership was to make an extrapolation from a temporary, conjunctural situation. If France had permanently become a semi-colonial country, that would have been another story. But it was a temporary situation, just an episode in the war. France remained an imperialist power, with imperialist structures, which continued through the Gaullist operation to exploit many colonial peoples and maintain its empire in Africa intact. To change one's attitude towards the bourgeoisie simply in the light of what happened over a couple of years on the territory of France was a premature move which contained within it the seed of major political mistakes.

In fact it did not lead to anything in practice. Those who say that the French Trotskyists 'betrayed' by making a bloc with the bourgeoisie in 1940-41 do not understand the difference between the beginning of a theoretical mistake and an actual treacherous intervention in the class struggle. There was never any agreement with the bourgeoisie, never any support for them when it came to the point. Whenever strikes took place the French Trotskyists were 100 per cent on the side of the workers. Whether it was a strike against French capitalists, German capitalists, or a combination of both, they were on the side of the workers every time. So where was the betrayal? It just confuses a possible political mistake and an actual theoretical one -- which eventually could perhaps have had grave consequences, but in actual fact never did. That it was a mistake I naturally do not deny. But I think the comrades of the POI minority who fought against it did a good job, and by 1942 it was reversed and did not come up again.

The sectarian mistake, however, was in my opinion much graver. Here the ultra-left wing of the Trotskyist movement denied any progressive ingredient in the resistance movement and refused to make any distinction between the mass resistance, the armed mass struggle, and the manoeuvres and plans of the bourgeois nationalist, social-democratic or Stalinist misleaders of the masses. That mistake was much worse because it led to abstention on what were important living struggles of the masses. Those comrades (such as the Lutte Ouvrière group) who persist even today in identifying the mass movements in the occupied countries with imperialism -- saying that the war in Yugoslavia was an imperialist war because it was conducted by nationalists -- are completely revising the Marxist method. Instead of defining the class nature of a mass movement by its objective roots and significance, they try to do so on the basis of its ideology. This is an unacceptable backward step towards historical idealism. When workers rise against exploitation and oppression with nationalist slogans, you say: 'The rising is correct; please change the slogans. You do not say: 'The rising is bad because the slogans are bad.' It does not become bourgeois because the slogans are bourgeois -- that is a wrong and absolutely unmaterialist approach.

Trotsky warned the Trotskyist movement against precisely such mistakes in his last basic document, the Manifesto of the 1940 emergency conference. He pointed out that they should be careful not to judge workers in the same way as the bourgeoisie even when they talked about national defence. It was necessary to distinguish between what they said and what they meant -- to judge the objective historical nature of their intervention rather than the words they used. And the fact that sectarian sections of the Trotskyist movement did not understand that, and took an abstentionist position on big clashes involving hundreds of thousands or even millions of people, was very dangerous for the future of the Fourth International.

To abstain from such clashes on ideological grounds would have been absolutely suicidal for a living revolutionary movement. But we had no section in Yugoslavia. And had we had one, it would happily not have been sectarian. Otherwise we could not address the Yugoslav Communists and workers with the authority which we have today. Our first intervention in Yugoslavia was only in 1948; it was a good one, and so now we can speak with an unblemished banner and considerable moral authority in Yugoslavia. But if the Lutte Ouvrière line had been applied in practice between 1941 and 1944 in Yugoslavia, and if Yugoslav Trotskyists had been neutral in that civil war, we would not be very proud today and we would certainly not be in a strong position to defend the programme of the Fourth International. As it is, some of the Yugoslav Communists who later became Trotskyists were heroes in the civil war, which gives them a certain standing and moral authority. It makes it easier for them and for us to discuss Trotskyism in Yugoslavia today. If we had to carry the moral blemish of passivity and abstention in a huge civil war, we would, to say the least, be in a very bad position today.

Postface: Who was Pierre Frank?
Ernest Mandel

Pierre Frank was born in Paris in 1905. His parents, of Russian origin, were employed as tailors. In the course of his studies as a chemical engineer, he participated in 1924-25 in the foundation of the General Union of Technical Students in Industry, Commerce and Agriculture (UGETICA), under the sponsorship of the Union of Technicians in Industry, Commerce and Agriculture (USTICA), the first union organisation of technicians created in France after the 1914-1918 war.

The political involvement of Pierre F'rank, which started when he was 15, led him to join the Communist Party 5 years later, in 1925. As a trade unionist he was active in USTICA and, for several years, in the Chemical Federation belonging to the Communist-led United General Confederation of Labour (CGTU).

In 1927, he saw the platform of the United• Opposition in the Communist Party of the Soviet Union (CPSU), led by Trotsky and Zinoviev, as the answer to the disastrous course being followed by the Stalin-Bukharin leadership. He supported the Opposition's theses, and was central in the creation of the first French Trotskyist publication La Verite (The Truth), of which he became man aging editor. His political position led to expulsion from the section of the CP in the industrial Paris suburb of Aulnay-sous-Bois.

A participant in the creation of the first Trotskyist organisation in France, the Ligue Communiste (Communist League) in 1930, Frank remained a member of its leadership until 1934. In May 1931 he became a member of the Inter national Secretariat of the international Trotskyist organisation led by Trotsky.

In July 1932 he went to Turkey to join Leon Trotsky, still in exile in Prinkipo, and was his secretary for a year.

Once back in France, he was in the forefront of all the political battles of the Trotskyists in 1934, at a time when the ranks of the working class were deeply divided faced with the fascist threat.

At the end of 1934, the Ligue Communiste publicly decided to send all its members into the Socialist Party (SFIo, Section Francaise de l'Internationale Ouvriere, French section of the Socialist International at the time). Within the party they formed the Groupe Bolchevik Leniniste (GB.L, Bolshevik Leninist Group). Pierre Frank was elected as alternate member of the Permanent Administrative

Commission of the SFIO at its June 1935 congress in Mulhouse. But in October 1935, along with other lea4ers of the GB-L, he was expelled from the party on the pretext of disciplinary infractions. The Socialist Party then became involved in constituting the Popular Front with the Communist Party.

Following the expulsion of the Trotskyists from the SFIO, divisions emerged in their ranks. In December 1935, Pierre Frank, with Raymond Molinier, created a new journal, La Commune, which stood for broad regroupment out side the SFIO. This was in contradiction with the line of the revolutionaries organised in the Jeunesses Socialistes Revolutionnaires (Revolutionary Socialist Youth) and supported by Trotsky. These differences led to the creation of the Parti Communiste Internationaliste (PCI, Internationalist Communist Party) alongside the GB-L in March 1936. After a fleeting reunification which led to the formation of the Parti Ouvrier Internationaliste (POT, Internationalist Workers Party), the PCI recommenced its own activity. This division of Trotskyist organisations in France lasted into the middle of the Second World War.

A warrant for Pierre Frank's arrest was issued in 1939. Sentenced in absentia to several years in prison, he went into hiding. Arrested in Britain in 1940, he was interned on the Isle of Man until 1943.

After the war ended he had to wait another year before being able to become freely active in France once more, but in 1946 he participated in the Fourth International conference that sealed the reunification of the Trotskyist forces. From that point on he was continuously in the top leadership of the International and its French section. After 1948 he alone represented the continuity with the pre-war generation of activists. He played a leading role in training the cadres of the movement internationally.

At the same time, Pierre Frank continued his activity in the French section, particularly during the fight against the Indochinese and Algerian wars. He was once again arrested and sentenced for his work in solidarity with the Algerian National Liberation Front.

The small nucleus that had carried on the tradition of militancy was given a new lease on life by the formation of the Jeunesse Communiste Revolutionnaire (Revolutionary Communist Youth) by those expelled from the Union des Etudiants Communistes and the Communist Party in 1966. At the end of June 1968, after the PCI and the JCR had been dissolved by the Gaullist government, Pierre Frank was yet again held in custody for ten days, for plotting against the security of the state.

After the fusion of the PCI and the JCR and the creation of the Ligue Communiste in April 1969, Pierre Frank continued his work as a leader for many years, before giving up all leadership responsibilities at the end of the 1970s. At the Eleventh World Congress of the Fourth International in 1979; he was elected a consultative member of the International Executive Committee, as recognition of his long and continuing contribution to the international leader ship.

Responsible for the publication of many of Trotsky's works, and having made the first sign of the anti-bureaucratic opposition in Poland (the Open Letter to the PUWP by Kuron and Modzelevski) known in France, he himself wrote several political works, particularly the *Histoire de l'Internationale Communiste* (not yet published in English), to which he devoted the last years of his life.

Declaration of the Fourth International and the Ligue communiste révolutionnaire

The United Secretariat of the Fourth International and its French section are in mourning.. With the death of Pierre Frank we have lost one of our most valiant members, one of our best leaders.

Pierre. Frank was a companion of Leon Trotsky and with him a co-founder of the Fourth International and of its French section. He was in the thick of every battle. His life is an example of a militant in the service of the revolution and the working class. He never faltered, right to the last, even during those terrible years when there was only an isolated handful of Trotskyists to denounce Stalin's crimes as well as the abominations of imperialism.

Pierre Frank, along with the generation of militants who shared his commitment, passed on to us an irreplaceable heritage — the heritage of Marxism and the revolutionary tradition of Lenin and Trotsky. Against the social democratic and Stalinist betrayals he was in the front ranks of those who kept alive the revolutionary experience which is the cornerstone of our struggle today. We benefited from his vast knowledge of the French workers movement and his acute understanding of its debates and traditions.

Throughout his life Pierre Frank placed internationalism and building the Fourth International at the centre of his political activity. In all the debates and when there were big political and organisational choices to be made he taught us that — as Rosa Luxembourg said — 'the centre of gravity of the class organisation of the proletariat rests on internationalism'.

CONTRIBUTIONS TO THE HISTORY OF THE FOURTH INTERNATIONAL

The United Secretariat of the Fourth International and its French section pay tribute to the memory of this workers' leader, this exemplary revolutionary leader. We call on our members and sympathisers to pay him solemn homage on Friday April 27. At this difficult time the LCR especially sends its militant solidarity to his companion Marguerite, who was deported to Ravensbruck for the same ideal and was at his side in all his battles.

Paris, April 18, 1984, 10:00 am
United Secretariat of the Fourth International
Political Bureau of the LCR

Notebooks for Study and Research

- 1 The Place of Marxism in History, Ernest Mandel (40 pp. € 5.)
- 2 The Chinese Revolution - I: The Second Chinese Revolution & the Shaping of the Maoist Outlook, Pierre Rousset(32 pp. € 5)
- 3 The Chinese Revolution - II: The Maoist Project Tested in the Struggle for Power, Pierre Rousset (48 pp. € 5.00)
- 4 Revolutionary Strategy Today, Daniel Bensaïd (36 pp. € 5)
- 5 Class Struggle and Technological Innovation in Japan since 1945, Muto Ichiyo (48 pp. € 5)
- 6 Populism in Latin America, Adolfo Gilly, Helena Hirata, Carlos M. Vilas, and the PRT (Argentina) introduced by Michael Löwy (40 pp. € 5)
- 7/8 Market, Plan and Democracy: The Experience of the So-Called Socialist Countries, Catherine Samary (64pp. € 5)
- 9 The Formative Years of the Fourth International (1933-1938), Daniel Bensaïd (48 pp. € 5)
- 10 Marxism & Liberation Theology, Michael Löwy (40pp € 5)
- 11/12 The Bourgeois Revolutions, Robert Lochhead (72pp. € 5)
- 13 The Spanish Civil War in Euzkadi and Catalonia 1936-39, Miguel Romero (48pp. € 5)
- 14 The Gulf War and the New World Order, André Gunder Frank and Salah Jaber (72pp. € 5)
- 15 From the PCI to the PDS, Livio Maitan (48pp. € 5)
- 16 Do the Workers have a Country?, José Iriarte "Bikila" (48pp. € 5)
- 17/18 October 1917: Coup d'état or Social Revolution, Ernest Mandel (64pp. € 5)
- 19/20 The Fragmentation of Yugoslavia: An Overview, Catherine Samary (60pp. € 5)
- 21 Factory Commitees and Workers' Control in Petrograd in 1917, David Mandel (48pp. € 5)
- 22 Women's Lives in the New Global Economy, Penny Duggan & Heather Dashner (editors) (68 pp. € 5)
- 23 Lean Production: Capitalist Utopia? Tony Smith (68 pp. € 5)
- 24/25 World Bank/IMF/WTO: The Free-Market Fiasco, Susan George, Michel Chossudovsky et al.
- 26 The Trade-Union Left and the Birth of a New South Africa, Claude Jacquin (92 pp., € 5)

CONTRIBUTIONS TO THE HISTORY OF THE FOURTH INTERNATIONAL

- 27/28 Fatherland or Mother Earth? Essays on the National Question, Michael Löwy (108 pp., €16, £10.99, $16)
- 29/30 Understanding the Nazi Genocide: Marxism after Auschwitz, Enzo Traverso (154 pp., €19.20, £12.99, $19.20)
- 31/32 Globalization: Neoliberal Challenge, Radical Responses, Robert Went (170 pp., €21.00, £13.99, $21.00)
- 33/34 The Clash of Barbarisms: September 11 & the Making of the New World Disorder, Gilbert Achcar (128 pp., €15, £10, $16)
- 35/36 The Porto Alegre Alternative: Direct Democracy in Action, Iain Bruce ed. (162 pp., €19.20, £12.99, $23.50)
- 37/38 Take the Power to Change the World, Phil Hearse ed. (144 pp., €9, £6, $12)
- 39/40 Socialists and the Capitalist Recession (with Ernest Mandel's 'Basic Theories of Karl Marx') Raphie De Santos, Michel Husson, Claudio Katz (196 pp., €9, £7, $12)
- 41 Living Internationalism: The history of the IIRE (108pp, €5)
- 42/43 Strategies of Resistance & 'Who Are the Trotskyists' Daniel Bensaïd (196 pp., £6, €8, $10)
- 44/45 Building Unity Against Fascism: Classic Marxist Writings, Leon Trotsky, Daniel Guérin, Ted Grant (164 pp., £6, €8, $10)
- 46 October Readings: The development of the concept of Permanent Revolution, D. R. O'Connor Lysaght ed. (110pp, €5)
- 47 The Long March of the Trotskyists, Pierre Frank (€9, £7, $12)
- 48 Women Liberation & Socialist Revolution: Documents of the Fourth International, Penny Duggan ed. (€9, £7, $12)
- 49 Revolution and Counter-revolution in Europe, Pierre Frank (280pp. €10, £9, $14)

Forthcoming

- Dangerous relationships, Marriage and divorces between Marxism and feminism, Cinzia Arruzza
- Marxism and Anarchism, Marx, Lenin, Trotsky et al.
- Returns of Marxism, Sara Farris and Antonio Carmona Baez eds.
- The conflict in Palestine, Cinzia Nachira ed.
- Towards a New Left: experiences from Europe, Bertil Videt et al.
- Women and the Crisis, Terry Conway ed.

Subscribe online at: http://bit.ly/NSRsub
To order, email iire@iire.org or write to International Institute for Research and Education, Lombokstraat 40, NL-1094, Amsterdam.

Further reading

The Formative Years of the Fourth International (1933-38)

Daniel Bensaïd
IIRE Notebook for Study and Research
no. 9
(48 pp. €2.75, £2, $3.25)

A new problem was posed to the movement for socialist democracy in the 1930s. To its fight against capitalism, it now had to add a fight against Stalinist bureaucracy in the USSR. In The Formative Years of the Fourth International, Daniel Bensaïd outlines the arguments that led part of this movement to found an independent international organization. He unravels the historical reasons, conjunctural prognoses and organizational choices behind the decision, showing in particular that the foundation of the Fourth International in 1938 concluded a prolonged attempt to regroup many anti-Stalinist, anti-fascist and anti-imperialist currents, beginning in 1933. Due to the concrete conditions of the 1930s, however, the regroupment failed to broaden the Fourth Internationalist current significantly.

Daniel Bensaïd was born in 1946. He was active in the French student and anti-imperialist movements that led up to May 1968. Drawing the lessons of the failure of the general strike, he emerged as one of the main advocates of building an independent radical left. He was an IIRE Fellow and taught sociology at the University of Paris until his death in 2010. His many published works include: Portugal: la révolution en marche (1975), Mai si! rebelles et repentis (with Alain Krivine, 1988), Le pari mélancolique (1997) and Les irréductibles: théorèmes de la résistance à l'air du temps (2001).

To order, email iire@iire.org or write to International Institute for Research and Education, Lombokstraat 40, NL-1094, Amsterdam.